The
CONSTITUTION

First published in 2013.
This edition published in 2019 by
The Welbeck Publishing Group
20 Mortimer Street
London W1T 3JW

ISBN: 978-1-83861-007-4

Library of Congress Cataloging-in-Publication Data available upon request.

Manufactured in Dubai.

10 9 8 7 6 5 4 3 2

The CONSTITUTION

THE STORY OF THE CREATION AND ADAPTATION OF
THE MOST IMPORTANT DOCUMENT IN THE HISTORY
OF THE UNITED STATES OF AMERICA

Gerry and Janet Souter

SEVENOAKS

CONTENTS

INTRODUCTION

The United States Constitution is America's instruction book. A faded, barely legible set of parchment pages, the original signed document was handwritten in iron gall ink with a feathered quill pen. Cast in eighteenth-century language and preserved in archival security, it is now available for public view and contemplation. The Constitution's present-day fragile appearance, however, masks the muscle and power of its carefully chosen words; forged at a time when life, death, and government rested in the ruling doctrine of divine right of kings.

Released from these frail pages, these revolutionary words have thundered through America's halls of justice and within its legislative bodies with a seemingly unstoppable, corporeal authority. Historians might all agree that the U.S. Constitution has been responsible for creating the most successful democratic republic ever envisioned. American citizens have lived by its commandments, stretched its implications, ignored its wisdom, tested its premises, assaulted its foundation, and interpreted the intentions of its framers to fit our changing decades of social, moral, and economic existence. Each new generation discovers the immutable strength and latent challenges behind those opening words, "We, the people…"

Government by the people can be subject to human imperfection. This book concentrates on challenges to our Constitution through generations of interpretation.

The foundation of this government was laid well before the first words were inked on parchment. British colonials who populated the Eastern Seaboard of North America had fought for their king and mother country against the French in the Seven Years' War, concluding their service with victory in 1763. On returning to their villages, farms, homesteads, and plantations, they settled in once again governed by British rule of law. The British, however, faced debts run up by the long war and needed additional revenue. New taxes were levied on the colonies without extending representation to them in the Houses of Parliament. The Crown felt entitled to these taxes as payment for government, security, banking, and trade. The colonial congresses petitioned for relief, but when one tax was withdrawn, another appeared. Garrison troops were harassed, commerce was disrupted. In 1776, fueled by the lure of independence, the colonies met in common congress and drafted a declaration that set in motion a revolution and announced the reasons for such a treasonous act to the world.

We begin this journey when memories of treason's noose were still fresh and the country was young and still encumbered with Old World customs. The act of separation produced a government of and for the people to achieve and preserve new freedoms. Even as the struggle to secure those freshly claimed liberties raged across fields and towns, the Continental Congress was, quite literally, kept on the move in order to stay ahead of the British Army while working to hammer out a government for its new citizens. This assumed, of course, that we were going to win. Ratified in 1781, before the deciding battle at Yorktown and our shaky birth as a new nation, the Articles of Confederation that emerged from this effort demonstrated our national spirit.

The first steps toward unified self-government, these articles necessitated constant rethinking as to just what it was the representatives were trying to build. Finally, after six years of trial and error, of experimenting and often painful discovery, the independent states of America decided to work toward the stability of a strong central government.

Our founders spent the summer of 1787 creating a new constitution, a "revised edition" of the original, not as an ivory-tower theory but in spare prose demanding ratification by all thirteen of the United States. In the coming years, as our population expanded and then exploded across the continent, each generation tested this bold experiment in statehood in ways perhaps never envisioned by its framers. The demands of politics, commerce, industry, society, and geography have challenged the translations of this eighteenth-century wisdom enacted through two hundred years of revisions: articles, sections, acts, bills, and amendments.

We look at many of those demands over the decades of change from colonial times to the twenty-first century and see, through a series of eleven thematic chapters, how challenges were met by a variety of generations. The aim is to understand that what's required of today's world can resonate with similar needs made apparent and solutions put forth in response a hundred years ago.

Only twenty-seven changes have been admitted to the original document from roughly two thousand proposed amendments to the Constitution since its creation. We'll see how the mechanics of change, insightfully built into the Constitution, have been employed as we have experienced collisions of events and philosophies over the decades and centuries. The speed of communication, revelations in the spheres of social and physical science, and our participation in a growing global community have demanded answers to never-imagined questions. Volumes have been written examining the tangle of constitutional interpretation to address these various and evolving challenges. What is the future of our founding principles and rules of law? The authors argue here that an examination of its past clearly suggests how today's Constitution maintains considerable influence and legitimacy with which to inform generations to come.

OPPOSITE: The United States Capitol in Washington, D.C., is the seat of the nation's legislature. Congress first met in this building in November 1800.

1 | THE NOVEL IDEA OF GOVERNMENT BY THE PEOPLE

THE DEMAND FOR REPRESENTATIONAL GOVERNMENT IN THE DECLARATION OF INDEPENDENCE

The Constitution of the United States of America was shaped and fashioned on the forge of great ideas. It is the product of a succession of intellectual leaps that became known as the Age of Enlightenment in the eighteenth century. The German philosopher Immanuel Kant (1724–1804) defined this period in human evolution as "man's release from his self-incurred tutelage," tutelage being "man's inability to make use of his understanding without direction from another." The English-born American émigré and firebrand journalist Thomas Paine (1737–1809) called it the Age of Reason. At a time when the ability to rule men's lives lay in the divine right of kings, where monarchical decree controlled life, death, liberty, and freedom of speech, and birthright condemned the rise of a person regardless of his or her ability, some men of letters turned their thoughts to the question "Why?"

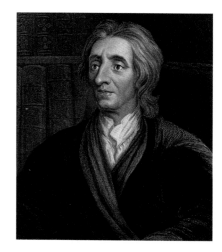

Government managed by the ancient Greeks' democracy, or the Romans' republic—with the power of the citizens' vote, or political representation of the citizens' need—had long been suppressed. But the printed and published words of those referred to in their time as the "substitute aristocracy"—learned men such as John Jacques Rousseau (1712–78), "I prefer liberty with danger than peace with slavery," or John Locke (1632–1704), "Being all equal and independent, no one ought to harm another in his life, health, liberty, or possessions"—gained acceptance during a period when people believed they were oppressed.

ABOVE: English philosopher John Locke (1632–1704), the "Father of English Empiricism," whose written works on the rights of man helped colonials consider independence from Great Britain.

THE SALONS OF EUROPE SPREAD THE AGE OF ENLIGHTENMENT

Informal conversations among learned persons held in private homes and public rooms were the main activity of the salons. These intellectual exchanges often resulted in the spreading of the Enlightenment into the public arena through personal, copied, circulated, and published letters as well as letters to the editors of widely distributed gazettes and magazines. These new ideas of social and political change reached a wide audience through this emerging periodical press. In Boston, Philadelphia, and other major cities in the colonies, the book *The Age of Reason* and pamphlet *Common Sense* by Thomas Paine were being read and debated in public houses, church meetings, and in local newspapers.

RIGHT: A recitation of Voltaire's tragedy *L'Orphelin de la Chine* at Madame Geoffrin's salon in Paris.

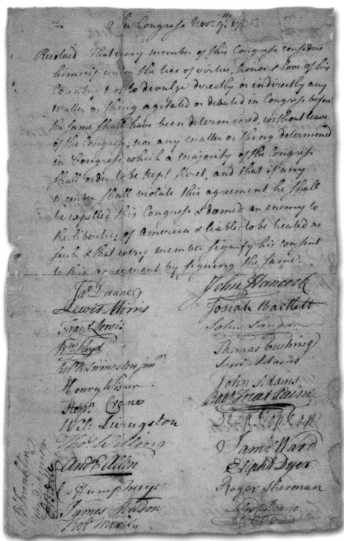

Isolated from the Old World's tyranny, the American colonies felt cut off from representation by their mother country, Great Britain. The colonists had come to this wild and vast new world on the east coast of North America and had worked hard to support themselves and become valuable trading partners as loyal subjects of their king. British acts against Americans' liberty and levies against commerce were becoming intolerable. As treasonous threats and autocratic demands sailed back and forth between American and English ports, new ideas and enlightened thoughts were being born in the salons and cafés of Europe. These entitlements spoke of the people's inalienable rights and representational government shaped by their own hands.

Provocations and demands on the colonies such as the Stamp Act, the Townshend Acts, and boarding British troops in private Boston homes demanded an immediate declaration of independence in 1775. A more moderate group, led by John Dickinson of Pennsylvania, appealed for a final letter to be extended directly to the Crown seeking a peaceful solution. This so-called Olive Branch Petition placed all the guilt on Parliament, which the colonies presumed had acted without the king's knowledge. George III refused to accept it. He called down the wrath of the empire on every colonist who dared sign such a document.

On November 9, 1775, three months after the Olive Branch Petition had been rejected and every signatory branded a traitor with a reward on their heads, the Continental Congress created an agreement of secrecy to protect these fugitives from the death penalty. It was eventually signed by eighty-seven delegates.

ABOVE LEFT: King George III of Great Britain (1738–1820) in coronation robes in a 1754 portrait. He refused to consider independence for the colonies.

ABOVE RIGHT: Revolutionary War agreement of secrecy signed by the delegates to the congress, knowing they were committing treason against the Crown.

THE DECLARATION OF INDEPENDENCE

With all diplomatic channels exhausted, all that remained was separation from the mother country and the turning of thirteen colonies into independent states. This decision almost certainly meant going to war with the greatest military power in Western civilization. To earn support from the majority of citizens in this shaky new republic would require a lot of explaining. A formal declaration stating the reasons for such a drastic step was deemed a necessity.

By this time, Thomas Paine's pamphlet *Common Sense,* which advocated a republican government and repeated the themes of the Enlightenment, had stirred public debate beyond the legislative arenas, consolidating considerable public support for separation and independence. Much of this sentiment took the form of local declarations—more than ninety from April to July of 1776 according to historian Pauline Maier. These sentiments were expressed with instructions to colonial delegations and carried out with official legislative acts stipulating the dissolution of all ties with Great Britain.

On May 15, 1776, Richard Henry Lee, a delegate from Virginia, received instructions to approve separation and the severing of all ties with Britain. In response, he placed the following resolution before Congress:

> Resolved, that these United Colonies are, and of right ought to be, free and independent States, that they are absolved from all allegiance to the British Crown, and that all political connection between them and the State of Great Britain is, and ought to be, totally dissolved.

The resolution was roundly debated, but also acted as motivation to produce a necessary explanation of why the colonies were to become independent states. Benjamin Franklin, John Adams, Robert R. Livingston, and Roger Sherman were tasked by Congress with creating a formal draft of this explanation. Once the general outline was established, Jefferson was persuaded to write the first draft, which he did, working on the second floor of a boarding house using a portable writing desk he designed and built. Franklin and Adams contributed scores of suggestions and corrections in the margins of that first draft. A second, clean draft was presented to Congress and they ruthlessly edited it ("mangled it" in Jefferson's words) according to local concerns and prejudices. For example, between July 2 and final ratification, the sentences condemning the slave trade were cut, fearing loss of the Southern states' votes.

On July 4, 1776, the final form of the document was approved with the signatures of fifty-six delegates—all of whom faced hanging if arrested by the British for doing so. It was then sent to the printers to be distributed and read throughout the newly minted United States of America.

ABOVE: *Writing the Declaration of Independence* by Jean-Leon Gerome Ferris: Thomas Jefferson (standing), supervised by Benjamin Franklin and John Adams, in Jefferson's apartments at Seventh and Market Street in Philadelphia.

OPPOSITE TOP LEFT: On July 4, 1776, members of the Second Continental Congress leave Philadelphia's Independence Hall after adopting the Declaration of Independence.

OPPOSITE TOP RIGHT: Declaration of Rights to the Virginia Constitution, written by George Mason and adopted in June 1776, which granted "certain inherent rights and enjoyment of life and liberty."

FRIDAY, June 14, 1776. } POSTSCRIPT. { No. 72.

IN CONVENTION.

JUNE 12, 1776.

A DECLARATION of RIGHTS made by the representatives of the good people of Virginia, assembled in full and free Convention; which rights do pertain to them, and their posterity, as the basis and foundation of government.

1. THAT all men are by nature equally free and independent, and have certain inherent rights, of which, when they enter into a state of society, they cannot, by any compact, deprive or divest their posterity; namely, the enjoyment of life and liberty, with the means of acquiring and possessing property, and pursuing and obtaining happiness and safety.

2. That all power is vested in, and consequently derived from, the people; that magistrates are their trustees and servants, and at all times amenable to them.

3. That government is, or ought to be, instituted for the common benefit, protection, and security, of the people, nation, or community; of all the various modes and forms of government that is best, which is capable of producing the greatest degree of happiness and safety, and is most effectually secured against the danger of mal-administration; and that whenever any government shall be found inadequate or contrary to these purposes, a majority of the community hath an indubitable, unalienable, and indefeasible right, to reform, alter, or abolish it, in such manner as shall be judged most conducive to the publick weal.

4. That no man, or set of men, are entitled to exclusive on separate emoluments or privileges from the community, but in consideration of publick services; which, not being descendible, neither ought the offices of magistrate, legislator, or judge, to be hereditary.

5. That the legislative and executive powers of the state should be separate and distinct from the judicative; and that the members of the two first may be restrained from oppression, by feeling and participating the burthens of the people, they should, at fixed periods, be reduced to a private station, return into that body from which they were originally taken, and the vacancies be supplied by frequent, certain, and regular elections, in which all, or any part of the former members, to be again eligible, or ineligible, as the laws shall direct.

6. That elections of members to serve as representatives of the people, in assembly, ought to be free; and that all men, having sufficient evidence of permanent common interest with, and attachment to, the community, have the right of suffrage, and cannot be taxed or deprived of their property for publick uses without their own consent, or that of their representatives so elected nor bound by any law to which they have not, in like manner, assented, for the publick good.

7. That all power of suspending laws, or the execution of laws, by any authority without consent of the representatives of the people, is injurious to their rights, and ought not to be exercised.

8. That in all capital or criminal prosecutions a man hath a right to demand the cause and nature of his accusation, to be

THE LEVERAGE OF NEW IDEAS

The Seven Years' War (1754–63) between Great Britain and France had drained the British treasury. To raise revenue, Parliament voted to extract additional taxes from their colonies. The Americans objected, citing they were not represented in the British legislature; therefore Parliament had no right to levy taxes. The British, however, saw the question from the point of view of the Glorious Revolution of 1688, which had established Parliament as the supreme authority (in the monarchical sense), meaning that any laws they enacted were wholly constitutional. During the Age of Enlightenment, however, so-called natural rights were deemed not dependent upon any culture, government, or king and were, as such, universal and unalienable. Natural law, as interpreted by the Enlightenment, challenged the divine right of kings and became the basis for a newly proposed social contract, positive law, and government—thus becoming legal rights. Steered by the writings of influential colonialists such as Samuel Adams, James Wilson, and Thomas Jefferson, Americans argued that Parliament was merely the legislature for Great Britain, while the colonies, with their own legislatures, were tied to the British only by their allegiance to the Crown. Soon, these ideas inspired clandestine meetings of influential and politically active Americans where the discussion turned to separation from Great Britain and independence for the colonies.

LEFT: Cartoon of Thomas Paine (1737–1809), American author, writing out his principles of republicanism in the pamphlet *Rights of Man*—he was called "Mad Tom" by the British.

MAD TOM.
or the MAN of RIGHTS.

DECLARATION OF INDEPENDENCE

Signed copy of the Declaration of Independence, July 4, 1776, written
primarily by Thomas Jefferson, and edited by committee members
including John Adams and Benjamin Franklin.

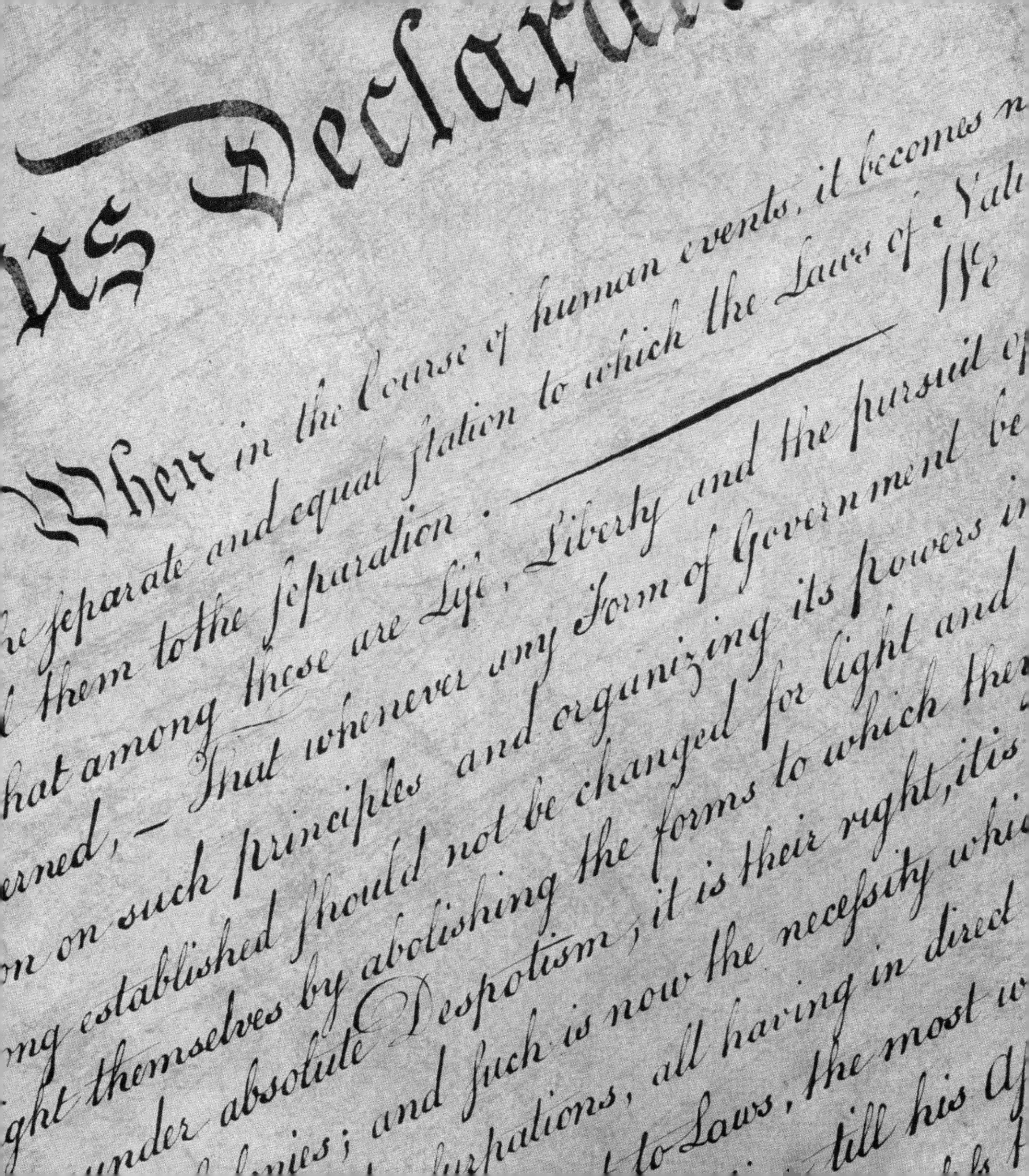

us Declarati

When in the Course of human events, it becomes n

he separate and equal station to which the Laws of Natu

l them to the Separation . — We

hat among these are Life, Liberty and the pursuit of

ered, — That whenever any Form of Government be

on on such principles and organizing its powers in

ng established should not be changed for light and

ght themselves by abolishing the forms to which the

under absolute Despotism, it is their right, it is

onies; and such is now the necessity whic

xations, all having in direct

to Laws, the most w

till his A

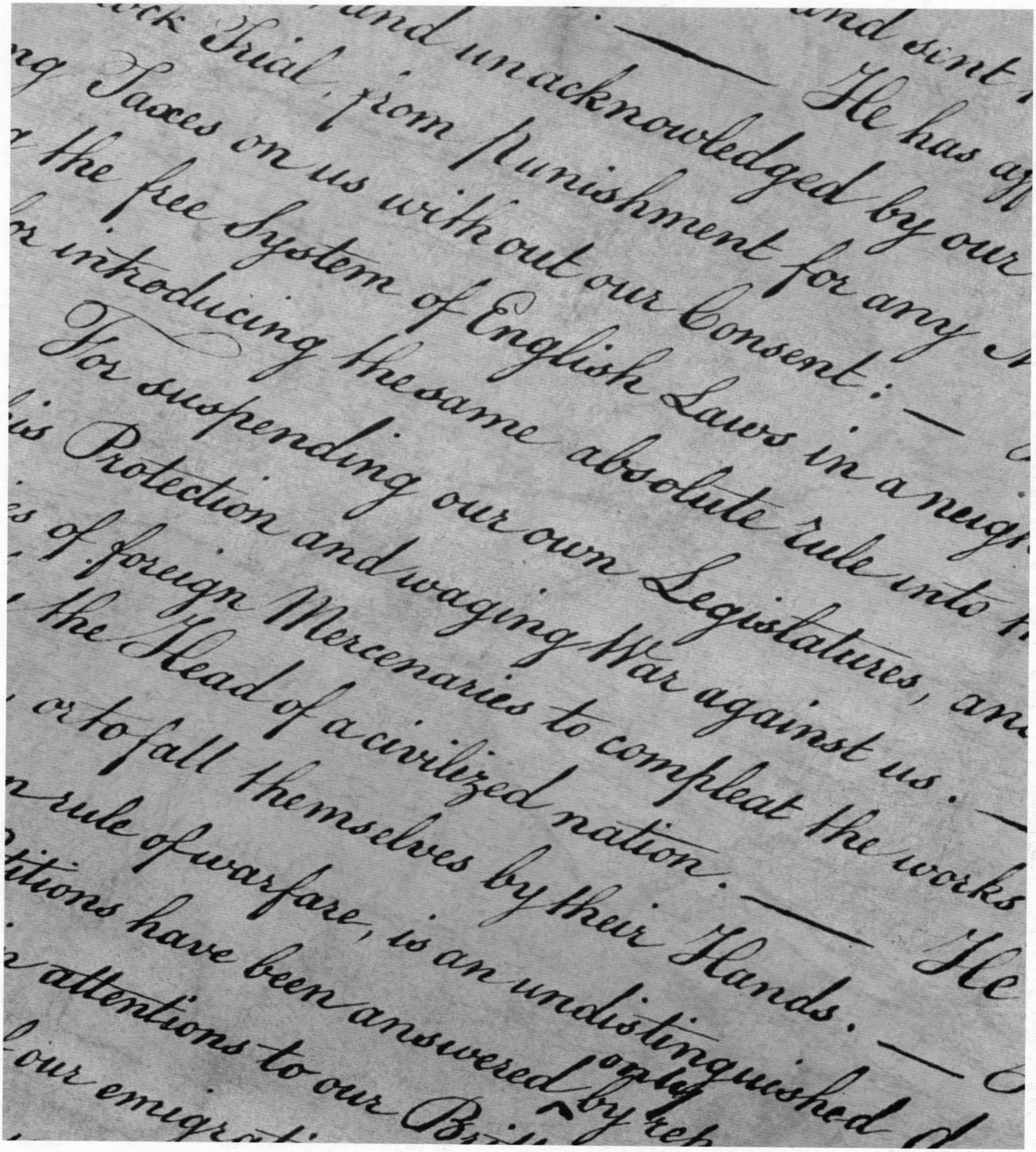

...and sent... *He has a...*

...ock Trial, from Punishment for any... *unacknowledged by our...*

...ng Taxes on us without our Consent:

...the free System of English Laws in a neigh...

...introducing the same absolute rule into...

...suspending our own Legislatures, and...

For...foreign Mercenaries to compleat the works... *Protection and waging War against us.* *...the Head of a civilized nation.* *He...*

...or to fall themselves by their Hands.

...rule of warfare, is an undistinguished...

...tions have been answered by rep...

...attentions to our Bri...

...our emigr...

Peace, contain

a firm reliance on the protection

John Hancock

Rob Morris

Benjamin

Benj. Frank

Samuel Chase

John Mo

Wm Paca

Geo Clymer

Tho. Stone

Jas.

Charles Carroll of Carrollton

Geo.

James

Ge

George Wythe

Richard Henry Lee

Casar Ra

Geo

Th Jefferson

Tho M

Harrison

THE BEGINNING OF A NEW ORDER

The war began with the "shot heard 'round the world" fired at Lexington and Concord on April 19, 1775, when 700 British Army regulars marched out from Boston to confiscate a pair of brass cannons as well as ammunition and capture revolutionary ringleaders Samuel Adams and John Hancock. Colonial militias from the surrounding villages responded to the raid, and their performance showed General George Washington (who would later command the Continental Army) that he had a long way to go before he had professional soldiers with which to fight the redcoats.

The struggle for independence began rather well. The Continental Congress authorized a quickly assembled army under the command of General Washington. Their enthusiasm for the task enabled this band of civilian soldiers to bottle up the British garrison aboard their ships in Boston Harbor. Startled redcoats saw barricaded trenches and artillery appear virtually overnight, aiming directly down into their ships. With Boston bursting at the seams from flocks of colonial volunteers flooding in, eager to get a piece of the action before the war was finished, the British hoisted sail and decamped. A big hurrah went up.

With this victory in hand, even as General Washington struggled to whip his slovenly soldiers into military shape, enflamed revolutionaries such as Thomas Paine reminded the celebrating Congress that the sovereigns who ruled the rest of the world still considered this shameful

BELOW: Colonial militias called out to prevent the capture of weapons and two cannons confront British regulars on the road through Concord, Massachusetts, on April 19, 1775.

business an insult to a legitimate monarch by undeserving rebels. The budding independent state needed evidence of its sincerity, unity, and resolve. To have the United States of America considered a legitimate government that could trade and deal with the likes of Spain, France, Italy, and the Netherlands, Congress had to rapidly craft a manifesto or declaration of independence: a model treaty to collect signatures and good will and a structure connecting the thirteen free and independent states into an entity that could conduct domestic and foreign affairs.

On June 7, 1776, while Boston was celebrating victory and the absence of redcoats in the streets, the Second Continental Congress agreed that the Declaration of Independence had to be linked with the workings of a functioning, centralized government that could deal uniformly with international affairs. Richard Henry Lee of Virginia urged Congress to prepare a plan of confederation of these newly independent states. Three overlapping committees were created to draw up the declaration, the treaty, and these new Articles of Confederation, linking the independent states together.

ABOVE: The statue of King George III is pulled from its pedestal in New York by the Sons of Liberty, to be melted down into shot and cannonballs.

LITERACY IN THE COLONIES

No country on the face of the earth can boast of a larger proportion of inhabitants, versed in the rudiments of science, or fewer, who are not able to read and write their names, than the United States of America.

THE COLUMBIAN PHENIX (SIC) AND BOSTON REVIEW, 1800

In 1762, the American colonies supported about 500,000 colonial citizens. By 1790, the United States of America had doubled its population to one million. Between 1787 and 1795, estimates of literacy—the ability to read and sign one's name—stood at 90 percent. Education was prized and respected in a society that had only a rudimentary knowledge of hygiene and sanitation, and preferred rum, whiskey, and beer to water from tainted wells. Life was as rough as the homespun cloth on their backs and the filth in their streets; understanding the written word was a passport to the future. The printing press was the internet of the eighteenth century. Farm children were homeschooled in their letters and numbers once the cows were bedded down and a fresh supply of wood stood by the hearth. Reading and writing were considered a basic part of women's domestic responsibilities; they often became teachers once the day's chores were done. By the revolutionary period, many colonial women also had a literacy rate of 90 percent. Families brought their Bibles from the old country and attended churches that offered lessons on wilderness life and their new English language.

As early as the seventeenth century, New England, for example, passed an "Old Deluder's Act" requiring the establishment of grammar

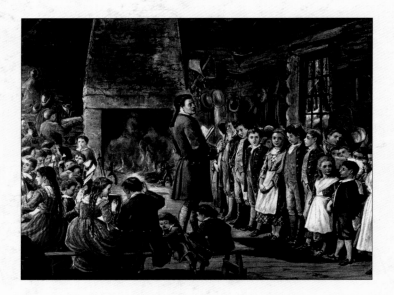

schools to thwart "one chief product of that Old Deluder, Satan, to keep men from knowledge of Scriptures. See that all youth under family government be taught to read perfectly in the English tongue." To these colonists, the written word seasoned their daily work with ideas that inspired discourse and, when the time came, joined a diverse people into a common purpose.

ABOVE: Interior of an eighteenth-century American one-room schoolhouse. Literacy was prized in the colonies and taken west as the country grew.

ARTICLES OF CONFEDERATION

While the articles sounded good on paper, the reality was fraught with conflicting priorities and points of view. After years of living under what they considered a tyrannical central Crown government, the state legislators and delegates to Congress had little appetite for the idea of giving up their rights to some misguided melting pot of other states' interests. So, while the congressional delegates debated and made demands which, in varying degrees, would ensure the retention of their individual sovereignty, the Declaration of Independence committee, under Thomas Jefferson, obtained the necessary approvals for states' signatures by July 4, 1776. That same day, unfortunately, John Dickinson's draft of the National Constitution (later known as the Articles of Confederation) received virtually no support. To make matters worse, the undeterred British had returned.

While the Royal Navy ships of the line pounded New York City, and as the disgorged crack infantry, marines, artillery, and Highlanders were double-timing across Long Island, the Congress of the United States

THOMAS JEFFERSON: AN INTELLECT WRAPPED IN ENIGMA

The Virginian Thomas Jefferson, born April 13, 1743, was not a brilliant orator, yet he is the acknowledged author of the Declaration of Independence. An accomplished scholar, he spoke five languages, was a gifted writer, inventor, philosopher, and naturalist, and assembled a collection of books that became the embryonic Library of Congress. During the revolution, and later as the Constitution was being debated, he served the country as an ambassador in France, and served as the nation's third president from 1801 to 1809.

ABOVE: In 1773, Thomas Jefferson, Richard Henry Lee, Patrick Henry, and Francis Lightfoot meet at the Raven Tavern to establish the Committee of Correspondence.

LEFT: American troops keeping warm during December 1777 at Valley Forge, Pennsylvania, as Congress struggled to feed, house, and clothe them.

FIGHTING FOR FREEDOM WITH THE CONTINENTAL INSURGENCY

The Revolutionary War (1775–83) was fought by the British Army against a "Continental insurgency." Not until the virtual conclusion of the conflict did the American fighting force coalesce into anything like a professional field army. They began with raw militia of farmers, greengrocers, and tinsmiths recruited from towns and villages, mostly without uniforms, with no training in marching, rifle and bayonet drills, or experience with field logistics. Their fighting style imitated the Native Americans, shooting from cover and relying on ambush and hit-and-run tactics to open-field confrontation. Militia enlistments were governed by planting and cattle herding seasons, causing whole regiments to disband and go home to tend to their fields in the middle of a campaign. Militia members received no pay except for their weapons, food, and forage for their personal horses. They paid a fine if they failed to show up for muster. Regular soldiers received a bounty for enlisting and Continental paper script for pay, which eventually became useless as it devalued due to lack of gold in the treasury. The Continental chief of artillery (Knox) was a former bookseller who learned his military skills from published writings and immediate experience.

The Continental insurgency showed such poor marksmanship with muskets, Washington had them fire shotgun loads of three .40-caliber buckshot and one .69-caliber ball in each musket cartridge. The British considered these cartridges to be a war crime and retaliated with harsh treatment of prisoners. The majority of American muskets and bayonets were smuggled through the British

blockade into American ports by agents of foreign countries. Officers from foreign armies led many of our troops in battle and taught our ranks how to fight and drill as our soldiers were pursued from one end of the country to another. Near the end of the war, the French committed a surge of infantry, cavalry, and artillery to help Washington achieve his ultimate victory at Yorktown in 1783.

ABOVE: The surrender of Lord Cornwallis' army at Yorktown, Virginia, in 1781 to the American-French Alliance, effectively ending the revolution begun in 1775.

packed its bags and spare wigs and ran for their lives. By November 1777, as they began their seven-year war on the run, they had cobbled together a workable Articles of Confederation for their home legislatures to consider.

Our government-on-the-run continued to revise the articles until 1781, slowed mostly by some states' land disputes, which carried on during the war and in the years directly after. These "landed states" had extended their western borders well past the original surveyed boundaries, back to the Mississippi River and edging up to Spanish Louisiana. By 1787, however, Virginia, South Carolina, North Carolina, Georgia, New York, and Connecticut relinquished their claims, given that the newly formed articles allowed each state only one vote, and size didn't matter. With these articles begrudgingly ratified, states began printing their own money, creating their own trade tariffs, and requiring foreign governments

to present credentials to each state legislature in order to be recognized as a trading and diplomatic partner of that state.

The Articles of Confederation were considered a "league of friendship"—a club of sorts with individual members, each with a personal agenda. Article Two defined the distribution of power: "Each state retains its sovereignty, freedom, and independence, and every Power, jurisdiction, and right, which is not by this confederation expressly delegated to the United States in Congress assembled."

Each state also raised its own militia, mostly a ragged collection of volunteers handling a mix of shoulder weapons, from captured British Brown Bess muskets to Kentucky long rifles. They elected their own officers and came and went from the ranks as the planting seasons demanded they return home.

ARTICLES OF CONFEDERATION

The Articles were created out of a need to have "a plan of confederacy for securing the freedom, sovereignty, and independence of the United States."

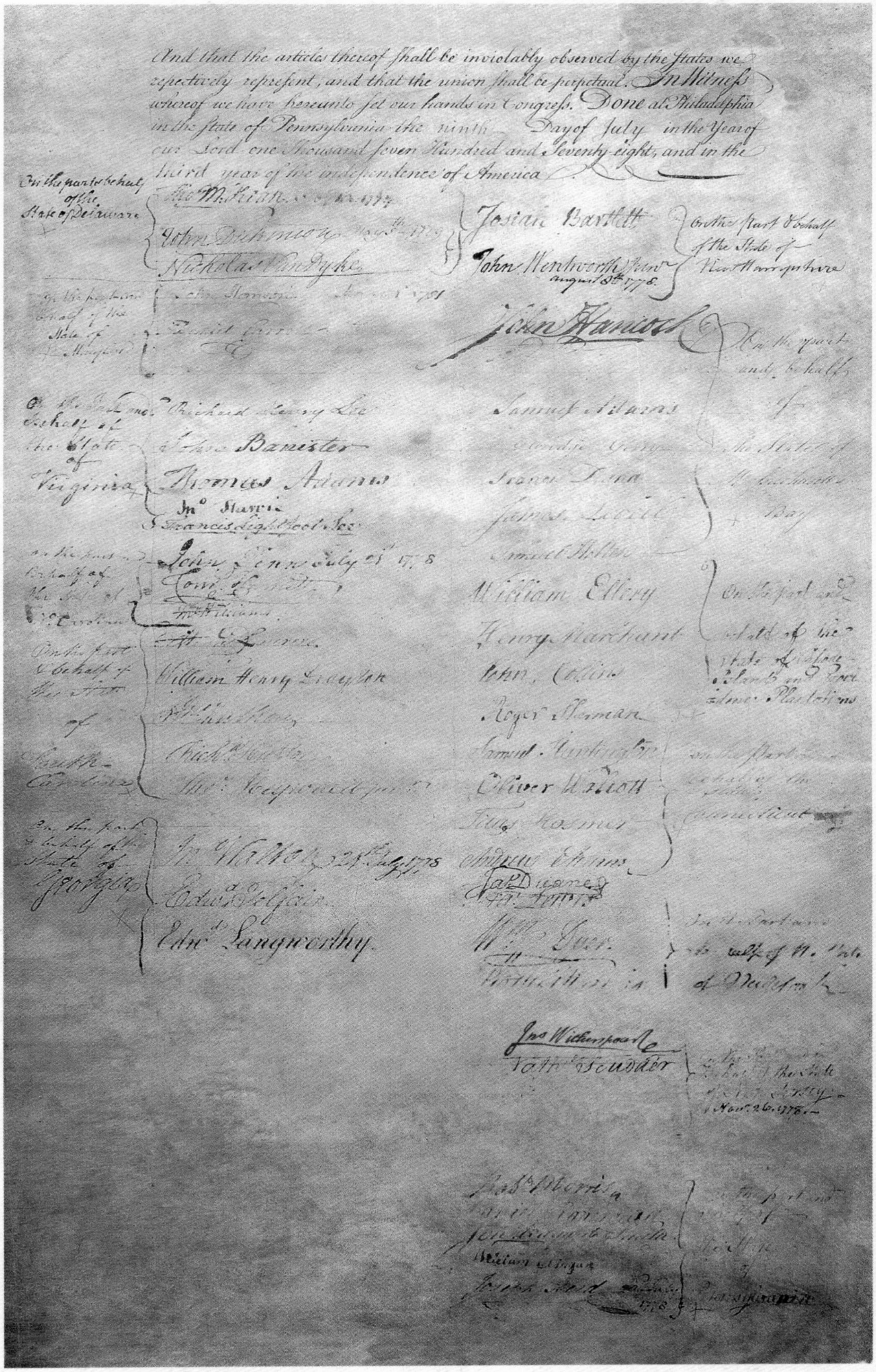

And that the articles thereof shall be inviolably observed by the states we respectively represent, and that the union shall be perpetual. In Witness whereof we have hereunto set our hands in Congress. Done at Philadelphia in the state of Pennsylvania the ninth Day of July in the Year of our Lord one Thousand seven Hundred and Seventy eight, and in the third year of the independence of America

On the part & behalf of the State of Delaware

Tho M Kean Feb 12 1779
John Dickinson May 5th 1779
Nicholas Van Dyke

On the part and behalf of the State of Maryland

Josiah Bartlett
John Wentworth Junr August 8th 1778

On the part & behalf of the State of New Hampshire

John Hancock

On the part and behalf of

On the part and behalf of the State of Virginia

Richard Henry Lee
John Banister
Thomas Adams
Jno Harvie
Francis Lightfoot Lee

Samuel Adams

the State of

On the part and behalf of the State of North Carolina

John Penn July 21 1778
Corns Harnett
Jno Williams

Samuel Huntington

On the part & behalf of the State of South Carolina

William Henry Drayton
Jno Mathews
Richd Hutson
Thos Heyward junr

William Ellery
Henry Marchant
John Collins
Roger Sherman
Samuel Huntington
Oliver Wolcott
Titus Hosmer
Andrew Adams

On the part and behalf of the State of Rhode Island and Providence Plantations

On the part & behalf of the State of Connecticut

On the part & behalf of the State of Georgia

Jno Walton 24th July 1778
Edwd Telfair
Edwd Langworthy

Jas Duane
Fra Lewis
Wm Duer
Gouv Morris

On the part and behalf of the State of New York

Jno Witherspoon
Nathl Scudder

On the part & behalf of the State of New Jersey Novr 26 1778

Robt Morris
Daniel Roberdeau
Jona Bayard Smith
William Clingan
Joseph Reed 22d July 1778

On the part and behalf of the State of Pennsylvania

A Growing Nationalism

The individual states also failed to contribute money requested by Congress to pay off war debts, back pay to shoeless veterans and threadbare officers pawning their swords for bread money. The government printed more than $240 million in cash—the bills were called "Continentals," designed by Benjamin Franklin. The states added another $200 million of their own paper notes. Within a short time, foreign governments began demanding that the eight million in gold they had put into the pot be returned. This new republic was quickly considered to be the "sick sister" of the world powers who would soon be returning to Great Britain's colonial fold.

Though Congress had established departments for Foreign Affairs, War, and Finance with "superintendents" manning each post, the central government was, by design, kept weak and dependent upon the states' tolerance. However, amid the flurry of state constitutions penned during the life of the articles, some interesting issues were dealt with. While the power of governors and judges were severely limited due to bad past experience with the Crown's heavy hand, the people came to rely on their legislatures for representation. These bodies could also declare war, control the courts, conduct foreign relations, and invoke bills of rights that both protected the people and closely monitored their representatives as well. Virtually every step in the chain of government was seasoned with a universal distaste for outside control.

A broad spectrum of advances in political and civic life began to unfold. Many of the states, for example, took advantage of their new freedoms and plunged into social reform. Thinly populated western counties were apportioned equal representation. Freedom of religion and separation of church and state found support in law by such devices as Thomas Jefferson's 1786 Statute of Religious Liberty, "Truth is great and will prevail if left to herself." By 1780, most of the northern states had abolished slavery, though New York's emancipation waited until 1799 and New Jersey stalled until 1804. Their economic reliance on the work of slaves in the mills and fields of the southern states continued, however, until the end of the 1861–65 Civil War.

By the conclusion of the revolution, as with all wars, women stepped up to manage large farms, stores, and businesses while the men were away. These new responsibilities altered the balance of power in many households and estates. The novelty of female education caught on as their abilities were recognized and, though voting rights were a few generations away, American women's days devoted exclusively to the domestic sphere were waning.

If the Articles of Confederation had any redeeming characteristics, the foremost had to be the growth of American nationalism. The revolution was fought not because all the states were driven by a national desire to come together. Quite the opposite; the separate colonies came together in order to slip from under the thumb of British rule. Only during the conflict did a sense of real unity develop that held them together when Great Britain washed its hands of the whole business owing to the cost and a lack of popular support at

---

ABOVE: Independence Hall, Philadelphia, in 1778, where the Declaration of Independence was signed in 1776 and the Constitutional Convention was held in 1787.

DANIEL SHAY SAVES THE U.S.A.

In 1786, a mob of disgruntled farmers staged "a little rebellion," as described by Thomas Jefferson while at a safe distance in Paris. This band of angry tax dodgers also managed to save the fragile United States from itself. Daniel Shay, a Revolutionary War veteran from Pelham, who fought at Ticonderoga, Bunker Hill, and Saratoga, assumed leadership of these Massachusetts farmers who felt they were footing an unjustly onerous tax bill so their state could balance its budget.

In August, mobs of indignant taxpayers closed the courts of several towns such as Pittsfield and Northampton. Following Shay, they marched to the capitol at Springfield to present their grievances to the legislature. Seeing this mob turn up on their doorstep, the resident lawmakers sent for local troops. Shay and his followers stormed the arsenal to arm themselves and battle was joined. The state militia killed three of the protestors with cannon shot, routing the farmers and ending the rebellion.

The story did not end there. This dustup reached many state halls of government and the cry of "liberty gone mad!" went up. Even George Washington remarked, "We are fast verging on anarchy and confusion!" The general lesson seemed to be that liberty had become an invitation to home rule, and a stronger central government was needed to keep a firm hand on the fledgling American ship in its labored process of creating a new state.

RIGHT: A colored nineteenth-century engraving illustrates a fight outside the courthouse at Springfield between opposing factions in Shay's Rebellion.

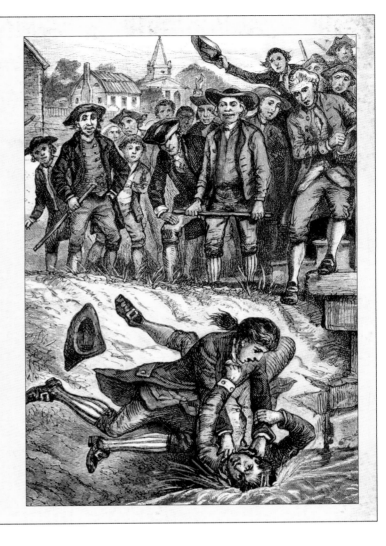

home, with little prospect for a decisive conclusion, and resistance buttressed by the Continental alliance with the French and Dutch. The Articles of Confederation was a conflicted first pass at a representative government that was, by design, not too central, too powerful, or too heavy-handed. It was written by brilliant men of hearty stock who were looking to craft new rules for changing times, inspired by fresh theories recently penned over brandy and cigars by their counterparts in the cafés and salons of Europe.

In 1786, stirred by discord among the states, a group gathered in Annapolis, Maryland, to attend the Meeting of Commissioners to Remedy Defects of the Federal Government. Twelve delegates from five states showed up: New York, New Jersey, Pennsylvania, Delaware, and Virginia. Ostensibly the discussion was aimed at trade barriers that interfered with commerce between the revenue-hungry individual states. When they found the room mostly empty, the assembled commissioners remained for three days, finally deciding a more inclusive convention was necessary to create any substantive agreement. The agenda lurking beneath talks about import-export tariffs on potatoes and calico cloth was the deconstruction of the failed Articles of Confederation.

The most determined plotter in this shadow scheme was Alexander Hamilton, the Federalist firebrand of the New York delegation. He was a strong supporter of an independent federal government that represented all the states. His resolution in the report submitted from the Annapolis convention to the central government offices in New York City and the state legislatures suggested a more representative meeting to be held in May 1787 in Philadelphia. Their stated goal was to smooth out the rough spots, loopholes, and friction points in the Articles of Confederation, making the rules of the game more fair and equitable to all the states.

Within this straightforward review-and-repair project, gears began turning within gears, and in May virtually every one of the delegates arrived with the goal of throwing out the articles and drawing up a new constitution. A cloak of secrecy was dropped over the proceedings in Philadelphia's Independence Hall—formerly the State House—so freely expressed ideas, appeals, rejections, and tantrums could be uttered without fear of public backlash, ridicule, or misinterpretation.

2 | A DOCUMENT WHOSE TIME HAD COME

DELEGATES GATHER FOR A CONSTITUTIONAL CONVENTION

Delegates to the Constitutional Convention meeting in May 1787 had a formidable task ahead of them. Shy and soft-spoken James Madison, a Virginia legislator and delegate to the Continental Congress in 1780, became the major force in fashioning the new charter. So concerned that their efforts would not fail, he arrived two weeks before the other delegates and drafted his Virginia Plan, which became the basic outline for the final Constitution.

In addition to Madison, the delegates included other colonial "celebrities."

George Washington, elected president of the convention, had distinguished himself in the French and Indian War (Seven Years' War) and had led the United States to victory in the Revolutionary War. Revered by his fellow delegates, he became the obvious choice to preside over the convention as they drafted the Constitution during that hot summer in 1787. He had a calm demeanor as he observed the proceedings, yet in his quietude, the members sensed his strength. In most debates he made it clear he favored a strong central government.

Benjamin Franklin, inventor, author, politician, and philosopher, had aged considerably by the time of the Constitutional Convention. As ambassador to France he had negotiated a military alliance with the French during the critical days of the American Revolution. Despite his advanced years, his zeal for building a nation dedicated to preserving freedom for all its citizens still burned in his heart. He served as an honorary delegate to the convention and was an outspoken advocate for the common people.

Alexander Hamilton, born in the British West Indies of illegitimate parentage, was educated in the United States and served as aide-de-camp to George Washington during the revolution. Later, he sought to revoke the Articles of Confederation in favor of a document outlining a strong central government with taxing bodies and a court system. His persuasive rhetoric at the Annapolis convention—a gathering of politicians who were concerned about navigation on the Potomac River—helped generate support for Congress to call for a constitutional convention.

Gouverneur Morris from Philadelphia was one of the convention's more boisterous delegates, in spite of struggling with physical problems—a peg leg and shriveled arm—and wrote several sections of the Constitution, including the Preamble.

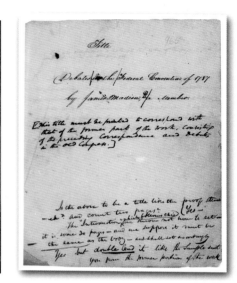

ABOVE LEFT: James Madison, fourth president of the United States, also known as the "Father of the Constitution."

ABOVE RIGHT: John C. Payne's copy of James Madison's "Original Notes on Debates in the Federal Convention" of 1787. Madison's notes were considered the most complete record of the convention's proceedings.

OPPOSITE: American general George Washington presides over the Constitutional Convention, which took place from May 25 through September 17, 1787.

CLOAKED IN SECRECY

The delegates to the Constitutional Convention actually met in secret, fearing that if the word spread that they were redoing the laws of the land, citizens might protest to prevent the subversive establishment of another monarchy. At the time they didn't even use the word "convention." When delegates corresponded with friends, they chose their words carefully. People believed that they were simply making changes to the Articles of Confederation. Most Americans felt that the Articles of Confederation sufficed as a governing document, but few realized that the articles failed to establish a system of collecting taxes, defending the country, and paying debts.

From May through September 1787, the delegates debated, fought, shouted, and pondered. The Articles of Confederation had proved weak and clumsy, giving more power to the states (who often fought among themselves) and little to the national government. The country had no way to regulate commerce, no taxing power, no way to enforce congressional acts, etc. The United States needed a stronger central government. It was difficult to agree on some issues, although with few exceptions, they all knew they must establish a strong federal system with limited powers—yet one that could work with independent state governments—and the group had loosely divided itself between Federalists and those who favored states' rights to protect against a possible despotic central government.

But it was Madison who contributed the most to the Constitution and later argued for the Bill of Rights (the Constitution's first ten amendments) to be added. The Virginia state constitution, written by George Mason in early 1776, became the guide for the final U.S. Bill of Rights. Of the seventy-four delegates named to the convention, fifty-five attended. Rhode Island sent no delegates.

NOTICEABLE BY THEIR ABSENCE

At the time of the Constitutional Convention, Thomas Jefferson, author of the Declaration of Independence, was situated in Paris, negotiating commerce treaties and loans to convince the European countries that the United States was solvent and trustworthy. Nevertheless, he managed to supply Madison with a wealth of material on political theory to help guide him in his efforts. John Adams, a Federalist and respected Founding Father who had helped draft the Declaration of Independence, was serving as diplomat to Britain at the time of the convention. Although his fellow Americans missed him, they were bolstered by his letters of encouragement, and his book *A Defence of the Constitutions of Government of the United States of America* was circulated through the members. Delegates praised or censured it depending on their view of Federalism.

THE U.S. CONSTITUTION

Constitution of the United States. After the Constitution was approved by the delegates in
1787, it was sent to the thirteen states for ratification and became law in 1788.

United States; If he approve he shall sign it, but if not he shall return it, with his Objections to that House in which it shall have originated, who shall enter the Objections at large on their Journal, and proceed to reconsider it. If after such Reconsideration two thirds of that House shall agree to pass the Bill, it shall be sent, together with the Objections, to the other House, by which it shall likewise be reconsidered, and if approved by two thirds of that House, it shall become a Law. But in all such Cases the Votes of both Houses shall be determined by yeas and Nays, and the Names of the Persons voting for and against the Bill shall be entered on the Journal of each House respectively. If any Bill shall not be returned by the President within ten Days (Sundays excepted) after it shall have been presented to him, the Same shall be a Law, in like Manner as if he had signed it, unless the Congress by their Adjournment prevent its Return, in which Case it shall not be a Law.

Every Order, Resolution, or Vote to which the Concurrence of the Senate and House of Representatives may be necessary (except on a question of Adjournment) shall be presented to the President of the United States; and before the Same shall take Effect, shall be approved by him, or being disapproved by him, shall be repassed by two thirds of the Senate and House of Representatives, according to the Rules and Limitations prescribed in the Case of a Bill.

Section. 8. The Congress shall have Power To lay and collect Taxes, Duties, Imposts and Excises, to pay the Debts and provide for the common Defence and general Welfare of the United States; but all Duties, Imposts and Excises shall be uniform throughout the United States;

To borrow Money on the credit of the United States;

To regulate Commerce with foreign Nations, and among the several States, and with the Indian Tribes;

To establish an uniform Rule of Naturalization, and uniform Laws on the subject of Bankruptcies throughout the United States;

To coin Money, regulate the Value thereof, and of foreign Coin, and fix the Standard of Weights and Measures;

To provide for the Punishment of counterfeiting the Securities and current Coin of the United States;

To establish Post Offices and post Roads;

To promote the Progress of Science and useful Arts, by securing for limited Times to Authors and Inventors the exclusive Right to their respective Writings and Discoveries;

To constitute Tribunals inferior to the supreme Court;

To define and punish Piracies and Felonies committed on the high Seas, and Offences against the Law of Nations;

To declare War, grant Letters of Marque and Reprisal, and make Rules concerning Captures on Land and Water;

To raise and support Armies, but no Appropriation of Money to that Use shall be for a longer Term than two Years;

To provide and maintain a Navy;

To make Rules for the Government and Regulation of the land and naval Forces;

To provide for calling forth the Militia to execute the Laws of the Union, suppress Insurrections and repel Invasions;

To provide for organizing, arming, and disciplining, the Militia, and for governing such Part of them as may be employed in the Service of the United States, reserving to the States respectively, the Appointment of the Officers, and the Authority of training the Militia according to the discipline prescribed by Congress;

To exercise exclusive Legislation in all Cases whatsoever, over such District (not exceeding ten Miles square) as may, by Cession of particular States, and the Acceptance of Congress, become the Seat of the Government of the United States, and to exercise like Authority over all Places purchased by the Consent of the Legislature of the State in which the Same shall be, for the Erection of Forts, Magazines, Arsenals, dock-Yards, and other needful Buildings;—And

To make all Laws which shall be necessary and proper for carrying into Execution the foregoing Powers, and all other Powers vested by this Constitution in the Government of the United States, or in any Department or Officer thereof.

Section. 9. The Migration or Importation of such Persons as any of the States now existing shall think proper to admit, shall not be prohibited by the Congress prior to the Year one thousand eight hundred and eight, but a Tax or duty may be imposed on such Importation, not exceeding ten dollars for each Person.

The Privilege of the Writ of Habeas Corpus shall not be suspended, unless when in Cases of Rebellion or Invasion the public Safety may require it.

No Bill of Attainder or ex post facto Law shall be passed.

No Capitation, or other direct, Tax shall be laid, unless in Proportion to the Census or Enumeration herein before directed to be taken.

No Tax or Duty shall be laid on Articles exported from any State.

No Preference shall be given by any Regulation of Commerce or Revenue to the Ports of one State over those of another: nor shall Vessels bound to, or from, one State, be obliged to enter, clear, or pay Duties in another.

No Money shall be drawn from the Treasury, but in Consequence of Appropriations made by Law; and a regular Statement and Account of the Receipts and Expenditures of all public Money shall be published from time to time.

No Title of Nobility shall be granted by the United States: And no Person holding any Office of Profit or Trust under them, shall, without the Consent of the Congress, accept of any present, Emolument, Office, or Title, of any kind whatever, from any King, Prince, or foreign State.

Section. 10. No State shall enter into any Treaty, Alliance, or Confederation; grant Letters of Marque and Reprisal; coin Money; emit Bills of Credit; make any Thing but gold and silver Coin a Tender in Payment of Debts; pass any Bill of Attainder, ex post facto Law, or Law impairing the Obligation of Contracts, or grant any Title of Nobility.

No State shall, without the Consent of the Congress, lay any Imposts or Duties on Imports or Exports, except what may be absolutely necessary for executing its inspection Laws: and the net Produce of all Duties and Imposts, laid by any State on Imports or Exports, shall be for the Use of the Treasury of the United States; and all such Laws shall be subject to the Revision and Controul of the Congress.

No State shall, without the Consent of Congress, lay any Duty of Tonnage, keep Troops, or Ships of War in time of Peace, enter into any Agreement or Compact with another State, or with a foreign Power, or engage in War, unless actually invaded, or in such imminent Danger as will not admit of delay.

Article. II.

Section. 1. The executive Power shall be vested in a President of the United States of America. He shall hold his Office during the Term of four Years, and, together with the Vice President, chosen for the same Term, be elected, as follows:

Each State shall appoint, in such Manner as the Legislature thereof may direct, a Number of Electors, equal to the whole Number of Senators and Representatives to which the State may be entitled in the Congress: but no Senator or Representative, or Person holding an Office of Trust or Profit under the United States, shall be appointed an Elector.

The Electors shall meet in their respective States, and vote by Ballot for two Persons, of whom one at least shall not be an Inhabitant of

THE GREAT COMPROMISE

Two issues dominated the convention: What powers should be given to the national government, and who should control this government? They could all agree on the first question: Congress should levy taxes, control commerce, issue money, make treaties, maintain an army, and suppress insurrection. The second caused several weeks of heated discussion. Larger states favored the Virginia Plan: representation determined by population. Smaller states wanted the New Jersey Plan, which allowed for equal representation. Day after day the arguments raged on, and one delegate feared that if there were no concessions, "Our business must soon be at an end." After the larger states threatened to walk out, cooler heads prevailed and the delegates adopted the Great Compromise. The new legislature would have the number of legislators in the lower house—the House of Representatives—based on population and elected by popular vote. The members in the Senate—the upper house—would have two members, chosen by the legislators. (This was changed in 1913 with the Seventeenth Amendment. It stated that two senators would be elected from each state to serve for a period of six years.)

Then there was the problem of slaves. At that time, about one in seven Americans was a slave. The northern states felt that each slave should be counted as one in order to determine the amount of taxes a state should pay. Naturally, where taxes were concerned, the southern states wanted to delete slaves from the count, but thought slaves could be included when it came to determining representation. The Three-Fifths Compromise settled the question; slaves were considered only three-fifths of a person, for both taxes and representation.

The method for choosing a president proved to be far more cumbersome. No one had any experience in electing a leader and giving him the power to command the armed forces, deal in international relations, appoint judges, or veto laws passed by Congress. Each state would choose electors, equal to the number of representatives it had in Congress. These electors would vote for two persons for president. The person receiving the most votes would become president; the one with the next highest number of votes would be vice president. In 1804, the

TOP RIGHT: Image of George Mason, author of the Virginia Declaration of Rights, which provided the basis for the Bill of Rights.

BOTTOM RIGHT: George Washington's copy of the first printed draft of the United States Constitution, August 6, 1787, with corrections in Washington's hand.

OPPOSITE: Hand-colored engraving, *In the Reading Room of an 18th Century New York Coffee House.* The Constitution was perused in taverns, coffee houses, homes, and other places where people gathered.

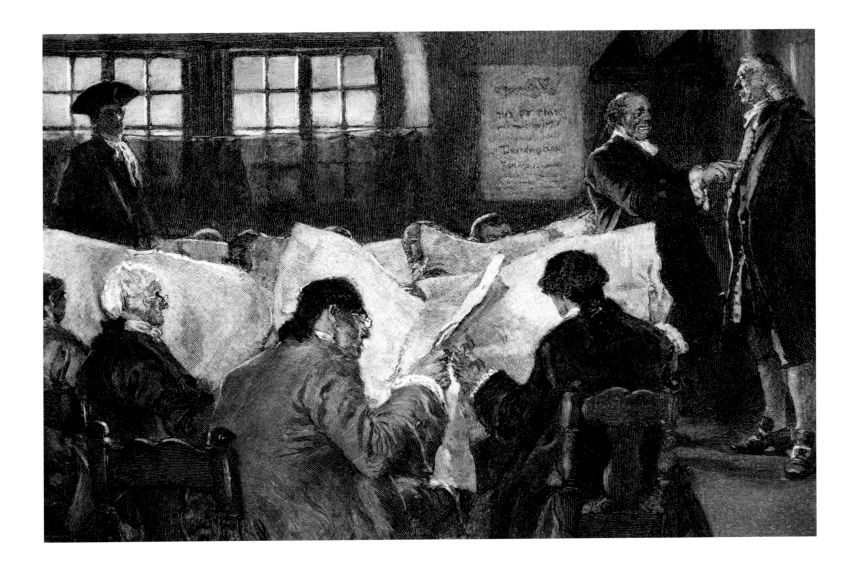

Twelfth Amendment determined that electors should vote separately for president and vice president. Not long after, the country evolved into a two-party system, and now the presidential and vice presidential candidates campaign for office together. The Electoral College still determines the election outcome, and if there is a dispute, the House of Representatives determines the outcome. The Supreme Court was established to adjudicate laws and treaties of the United States, something that did not appear in the Articles of Confederation. Congress didn't say that the court could declare a state or federal law void, but over the years, the court has used its judicial review rights in determining certain cases.

This system of checks and balances has served the country well, even during the most difficult periods, when our nation's government might have dissolved. The document that would determine whether America's new political system would survive a few decades or far into the twenty-first century was completed on September 17, 1787. But their job wasn't over. Now they had to sell it to the rest of the country.

THE SLAVERY ISSUE

It would seem that a country that had so recently secured its freedom would draft a document granting release for its own slaves. At the time, slaves were considered a commodity and Congress had the right to establish import taxes on them. It was agreed that these taxes would be limited to ten dollars a head and in return the southern states agreed to stop the import of slaves by 1808. In the end, economy was the driving force in the slavery issue, and since it was considered a commodity, Congress controlled the slave trade. Still, many delegates voiced vehemently against the slavery system, including the blustery Gouverneur Morris, shouting while balancing himself with his cane, "Wretched Africans! The vassalage of the poor has ever been the favorite offspring of aristocracy!"

3 | ONE SIZE FITS ALL

SELLING THE CONSTITUTION AND THE PROMISE OF A BILL OF RIGHTS

John Jay said it best: "Let Congress Legislate, let others execute, let others Judge." Following the Constitution's dictates in Article VII ("the Ratification of the Convention of nine States, shall be sufficient for the Establishment of this Constitution…"), the document's framers now needed ratification by state conventions. Copies were loaded into saddlebags and taken by coach down winding dirt roads for delivery to delegates in each state, who voted to accept or reject it. Those who opposed it were known as Anti-Federalists and these generally consisted of farmers, debtors, and laborers; in other words, people who valued their new liberties and feared the country might evolve into a monarchy. The Federalists, usually men of wealth and position, desired a stable, central, and efficient body of lawmakers.

The promise of adding amendments that clearly gave certain powers to the states—such as the power to enact laws not in conflict with the Constitution—helped sell the Constitution in most states. Over the next few months, the conventions held in Delaware, Pennsylvania, New Jersey,

Georgia, and Connecticut quickly voted to ratify this new document. Others soon followed, and by June 1788, nine states had voted in favor, making the Constitution legal.

New York, however, had yet to accept the Constitution as it stood. The majority of laborers and merchants in New York City favored the Constitution, but the rural population in outlying areas wasn't so certain it would work. Although Alexander Hamilton hadn't been a proponent of the new document, he, along with John Jay and James Madison (all using

---

OPPOSITE: Table of contents and first page of the first edition of *The Federalist*, a series of essays in favor of a federal constitution. The papers were published in newspapers and later into books.

BELOW: *The Scene at the Signing of the Constitution*, with George Washington presiding. The official journals and papers of the convention were given to Washington for safekeeping until the Constitution was officially ratified.

the common name "Publius"), created the Federalist Papers, essays explaining the need for a strong central government while pointing out that the system of checks and balances could work. Hamilton launched a nearly one-man campaign across the state, plying some opponents with free meals or threats to have New York City secede if they didn't go along with the rest of the country. It worked. In July 1788, New York ratified the Constitution.

The promise of a second convention to draft amendments clearly defining civil liberties also helped Virginia, Rhode Island, and North Carolina sign on. By May 1790, all thirteen states had ratified the Constitution.

By April 1789, once the old Congress had slipped away, the new one gathered in New York and managed to hammer out the first of many issues, namely, how to address the country's leader. John Adams thought "His Elective Highness" or "His Excellency" had a nice ring to it. After three weeks, Washington himself settled the issue. He didn't want to appear as a "king" or "monarch," which might imply despotism. Instead, he preferred "president." The Electoral College met and unanimously chose George Washington as president of the new nation, with John Adams as vice president. On April 14, 1789, Washington, with some trepidation about the momentous task before him, left Mount Vernon for the trip to New York, the nation's temporary capital. He was inaugurated on April 30. Knowing that most of his actions could set a precedent for future leaders, he said, "The eyes of Argus are upon me and no slip will pass unnoticed." He began by choosing a group of advisors, known as his cabinet, an action that presidents have followed to the present day. He appointed Thomas Jefferson as Secretary of State, Alexander Hamilton as Secretary of the Treasury, and General Henry Knox as Secretary of War.

After settling in, the new congressional leaders set to work drafting the promised series of amendments, later known as the Bill of Rights, spelling out in greater detail the purpose of the Constitution, guaranteeing U.S. citizens certain personal and property rights. They also lost no time in appointing a postmaster general and passing a Judiciary Act that established thirteen federal district courts. In one of his first duties as president, George Washington appointed John Jay as Chief Justice of the Supreme Court.

THE

FEDERALIST:

ADDRESSED TO THE

PEOPLE OF THE STATE OF NEW-YORK.

NUMBER I.

Introduction.

AFTER an unequivocal experience of the inefficacy of the subsisting federal government, you are called upon to deliberate on a new constitution for the United States of America. The subject speaks its own importance; comprehending in its consequences, nothing less than the existence of the UNION, the safety and welfare of the parts of which it is composed, the fate of an empire, in many respects, the most interesting in the world. It has been frequently remarked, that it seems to have been reserved to the people of this country, by their conduct and example, to decide the important question, whether societies of men are really capable or not, of establishing good government from reflection and choice, or whether they are forever destined to depend, for their political constitutions, on accident and force. If there be any truth in the remark, the crisis, at which we are arrived, may with propriety be regarded as the æra in which

A   that

HE KNEW HIS ROLE

As president, George Washington took the limits of his power seriously. He left Congress to its own devices and never expressed criticism or praise for a member of the legislature. A veto, he believed, should be employed only if a law in some way violated the Constitution, and he never discussed any proceedings going on in Congress. This did not prevent him from an occasional display of temper. At a cabinet meeting where he was subject to some criticism, he shouted that he would rather "be on his farm than to be made emperor of the world."

ABOVE: George Washington, leader of the Continental Army and the nation's first president.

ESTABLISHING A FINANCIAL SYSTEM

As with all nations, the United States needed money. The country had accumulated some $52 million in debt to foreign countries and other Americans, not including state debts, which added about $25 million to the total. Congress set up a system of tariffs on imported goods and the Tonnage Act, which, while taxing Americans a small amount, set much higher rates for foreign ships. Alexander Hamilton proposed a complicated funding structure to pay back American speculators who had purchased IOUs to help finance the revolution. Essentially, the IOUs would be exchanged for interest-bearing bonds. He felt that if a federally chartered banking corporation received capital from the Treasury and private investors, it could then lend money to businessmen, which in turn would stimulate commerce and manufacturing. Hamilton envisioned an industrial America, providing jobs for everyone, thus giving the country a stable and growing economy. However, this bold plan didn't gain supporters easily, since the continued fear of "centralization" prevailed. James Madison and Secretary of State Thomas Jefferson were its harshest critics. Jefferson, in particular, foresaw industrialization breeding clusters of great cities full of

THE WHISKEY REBELLION

After Alexander Hamilton's Whiskey Tax was passed, farmers in western Pennsylvania protested, flatly refusing to pay it. During that time they also burned the homes of revenue agents and finally, in 1794, 7,000 men descended on Pittsburgh with the intention of burning down the town. It took only the sight of artillery and the promise of whiskey to mollify them. However, George Washington insisted on enforcing the law. Militiamen, numbering 13,000, stormed into western Pennsylvania. The rebels knew they were outnumbered and fled. In the end, most Pennsylvanians (especially non-distillers) agreed that the tax, though disliked, should be paid. Ironically, during Thomas Jefferson's presidency, the Whiskey Tax was repealed.

AN EXCISEMAN. Carrying off two Kegs of Whiskey, is pursued by two farmers, intending to tar and feather him. he runs for 'Squire Vultures to divide with him; but is met on the way by his evil genius who claps an hook in his nose. leads him off to a Gallows, where he is immediately hanged.

corruption and crime. Madison, a southerner, felt the plan benefited speculators from the North. Hamilton finally struck a deal with Madison and Jefferson. He told Jefferson that unless Congress passed the proposal, the Union was in danger of collapse. To satisfy Madison, a Virginian, Hamilton suggested that the capital be moved temporarily to Philadelphia, then to an area between the two southern states: Virginia and Maryland. The bill to charter a national bank was shoved through Congress, but again it took a considerable amount of urging by Hamilton to convince President Washington (who feared that the Constitution did not allow for the government to exercise this power) to sign it.

The Whiskey Tax was passed in 1791. This was an excise on distilled liquors, which in turn paid interest on funded debt, but would later cause one of the first tests of the new Constitution. The Coinage Act the following year erased the specter of the old Continental and established the dollar, composed of dimes and cents and backed by gold or silver.

Washington exercised his presidential prerogative of negotiating treaties when he sent John Jay to England to settle some still-outstanding problems between the two countries. Among these were Great Britain's occupation of Western military posts, a boundary issue with Canada, and the seizing of American ships on the high seas. The British agreed to meet with Jay, fearing that the United States might align itself with France's new republic. Yet Great Britain had recently enjoyed some victories against other European countries, so they could afford to refuse some of America's requests. Jay was received graciously and returned with many concessions. The British would depart from its Western posts and pay American ship owners for the ships they'd taken in the West Indies. They would not, however, honor American neutrality rights on the high seas. There were several restrictions on American commerce in the West Indies, for example. Jay agreed that the country would pay pre-Revolutionary War debts owed to British merchants, making some states angry, especially when the British refused to pay for slaves that they had "abducted." Although a storm of protest arose among the population, Washington accepted the treaty and, after a long and contentious deliberation, it was ratified by the Senate in June 1795. For the time being, another war, which neither nation could afford, was averted.

By the end of Washington's administration, the country had started the first of many westward movements. "I believe scarcely anything short of a Chinese Wall or a line of Troops will restrain…the Encroachment of Settlers," Washington said in 1796, his last full year in office.

OPPOSITE: An antigovernment cartoon of 1794 siding with the Pennsylvania organizers of the Whiskey Rebellion who opposed the taxation power of Congress.
TOP RIGHT: The Coinage Act, signed March 3, 1791, establishing the United States Mint.
BOTTOM RIGHT: Nineteenth-century color engraving of Thomas Jefferson's followers burning John Jay in effigy following the treaty with England of 1794. Many felt the treaty gave too many concessions to the British.

Congreſs of the United States:

AT THE THIRD SESSION,

Begun and held at the City of Philadelphia, on Monday the ſixth of December, one thouſand ſeven hundred and ninety.

———

RESOLVED by the SENATE and HOUSE of REPRESENTATIVES of the United States of America in Congreſs aſſembled, That a mint ſhall be eſtabliſhed under ſuch regulations as ſhall be directed by law.

Reſolved, That the Preſident of the United States be, and he is hereby authorized to cauſe to be engaged, ſuch principal artiſts as ſhall be neceſſary to carry the preceeding reſolution into effect, and to ſtipulate the terms and conditions of their ſervice, and alſo to cauſe to be procured ſuch apparatus as ſhall be requiſite for the ſame purpoſe.

FREDERICK AUGUSTUS MUHLENBERG,
Speaker of the Houſe of Repreſentatives.

JOHN ADAMS, *Vice-Preſident of the United States,*
and Preſident of the Senate.

APPROVED, March the third, 1791.

GEORGE WASHINGTON, *Preſident of the United States.*

4 | IT'S PERFECT—LET'S CHANGE IT

INTERPRETING THE CONSTITUTION AND THE PROCESS OF AMENDMENTS

The Constitution's working structure, at times complex when one is forced to interpret certain passages, is also one of the shortest written constitutions in the world at a little over 4,000 words. It is also the oldest written constitution of any major government that is still in use today. It consists of a preamble (introduction), seven articles, and twenty-seven amendments, the first ten of which are known as the Bill of Rights.

The Constitution works because it has the flexibility to allow for changing times, attitudes, and even technology. Our leaders add to it, after much deliberation, following the guidelines set by the Founding Fathers.

A bill (a proposed law) is introduced in the House of Representatives and given a name and number, then given to committee. The committee may decide it's unnecessary and reject it. If approved, it goes to a hearing, where representatives listen to facts about it and make possible changes. A vote is taken and, if favorable, it is sent back to the House to be read again. Members may make changes or offer amendments. The bill is read yet again, but only by title, followed by a vote. If approved, it goes to the Senate for another vote, possibly with amendments added. If defeated, the bill dies, but if approved with amendments, it then goes to a joint congressional committee to smooth out the differences and is voted on again. If the bill is passed, it is sent to the president, who signs

it into law or vetoes it. If vetoed, the president sends the bill back to the house of origin with the reasons why it was vetoed. The bill is debated and goes up for another vote. If it receives less than two-thirds approval, the bill dies. If it receives more than two-thirds, it is voted on again by the other house. If that passes, Congress has successfully overridden the president's veto and the bill becomes law.

The president will have certain legislative goals he would like to reach during his administration (such as the Civil Rights Bill, which was initiated by Kennedy and continued by President Johnson after Kennedy's death), but he cannot introduce a bill himself. He will call upon a congressman who has a sympathetic viewpoint on the chief executive's policy to introduce the bill to the House. He may also call upon the vice president or lobbyists to campaign for his agenda on Capitol Hill. However, a president from time to time can issue an "executive order," which has the same strength as a law. (President Truman's order desegregating the military is a good example.) In rare cases, Congress can pass a bill which will cancel an executive order, which the president may veto. In that case Congress may override that veto.

The Supreme Court portion of the Constitution engendered the least amount of controversy. The delegates provided for a Supreme Court, life tenure, and a salary for the judges.

OPPOSITE TOP: President Barack Obama takes the oath of office during the 57th Presidential Inauguration ceremonial swearing-in at the United States Capitol on January 21, 2013.

OPPOSITE BOTTOM: Speaker of the House John Boehner, R-Ohio, swears in the 113th Congress on the House floor in 2013. The House of Representatives elects its speaker on the first day of every new Congress.

ABOVE: The justices of the United States Supreme Court, led by Chief Justice Morrison Waite, hear a case. Waite served as Chief Justice from 1874 to 1888. Most of the Supreme Court's opinions during that period favored restricting federal authority in matters relating to Reconstruction.

IS IT A LAW OR AN AMENDMENT?

There are differences between a law and an amendment. A constitutional amendment may define our rights as citizens or government structure, requires a two-thirds vote in both houses of Congress, and must be ratified by three-quarters of the state legislatures. A law requires a majority vote in both houses.

FROM WASHINGTON.
JANUARY, 31, 1803.

" This day a debate took place of about four hours, in the senate, upon an application made by Mr. *Marbury* of this place, one of the *midnight appointments* of Mr. Adams, as justice of the peace, for a copy of such part of the executive record of the senate, as related to his nomination and approval by that body. In this debate all the orators on both sides spoke : we have not time to give the detailed debate, but the question was lost 13 to 15.

This business is connected with the celebrated *Mondamus* affair of last year ; Marbury being the person *used* by the *tories* to blow up this bubble.

The petition of the *dislocated judges* which was lately before the house of representatives, has been also before the senate. A committee consisting of all on one side was appointed to gratify them, e. g. *James Ross, Gouverneur Morris* and *Jonathan Dayton :*—it will be readily conceived that they have made a *thundering* report, and that it is up to the hub, and calculated to rescue the people from their worst enemies ! it is the order of the day for Wednesday next ; and the report goes that the New-York *Gouverneur* and our would be *Gouverneur* Ross and the would-be governor and clerk in chancery of Jersey, Ogden, are all to make a *great noise* on that day—they mean to shew themselves before the 4th of March and as the thief said at Tyburn, to die hard—die all, die nobly, die like demi gods.

The house of representatives sat with closed doors this day, on what business is not to be ascertained. It was reported that it was on a motion intended to go to the expulsion of *Rutledge* ; this is not however, so certain as that the public mind is much irritated at the length of time he has been suffered to sit in the house after the proofs have been brought so completely home to him. There are other circumstances concerning this man's *arts* of a similar nature that have been brought to light within a few days, and which shall be published very speedily if no steps are taken by the house of representatives to purify congress. Some of the members have shewn a very honorable sense of their own dignity, a very large number of the members declared their determination not to remain in the house should he be called to the chair in committee. This has had its due effect so far. There are others who do not appear to feel the same respect for themselves nor for the character of the government or the country which the forgeries were intended to dishonor."

The mission of Mr. Munroe to Euron-

LEFT: Account of the Supreme Court case of *Marbury vs. Madison*, which established the constitutional doctrine of judicial review, as reported in the *Philadelphia Aurora*, February 4, 1803.

ABOVE: Former Clerk of the House of Representatives William Tyler Page lecturing the newly elected members of the 71st Congress regarding their duties in 1929.

Justices would be nominated by the president, but they had to be confirmed by the Senate. The court also had the power to resolve some disputes among the states. The Judiciary Act was passed in 1789, creating the lower federal trial and federal appeal courts to comply with the Constitution, which stated that the "judicial Power of the United States shall be vested in one supreme Court and in such inferior Courts as the Congress may…ordain and establish."

Then, twelve years later, President John Adams put through the Judiciary Act of 1801, giving the president authority to appoint federal judges and justices of the peace. He also created six new circuit courts and appointed sixteen new federal judges and attorneys, marshals, and clerks. This Judiciary Act was designed to relieve the Supreme Court justices from the strain of serving as judges in a local circuit court. Most of these appointees (called "midnight justices" because Adams pushed through the appointments in the final hours of his administration) were also sympathetic to the Federalist causes. Since they were appointed for life, Adams hoped his actions would help keep some Federalist power alive in the upcoming Jefferson administration.

Shortly after Jefferson took office in 1801, Congress repealed Adams' Judiciary Act. Later, the Judiciary Act of 1802 was passed, restoring parts of the 1801 act and reorganizing the federal court structure. There are a few ways to add an amendment to the Constitution, and yet, although the framers allowed for flexibility, they wanted to be certain that changes weren't made without careful consideration. (One exception might be the Eighteenth Amendment, which had prohibited the manufacturing, transportation, and sale of alcohol in the United States—the only one to be repealed.)

The Senate or House of Representatives may propose an amendment. There must be enough representatives and senators present to form a quorum (the number of members needed to conduct business). If there are sufficient numbers for a quorum, then two-thirds of the House and two-thirds of the Senate who are present must vote "yes" for an amendment to get to the proposal stage. This joint proposal, or resolution, is sent to all the states for review; three-fourths of the states—thirty-eight total—must approve it. Each state decides the best method for voting on the amendment, but usually the proposal is debated by the state legislature and then put up for a vote. Once a state has voted in favor of an amendment, it cannot rescind its decision. However, if its legislature voted against it, then it can reverse the vote in favor of the amendment.

The Preamble of the Constitution states its purpose: "to form a more perfect Union, establish Justice, ensure domestic Tranquility, provide for the common defence, promote the general Welfare and secure the Blessings of Liberty…"

ARTICLE I explains the structure of the houses of Congress—the House of Representatives and the Senate—and how they are elected. Members of Congress collect taxes, pay debts, regulate trade, and declare war.

ARTICLE II deals with the presidency, the Executive Branch, and outlines the duties of the president and vice president, how they are elected and, when necessary, removed from office (later replaced by the Twelfth Amendment).

ARTICLE III establishes the judicial branch, known as the Supreme Court.

ARTICLE IV tells how the states relate to the federal government and their rights.

ARTICLE V outlines how the Constitution can be amended.

Articles VI states that the Constitution is the supreme law of the land. State legislatures may not make laws that conflict with rights in the Constitution.

ARTICLE VII covers ratification. The document must be ratified by nine states. It was ratified in 1788, and became the supreme law of the land even though four states had still not signed it.

MARBURY VS. MADISON

The first challenge to the Supreme Court came in 1801, in the *Marbury vs. Madison* case. Shortly after taking office, President Thomas Jefferson discovered that John Adams, in the last hours of his presidency, had pushed through appointments for judges sympathetic to Federalist causes. However, Adams had neglected to distribute a few of the judges' appointment certificates. Chief Justice John Marshall felt James Madison, Thomas Jefferson's Secretary of State, should have the "honor" of delivering the remaining documents, but Jefferson, angered at Adams' tactics, made certain that the deliveries were delayed, hoping to void the commissions. One of the appointees, William Marbury, petitioned the court to direct Secretary of State James Madison to give him his appointment. Chief Justice Marshall knew that Marbury had a strong case, but he also felt that Madison should not be *forced* to acquiesce.

Justice Marshall also claimed that a clause in the Judicial Act of 1789, which stated the Supreme Court had authority to rule on a case outside its jurisdiction, was unconstitutional. Therefore the court could not rule on Marbury's case nor force Madison to hand over the commission. This was the first congressional act to be partially struck down by the Supreme Court.

LEFT: American financier and politician William Marbury, the plaintiff in the *Marbury vs. Madison* case, 1803.

THE BILL OF RIGHTS

Now that the country had its essential government machinery in place, Congress met to draft the constitutional amendments, the first ten of which are known as the Bill of Rights. At the time, most leaders felt these rights were assumed, and didn't need further explanation. Years later, it is obvious that they are essential to interpreting the Constitution.

AMENDMENT I—Freedom to practice religious beliefs, the freedom of speech and the press, and freedom of peaceful assembly.

AMENDMENT II—A well-regulated militia, being necessary to give security to the people, provides for the right to bear arms.

AMENDMENT III—No quartering (hosting, lodging) of soldiers without the consent of the homeowner.

AMENDMENT IV—No unreasonable search or seizure of a person, his home, papers, or effects.

AMENDMENT V—A person has the right to refuse to be a witness against himself, and cannot be tried for the same crime more than once, nor be deprived of life, liberty, or property without due process of law.

Amendment VI—In all criminal prosecutions, the accused has the right to a speedy and public trial and the right to an attorney.

AMENDMENT VII—The right to a trial by jury in civil cases.

AMENDMENT VIII—Excessive bail shall not be required nor excessive fines imposed nor cruel and unusual punishment inflicted.

AMENDMENT IX—Certain rights shall not be construed to deny others not mentioned in the Constitution.

AMENDMENT X—Constitutional powers not delegated to the United States or denied to the states are reserved to the states or to the people.

An additional seventeen amendments have been added over the past two centuries. It is interesting to note that during the nineteenth century, only four amendments were added, three of which addressed the rights of African Americans.

TOP RIGHT: Bronze statue of the minuteman of Concord, Massachusetts, by Daniel Chester French, c.1876. In the eighteenth century, minutemen were a small force that would assemble to serve with the militia as needed, often at a moment's notice.

BOTTOM RIGHT: Exercising his right to free speech, Frederick Douglas speaks while a Boston mob and the police break up an abolitionist meeting on December 3, 1860.. The meeting commemorated the life of abolitionist John Brown, who had been executed for his raid on the arsenal at Harpers Ferry, West Virginia, the previous year.

OPPOSITE: An English officer in occupied Philadelphia questioning Mrs. Lydia Darrah in December 1777. The Darrah family was forced to house British soldiers during the Revolutionary War. The Fourth Amendment protects the right of privacy for all citizens.

Amendment XI, adopted 1798—Bars citizens' suits against states by residents and nonresidents in federal court.

Amendment XII, adopted 1804—Establishment of the Electoral College. (This replaced Article II, Clause 3, Section 1.) Electors meet in their respective states and vote for the president and vice president. Each elector submits two ballots: one for president and another for vice president. The votes are sent to the Senate and the House of Representatives, where they are counted. The candidate with the majority is elected. (Originally the Constitution stated that the candidate with the most electoral votes became president and the one with the next highest number of votes became vice president. Later, when the two-party system took hold, this resulted in the president and vice president representing two different parties.) The number of electoral representatives from each state is based on the state's population. Today, the candidates must garner at least 270 electoral votes for a majority. If neither candidate receives a majority in the Electoral College, the House of Representatives votes by state for the two receiving the most votes. If no decision is made, the new vice president takes on the presidential duties until the election is settled.

TERM PAPER BECOMES AN AMENDMENT

The story of the Twenty-seventh Amendment (which states that an increase or decrease in pay for congressional members is delayed until the next set of congressional terms in office) puts a modern spin on the concept of an ordinary citizen speaking up and inciting change. Originally included in the Bill of Rights, the amendment had been tabled, yet it was not altogether dead, since it had been proposed long before the seven-year limit went into effect. In 1982, a college sophomore stumbled upon the story of the amendment and decided to use it as a term paper subject, concluding that this amendment still had validity and could be brought up before Congress. Despite his professor's misgivings, the student persisted, and for the next several months wrote to state legislators, eventually convincing them to propose it to Congress. The amendment was ratified in 1992.

THE BILL OF RIGHTS

James Madison penned the first ten amendments to the Constitution not implicit in the
original document. They became the Bill of Rights.

S OF THE

and held at the City of New-Y

Fourth of March, one thousand seven hundre

THE Conventions of a number of the States, having at the time of their adopting the Constitution

tory and restrictive clauses should be added: And as extending the ground of public confidence in the Government, will

RESOLVED by the Senate and House of Representatives of the United States of America, in Congress

be proposed to the Legislatures of the several States, as amendments to the Constitution of the United States, all or any of which Art

to all intents and purposes, as part of the said Constitution; viz

ARTICLES in addition to, and amendment of the Constitution

the first enumeration required by the first article of the Constitution, there shall be one Representative for every thirty thousand,

which, the proportion shall be so regulated by Congress, that there shall be not less than one hundred Representatives, no

until the number of Representatives shall amount to two hundred, after which the proportion shall be so regulated by Congr

nor more than one Representative for every fifty thousand persons.

No law, varying the compensation for the services of the Senators and Representatives, shall take effect, until an election

to petition the Government for a redress of grievances.

shall with no law respecting an establishment of religion, or prohibiting the free exercise thereof; or abridgin

litia, being necessary to the security of a free State, the right of the people to keep a

now be quartered in any house, without the consent of the Owner; nor in

their persons, houses, papers, and effects, against unreasona

tion, and particularly, describing the place to be s

crime, unless on a present

nor shall any person b

liberty, or prop

Arti-cles.	Affirmative											
I.	N.H.		R.I	Y N.Y.	N.J	P.		M.	V.	N.C.	S.C.
II.				Y			D.	M.	V.	N.C.	S.C.
III.	N.H.		R.I	Y N.Y.	N.J	P.	D.	M.	V.	N.C.	S.C.
IV.	N.H.		R.I	Y N.Y.	N.J	P.	D.	M.	V.	N.C.	S.C.
V.	N.H.		R.I	Y N.Y.	N.J	P.	D.	M.	V.	N.C.	S.C.
VI.	N.H		R.I	Y N.Y.	N.J	P.	D.	M.	V.	N.C.	S.C.
VII.	N.H.		R.I	Y N.Y.	Y.J	P.	D.	M.	V.	N.C.	S.C.
VIII.	N.H.		R.I	Y N.Y.	N.J	P.	D.	M.	V.	N.C.	S.C.
IX.	N.H.		R.I	Y N.Y.	N.J	P.	D.	M.	V.	N.C.	S.C.
X.	N.H.		R.I	Y N.Y.	N.J	P.	D.	M.	V.	N.C.	S.C.
XI.	N.H		R.I	Y N.Y.	N.J	P.	D.	M.	V.	N.C.	S.C.
XII.	N.H		R.I	Y N.Y.	N.J	P.	D.	M.	V.	N.C.	S.C.

BILL OF RIGHTS TALLY, 1791

Thomas Jefferson's tally of the states' votes to ratify ten amendments that made up the Bill of Rights. Jefferson was serving as Washington's Secretary of State at the time.

Negative

N.H.		R.I. silent		N.Y.	N.J. silent	P. silent					

TOP RIGHT: An integrated jury in a Southern courtroom. The Constitution established the jury system as a protection against aggressive prosecutors or prejudiced judges.
BOTTOM RIGHT: "In Safe Waters at Last": a 1913 cartoon commenting on the passage of the Sixteenth Amendment to the U.S. Constitution, which permits Congress to tax individual incomes.
OPPOSITE TOP: Missouri governor Frederick Gardner signs the resolution ratifying the Nineteenth Amendment, granting women's suffrage in 1919.
OPPOSITE BOTTOM: Gerald R. Ford shakes hands with President Richard M. Nixon at Ford's vice presidential inauguration in December 1973. James Eastland, president *pro tempore* of the Senate, looks on. Nixon appointed Ford following Vice President Spiro Agnew's resignation.

Amendment XIII, adopted 1865—Slavery in the United States is abolished, and Congress has the right of enforcement. Some states refused to ratify it. In fact, Mississippi approved ratification in 1995, but did not formally approve it until 2013.

AMENDMENT XIV, adopted 1868—Grants African Americans, or anyone who was born in the United States, full citizenship, including those who were naturalized citizens. This amendment was ratified to eliminate discrimination which existed after the Thirteenth Amendment was enacted. In addition, it eliminated the "three-fifths of a person" ruling in the original Constitution.

AMENDMENT XV, adopted 1870—All citizens have the right to vote. States may set their own voting rules, but cannot prevent a person from voting because of his race, color, or former status as a slave.

AMENDMENT XVI, adopted 1913—Congress has the power to tax incomes. Prior to this, except during the Civil War, the federal government relied on excise taxes to fund projects.

AMENDMENT XVII, adopted 1913—reapportionment of the Senate: two from each state, elected every six years. When vacancies happen, it's up to the governor of the state to appoint a replacement. Prior to this, senators were appointed by legislators.

AMENDMENT XVIII, adopted 1918—Forbade the sale, manufacture, or transportation of intoxicating liquors. Supported by the law known as the Volstead Act, it gave rise to crime, murder, and corruption.

AMENDMENT XIX, adopted 1920—Granted women's suffrage.

AMENDMENT XX, adopted 1933—Changed the presidential inauguration from March 3 to January 20, to avoid an extended "lame duck" session in Washington.

AMENDMENT XXI, adopted 1933—Repealed the Eighteenth Amendment, which had caused more problems than it solved.

AMENDMENT XXII, adopted 1951—Established the two-term limit for presidents. Franklin D. Roosevelt had been elected to four terms, even though he was in poor health when elected for his last term in 1944. He died in office in 1945.

AMENDMENT XXIII, adopted 1961—Allowed for citizens who live in the District of Columbia to be represented in the Electoral College. Originally, D.C. was envisioned as a seat of government, not a place where people both worked and lived. This amendment gave D.C. citizens full voting rights.

AMENDMENT XXIV, adopted 1964—Outlawed poll tax in federal elections. Following the Civil War, the South established poll taxes as another way of preventing African Americans from voting.

AMENDMENT XXV, adopted 1967—Provided for presidential succession. Although Article II stated that if the president is unable to carry out his duties, the office "shall devolve upon the Vice President," it was not clear if the vice president was in fact the president, or acting president. This amendment stated that the vice president becomes a full-fledged president. It also allows for appointing a vice presidential replacement if that office becomes vacant. This amendment was tested only a few years later in 1973. Vice President Spiro Agnew resigned after he admitted to tax evasion. President Nixon appointed Congressman Gerald Ford as vice president. In 1974, President Nixon, rather than face impeachment, resigned in the wake of the Watergate scandal. Ford became president and named Nelson Rockefeller as his vice president.

AMENDMENT XXVI, adopted 1971—Lowered the voting age to eighteen years. During the Vietnam War, when young men were drafted into military service, they felt it was unfair not to have a say in voting for their president.

AMENDMENT XXVII, adopted 1992—An increase or decrease in pay for congressional members is delayed until the next set of terms in office. This amendment actually dates back to the 1700s, when the Bill of Rights was being drafted. However, only six of eleven states ratified it—not enough for it to pass.

Constitutional changes can also be enacted through a constitutional convention, but this proposal has never been put before Congress. There is now a seven-year time limit on amendments. If an amendment isn't ratified after seven years, it is considered dead and will not be brought before Congress again.

NO AMENDMENT IS EASY

The framers of the Constitution wanted to make any proposed revisions subject to intense scrutiny before ratification. Since 1789, thousands of amendments have been proposed in Congress. Over the past two centuries, thirty-three proposals garnered the required two-thirds vote in the legislature after which they were presented to the states for ratification. Of these, twenty-seven amendments were added to the Constitution.

DISTRIBUTION OF POWER

It had been relatively easy to choose the country's first president. George Washington was loved by the populace and retained respect within the halls of power. By 1800, however, the political climate reflected two points of view: Republicans (those who followed Jefferson's philosophy of a limited central government, with more power to the states) and Federalists (the Hamiltonians, including John Adams, who believed a stronger central government was essential to preserving national unity). John Adams had been elected president in 1796 over Thomas Jefferson, winning by a narrow margin of seventy-one electoral votes over Jefferson's sixty-eight. Jefferson served as Adams' vice president, and at this point it became obvious that a president and vice president with opposing philosophies created a somewhat unstable governing body. During Adams' administration there had been a danger of war with France when the French attacked American shipping, then in effect demanded money (bribes), during an episode known as the XYZ Affair. Adams refused to give in to France's demands and managed to avoid going to war with the nation that had once supported American independence. Fortunately, France never really wanted war with the United States, and eventually the issue faded.

However, fearing the possibility of European agitators infiltrating the country, the Federalists pushed through the Alien and Sedition Acts. The Alien and Enemies Act allowed the president to arrest or expel aliens during wartime if he felt they were a danger to the peace of the country. The Sedition Act made it a crime to "impede the operation of any law" or

HAMILTON AND BURR MEET AT DAWN

Alexander Hamilton was smart, perceptive, and aggressive, but his pride proved to be his undoing. In 1804, he learned of a treasonous plot supposedly engineered by Aaron Burr involving the formation of a separate union of northern states. Referring to Burr as an "unfit and dangerous man," Hamilton fought against Burr's bid for governor of New York. After Burr lost the election, he challenged Hamilton to a duel. To avoid humiliation, Hamilton felt he had to accept and the men faced off at dawn on July 11, 1804. Hamilton was mortally wounded and died the following day. Burr was indicted for murder, but was never tried.

RIGHT: Alexander Hamilton and Aaron Burr prepare to duel. Many men at the time, especially southerners, believed in dueling to preserve their honor.

instigate an insurrection; however, this included a section which forbade the publishing of any "false, scandalous and malicious" statements about the government. This did not sit well with Jefferson, since to him it violated the provisions of the First Amendment. He and James Madison initiated the Kentucky and Virginia Resolves, which stated that individual states could declare a law passed by Congress as unconstitutional. Kentucky and Virginia never tried to push these resolves through, but the resolves did help Jefferson put forth the issues for a presidential campaign in 1800.

In the election of 1800, Republicans Thomas Jefferson and Aaron Burr each received seventy-three electoral votes for president. This left the tie-breaking decision to the House of Representatives. After several deadlocks, Alexander Hamilton declared Jefferson the winner, although he and his fellow Federalists believed that Jefferson was somewhat obsessive regarding his faith in the rights of man and government by the people. However, Hamilton detested Burr even more, so in the end he persuaded Federalists to consider Jefferson for president. It is possible that Jefferson may have assured opponents that he would carry on Hamilton's financial system, and Washington and Adams' foreign policy. This drama resulted in the Twelfth Amendment, which, to avoid another impasse, allowed for two ballots in the Electoral College—one for president and another for vice president.

In true Republican fashion, Thomas Jefferson eschewed the ostentatious trappings that might smack of the hated "monarchism." In the spirit of this attitude, he walked to his inauguration at the new nation's capital, Washington, D.C. His blue coat, thick drab-colored waistcoat, green velveteen breeches, yarn stockings, and slippers gave the appearance of a leader determined to pay homage to the common man.

This election also showed that the United States Constitution had reached and overcome a significant hurdle. Power had passed peacefully and intelligently, from one political power to another. At the same time, a constitutional amendment was made to accommodate a new political climate. In choosing Jefferson, the country was ready to embrace individual freedom and let national power take a back seat. Yet Jefferson supported all the Federalist achievements, and in the years to come he would make significant strides of his own, in particular negotiating the Louisiana Purchase, which nearly doubled the size of the new nation.

OPPOSITE TOP: John Adams, second president of the United States and vice president under George Washington. Adams' argumentative demeanor led many to believe that he was the most independent-minded of all the presidents.
ABOVE RIGHT: Thomas Jefferson, the third president of the United States and primary author of the Declaration of Independence. Jefferson wrote a bill establishing religious freedom in Virginia in 1786.

RISE OF THE TWO-PARTY SYSTEM

The two-party system gained more prominence after Washington's administration ended. Politicians were now divided into the Federalists, who, in the Washington and Adams administrations, had given the country the strength of leadership needed to bring about a sound fiscal order, handle differences with Great Britain, and avoid getting embroiled in European conflicts. By 1800 the Federalists felt threatened by the party known as Democratic Republicans, who followed Thomas Jefferson's vision of a return to a simple, agrarian society free to govern itself and, by its simplicity, needing little governing by forceful politicians.

5 | GROWING THE COUNTRY

FROM THE LOUISIANA PURCHASE TO EXPLORING OTHER WORLDS

Thomas Jefferson, the third president of the United States, believed in an agrarian economy, states' rights, and small government. He was a scholar, an inventor, architect, and bibliophile who had an old-shoe lifestyle, answered the door if someone knocked, and made the unconventional decision to walk from his Washington apartment to his first inauguration. He was also, more notably, largely responsible for the biggest land grab in United States history—an action that appeared to challenge the powers of the president in the freshly minted Constitution.

For Jefferson, the Louisiana Purchase (the "grab") of 1803 was a colossal leap of faith for a small accretion of former colonies huddled largely on the eastern seaboard of the vast North American continent.

The whole shady business began with the vaguely disreputable attempt by Napoleon Bonaparte to peddle a plot of land he didn't own.

Originally, the millions of acres known as "Louisiana" were claimed by both France and Spain. The 1763 conclusion of the Seven Years' War in Great Britain's favor forced France to relinquish that claim, and Spain now officially owned the middle of the North American continent west of the Mississippi River down to New Orleans. The United States planned to pick away at this grand swath of territory, acquiring it over time.

For the moment, however, Spain controlled all traffic on the Mississippi. Pinckney's Treaty of 1795 provided Americans with the "right of transit" and use of New Orleans as an entry-exit port for goods to and from the interior east of the river. Following the 1783 Peace Treaty that forced British settlers out of the area, Americans rushed into this "Mississippi Territory."

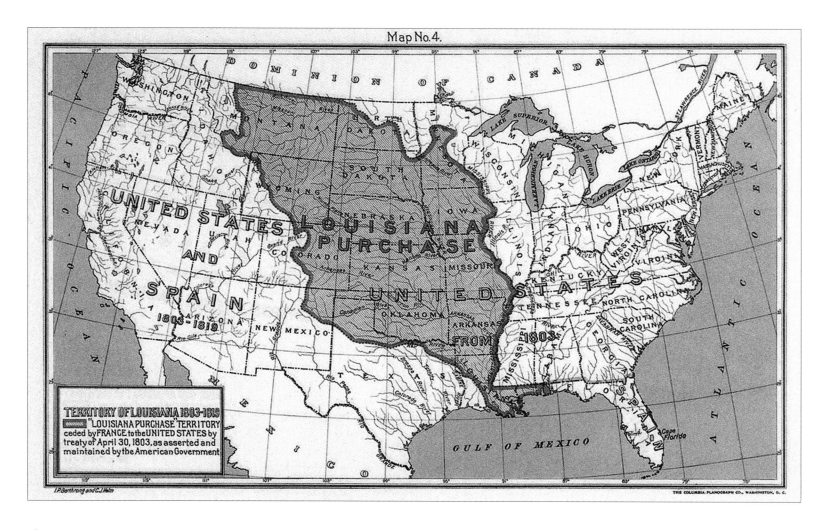

Map No. 4.

TERRITORY OF LOUISIANA 1803-1819
"LOUISIANA PURCHASE TERRITORY
ceded by FRANCE to the UNITED STATES by treaty of April 30, 1803, as asserted and maintained by the American Government

Meanwhile, Spain and France signed the Treaty of Ildefonso, which returned the Louisiana Territory back to France. This result of Napoleonic arm-twisting concluded on October 1, 1800, thus reopening the Mississippi to American trade. Tallyrand, the French foreign affairs minister, wrote: "The French Republic...will be the wall of brass forever impenetrable to the combined efforts of England and America."

It was some time before the United States government learned of this treaty. In 1802, not wanting to be bound by the interests of France and Spain, President Jefferson shipped James Monroe and Robert R. Livingston to Paris to negotiate with Napoleon for the purchase of the city of New Orleans. The aim was, at the very least, to guarantee use of the city's entry port into the Mississippi River.

Napoleon was in a mood to negotiate. He needed cash—lots of it—to finance his decision to cross Spain and crush Portugal. What's more, the slaves of French-owned Saint-Domingue (Haiti) had caused a revolution and massacred their local French government, allowing Saint-Domingue to become the first independent, former slave state in the world. This round of bad luck for the French meant the loss of sugar revenues and, combined with a future desire to invade Britain, forced Napoleon to trim off some real estate for a quick profit.

He made Monroe and Livingston an offer they couldn't refuse. The whole Louisiana Territory could be theirs for $15 million. The American negotiators had authority to pay up to $10 million for New Orleans and its environs, and while stupefied by Napoleon's offer, they managed to restrain themselves long enough to accept the deal and sign the purchase treaty without waiting for instructions.

While confident that the president would be pleased, Monroe and Livingston had forgotten about the U.S. Constitution. Jefferson's allies in government, including James Madison, were tarred with the same brush as hypocrites by Hamilton's strong central government Federalists. Making big land purchases without the advice and consent of Congress seemed at odds with the "Jeffersonian" style of small populist government. The House of Representatives approved the purchase by only two votes—against opposition by majority leader John Randolph—but the loudest cry against the real estate deal was the taint of being unconstitutional. Jefferson countered that the Constitution never mentioned the acquisition of any tract of land, and the government had the chance to evict France from America.

There were any number of weighty issues on the front burner of American politics during this period. An explosion of free and slave states, the racial stew of free black people, French and Spanish living in New Orleans being offered citizenship, dilution of the power of the Atlantic seaboard states, a huge new voting block of western farmers, and more indigenous Native American tribes to be "supervised" were sharply debated considerations. After considerable browbeating, all political challenges and attempted blockades faded away. All that remained which could prevent closure of the deal for Louisiana was Bonaparte's lack of a bill of sale from the Spanish.

James Madison tried to appeal to Spain's better nature and discovered there was none where Louisiana was concerned. All diplomatic avenues went nowhere, so the U.S. left France to sort out Spain and signed the final Purchase Treaty in 1803. Congress scraped together a down payment of $3 million in gold and paid off the rest with international banking houses, underwriting the deal so Bonaparte could quickly lay his hands on the money. The cash lasted until his Grand Armée was crushed by an international coalition at Waterloo in 1814.

OPPOSITE: The Louisiana Purchase virtually doubled the size of the United States. Jefferson dispatched three expeditions to see what he had bought for $15 million.
ABOVE: Slave rebellion on San Domingue (Haiti) established the first slave-created nation when the French were driven out, causing Napoleon to replace lost sugar revenues by selling off real estate.

ADDITIONAL ELBOW ROOM— THE LOUISIANA TERRITORY

The total area acquired in the 1803 Louisiana Treaty with France encompassed about 828,000 square miles. For that $15 million the U.S. took possession of land that would later become Arkansas, Missouri, Iowa, Oklahoma, Kansas, Nebraska, and parts of Minnesota. The U.S. also acquired most of North and South Dakota, northeastern New Mexico, northern Texas, and chunks of Montana, Wyoming, and Colorado east of the Continental Divide. Jefferson's purchase included Louisiana west of the Mississippi River and the city of New Orleans—the original goal of his modest request of France—as well as bits of future Canadian provinces Alberta and Saskatchewan. The tab came to about three cents an acre, or the equivalent of forty-two cents an acre today.

THE MISSOURI COMPROMISE

The Louisiana Territory gradually opened to settlement through a steady and growing westward flow of Americans from the crowded eastern seaboard. Along with their elected governments, these settlers brought their skills, commerce, and customs with them. The realities of an entrenched economic culture also traveled west. The United States' agrarian economy was largely slave-based. Shiploads of Africans had been literally kidnapped and brought to the U.S. packed into the holds of sailing ships to be sold in southern state markets like cattle and horses. And, like cattle, slaves were property to be traded, bought, sold, and worked without pay. While the Southern states controlled the slave market, Northern states benefitted from the low-cost labor of slaves who worked the Southern plantations—farms which provided highly profitable cotton and tobacco yields later shipped into Northern marketplaces and foreign markets.

The morality of the slave trade, its cruelty and oppression, was a harsh undercurrent in social, business, and religious circles in the growing United States. Pro- and antislavery factions were passionate and active in the federal government. The Constitution did not specifically mention the slave trade, and that sticking point had been cut from the final version to ensure passage by the Southern states. The Constitution, however, did guarantee the rights of all its citizens—just not the rights of all its "property."

Growing the country in this atmosphere of moral hypocrisy required a delicate balance of slave and free states be maintained as new states were added. In 1820, the Missouri Territory sought statehood, as did the northern tip of Massachusetts—an area which called itself "Maine." To

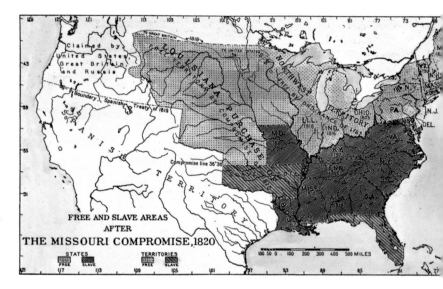

FREE AND SLAVE AREAS
AFTER
THE MISSOURI COMPROMISE, 1820

maintain the balance, Missouri was admitted as a slave state and Maine as free in the outline of the Missouri Compromise Act. Part of this act also specified that slavery would be prohibited above Missouri's northern border—the 36° 30' latitude. That provision lasted thirty-four years.

In 1854 Senator Stephen Douglas introduced a bill that resulted in the creation of the states of Kansas and Nebraska directly west of Missouri. Hewing to the states' demands for sovereignty, he suggested the settlers of these two new states decide if they wanted to be slave or free. Antislave factions raged that self-determination invalidated the Missouri

---

HOW A TERRITORY BECOMES ONE OR MORE STATES

An incorporated territory is a specific area over which the U.S. Constitution is applied to the territory's local government in the same manner as it applies to citizens and local governments that are part of the U.S.—an integral part rather than being "possessions." In the case of the Louisiana Territory, the Supreme Court eventually ruled:

"Owing to a new war between England and France being upon the point of breaking out, there was need for haste in the negotiations, and Mr. Livingston took the responsibility of disobeying his (Mr. Jefferson's) instructions, and, probably owing to the insistence of Bonaparte, consented to the 3d article of the treaty (with France to acquire the territory of Louisiana), which provided that 'the inhabitants of the ceded territory shall be incorporated in the Union

of the United States, and admitted as soon as possible, according to the principles of the Federal Constitution…' This evidently committed the government to the ultimate, but not to the immediate, admission of Louisiana as a state."

As borders to the individual states within the Louisiana Territory were surveyed and approved by the local governments, a petition was sent to Congress for admission to the United States. Congress passed an Enabling Act that authorized the people of the proposed state to draw up a constitution. Once ratified by the people's vote, this document was submitted to Congress. When approved by Congress, statehood legislation was sent on to the president for signature and issue of a formal proclamation.

BIRTH OF THE "GRAND OLD PARTY"

The GOP, or Republican Party, came into existence during the battle over the Kansas-Nebraska Act of 1854. Its base was composed of Northern antislavery supporters who wanted a stronger political voice in federal and state legislatures, and whose stated goal was both the emancipation of all slaves and nothing short of an end to that cruel institution. By 1858, they had won over members of the scattered Whig Party and the Free Soil Democrats.

Abraham Lincoln, the first Republican candidate for the presidency, won the 1860 election in a period when Southern states were beginning to secede from the Union. Lincoln led his party and the Union to victory in a bloody Civil War and the GOP went on to dominate American politics until the Great Depression and the 1932 election of Franklin Delano Roosevelt.

Compromise. Loud and vigorous debate followed in the federal legislature. Once again lacking constitutional guidelines to stand on, the compromise was successfully repealed by the Kansas-Nebraska Act. This trend went further when, in 1857, the Supreme Court ruled, in the *Dred Scott vs. Sandford* case, that Congress had no authority to prohibit slavery in the U.S. territories and declared the Missouri Compromise unconstitutional. Barring federal involvement or intervention, the remaining questions were attacked at the regional level: slave or free? After savage interstate guerrilla warfare between pro- and antislavery extremists, both Nebraska and Kansas joined the Union as free states.

Missouri, bordered by both free and slave states, was equally split. A constitutional convention voted, in a very close call, to remain a part of the Union. Generals, supplies, and troops flowed to both sides (approximately 110,000 state troops were committed to the Union army and about 40,000 to the Confederates) and the state was ravaged by bloody internecine warfare by "Free-Staters" and "Border Ruffians."

Such violent attempts to "balance" slave and free states while simultaneously seeking to dissolve the very institution of slavery itself eventually led to the Civil War of 1861–65. This war and the deep rifts which brought it about threatened to mortally wound the Constitution and destroy the hard-won Union.

ABOVE: One of the Lincoln-Douglas debates of 1858 that focused political attention on the emerging politician, "rail splitter" Abraham Lincoln, who lost this Senate election to Stephen Douglas.

OPPOSITE: The Missouri Compromise of 1820 shows the free and slave states maintaining a balance to avoid secession of Southern states to keep their slave economy.
ABOVE: "Bloody Kansas" earns its name with the sacking of "Free-Soil" capital Lawrence, Kansas, by proslavery raiders on May 21, 1856.

ACQUISITION BY CONQUEST

Even by presidential standards, James K. Polk was a go-getter. He made it perfectly clear when he ran for office in 1845 that, if elected, he would remain as president for exactly one term and then leave for home. And that's what he did. His four-year record as the United States' eleventh president won him respect as the strongest pre-Civil War chief executive. Having come up through Southern gentility as a slave owner and master of a cotton plantation, he married well and chose, as his

mentor, the indomitable Andrew Jackson. So close and successful was his relationship with "Old Hickory" that he came to be known as "Young Hickory." A wide flock of candidates ran for president in the 1844 election, but when the dust settled only Polk remained as the "dark horse" who took the field. His first task was to get all the federal money back into the treasury from private banks. Next, his top priority was to expand the Union, setting his sights on what was then known as the Oregon Territory.

THREE STAR-CROSSED GENERALS

The Mexican War (1846–1848) consisted of several short, sharp fights—brutal and bloody tests of courage on both sides. While the Mexican soldiers fought bravely, their officers and tactics were no match for the Americans. In almost every conflict the Mexicans outnumbered the American invaders, who, despite heat and disease, always managed to maintain the offensive. General Santa Anna, who had presided over the massacre of Texans and volunteers at the Alamo in 1836, was up against America's finest young and veteran commanders.

At the battle of Cerro Gordo, Santa Anna was routed by Major General Winfield Scott with the help of a party of engineers led by Captain Robert E. Lee. Together they hacked a path through the jungle which ultimately surrounded the Mexicans. A second lieutenant of infantry (Ulysses S. Grant) distinguished himself in this fight, even though he was opposed to the seizing of another country's land. Another West Point graduate, James Longstreet, won numerous brevet (field) promotions for bravery in the Mexican War. In the 1850s, he rose to the rank of major on the western frontier.

These three young officers helped lead the way to victory for America in 1848. They would meet again in the coming Civil War, led by General Lee, commander of the Confederate Northern Army of Virginia, along with General Longstreet at his side. Both were equally bent on destroying the Constitution. They faced off against Lieutenant General U.S. Grant at the head of the Union army, whose dictate as northern commander was to defend the freedoms guaranteed by that document.

Both Great Britain and the United States shared the spread of land that hugged the west coast and reached well up into the region of the 54th parallel. Polk whipped up Democratic members of Congress into a possessive fury, demanding "54-40 or Fight!" This bellicose posturing was a bluff and Great Britain was relieved when Polk "settled" for stopping the expansion at the 49th parallel—his original goal and today's border with Canada. That acquisition eventually included the states of Washington, Oregon, and Idaho, and parts of the states of Montana and Wyoming.

With Oregon in hand, he moved on the newly independent Texas (won from Mexico in 1836). It had been turned down for statehood repeatedly by Congress for fear of war with Mexico, but when Polk became president, the outgoing chief executive, John Tyler, tried, unsuccessfully, to annex the state. In a last grand attempt, Tyler suggested a "joint resolution" to finally bring Texas into the Union. A joint resolution is almost the same as a bill, and in the case of Texas it sped along the process—requiring only a simple majority vote in each house—rather than framing a joint treaty of annexation requiring a two-thirds acceptance by the Senate. Texas snapped up the offer.

With Texas in his pocket, Polk went back to a simmering Mexico to acquire northern California and New Mexico. Two succeeding Mexican governments had denied this purchase and Mexico City rejected Polk's offer out of hand. In 1845, Polk ordered General Zachary Taylor to bivouac 4,000 troops south of the Nueces River across from the city of Matamoros in claimed but contested Mexican territory. The president also sent John C. Frémont and a body of "engineers" armed to the teeth on a "scientific expedition" into California. When John Slidell, a Louisiana politician, arrived in Mexico to talk business, his reception was frosty. He reported to the Secretary of State, "Be assured, that nothing is to be done with these people until they have been chastised."

Polk decided to chastise the Mexicans to establish the Rio Grande River as the border between the two countries. On shaky constitutional ground, he demanded a declaration of war from Congress based on Mexico's failure to pay claims of U.S. citizens and for snubbing Slidell's diplomatic overtures. The same evening that his demand was walked over to Congress, an aggressive band of Mexican soldiers swept across the Rio Grande into an encampment and killed some American troops. Polk struck back like lightning, arousing Congress with the news that Mexico "had invaded our territory and shed American blood upon American soil." Unaware of Polk's behind-the-scenes maneuvering, Congress took the bait and, in 1846, cast off a declaration of war. Enflamed by the "invasion," thousands of American volunteers swelled the army's ranks and marched south.

As the war moved toward victory for the United States, antislavery abolitionists and Whig politicians—notably a freshman Illinois senator, Abraham Lincoln—excoriated Polk and his slave-owning Democrats who were, the opposition claimed, "looking for bigger pens to cram with slaves." Eventually, the Mexican army's last stand at the fortress of Chapultepec collapsed and the war ended. It was 1848. The U.S. acquired California and New Mexico and the Mexican government received $15 million for their trouble. James K. Polk's blatant grab for land by diplomatic maneuvering and conquest pushed the United States much closer to a politically divided nation, an abandoned Constitution, and a civil war.

OPPOSITE: U.S. Army storming Mexican troops entrenched in the Chapultapec Palace on September 13, 1847. This concluding battle decided U.S. victory in the Mexican War.

THE HOMESTEAD ACT

The Homestead Act of 1862 (granting acreage of federal lands to resident applicants) was nothing new. The practice of redistributing land to a growing population of small farmers dated back to 1787. In this case, however, timing was everything. Since the 1850s, slavery issues were heating up, and Southern congressmen saw government land distribution into the growing West as a threat to their slave-based agricultural economy. In 1858, the South rallied to defeat a proposed Northern, Republican-driven homestead bill by one vote, and in 1859, President James Buchanan killed a version of the Homestead Act with a veto, even though it had passed in both houses.

The secession of the Southern states during the 1861–65 Civil War handily eliminated this opposition and, with Abraham Lincoln's blessing, the Homestead Act passed into law on May 20, 1862. Under this act, farmers, laborers, and/or herders could sign up for a parcel of 160 acres of surveyed public land. Claimants were required to improve the plot by cultivating the acreage and building a dwelling upon it. After five years on the land, the original filer was entitled, for the price of a small registration fee, to own the property, free and clear. At the conclusion of the Civil War, Union soldiers could claim their 160 acres of land and deduct their time in service from the residency requirements. Those who were willing to pay $1.25 an acre could own their land in only six months.

To offer the widest possible opportunity to the flood of foreign immigrants pouring through the eastern seaboard and southern ports of entry who were filling wagons and heading west, the act further stipulated that "any adult citizen or intended citizen could claim 160 acres of surveyed government land." By the end of the Civil War, 15,000 land claims were filed. Hard cash, however, was rare among the settlers and not many were able to "prove up" on their property, buy seed and tools, or cultivate the land. Herders who demanded free range for their cattle discouraged small farm holdings from fencing their fields, and outbursts of violence between neighbors was not uncommon.

The act was also badly drawn, permitting speculators and "straw purchasers" to buy up contiguous parcels and turn them over to miners, lumbermen, cattle companies, and the railroads once the transcontinental railroad was approved under the Pacific Railway Act passed on July 1, 1862. Selling land along the tracery of railroads that spanned the continent made many millionaires. Many of the tracts could be resold when they proved to be unfriendly to cultivation. The General Land Office dispersed some 500 million acres between 1862 and 1904, but only eighty million were claimed, proved up, and held by homesteaders. Those claims continued into the twentieth century, but most of the small family holdings of the 1930s and 1940s were converted to larger, company-operated farms to profitably feed a growing nation.

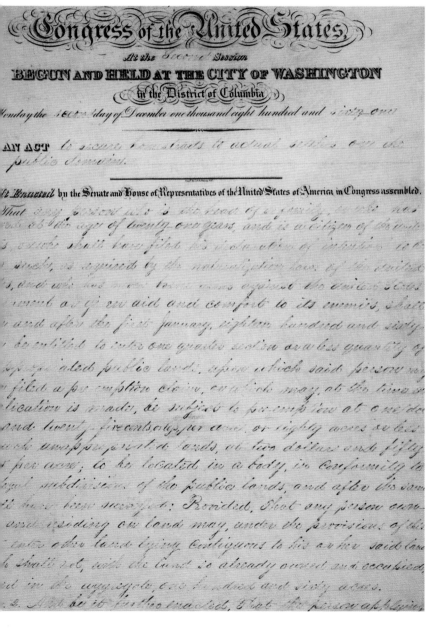

RAILROADS: KEY TO EXPANSION OF THE WEST

The Pacific Railway Act floated through Congress in 1862 on palms greased with land speculators' cash as the Civil War reached its most dangerous year. The South had achieved several victories, leaving the Union army stalled and European powers preparing to aid the Confederacy. With a southern route across the continent out of the picture, a northern route favorable to the Union became a reality. Passing this act through the Republican Congress only two months after passage of the Homestead Act was no coincidence. The two acts were conjoined to undermine the South's grip on the agrarian economy and to allow an explosion of northern capital to flow west on the shoulders of private enterprise while government dollars were tied up in the war. This show of Union confidence in the ultimate outcome also helped slow Europe's Confederate ambitions.

The act awarded twenty alternating sections—"checkerboards"— for each mile of track laid to rail companies that sprouted up from consortiums of investors. Along with the land went mineral rights, including coal to stoke the steam engines' fireboxes. These federal grants guaranteed the railroads unencumbered land on which to lay their track as well as plots saleable by the railroad companies to individual settlers for cash to offset railroad building expenses. Every tent city along the right-of-way had a land office peddling property to greenhorn homesteader families. Local banks offered high-interest loans and partnered with the land offices, reselling foreclosed parcels for profits.

Between 1862 and 1871, about 45,000 miles of track were laid. That number jumped to 170,000 from 1871 to 1900. The first railroad was completed on May 10, 1869, and a gold ceremonial spike joined the rails. Four more railroads spanned the continent by 1900.

The Homestead Act of 1862 was vulnerable to fraud as well, and the Pacific Railway Act favored large companies of speculators, leaving smaller companies to purchase track right-of-way from individual landowners for high prices—or be refused land use for trackage. Despite this venality and greed, the act worked. The railroads opened the West to settlement and greatly expanded the American economy.

OPPOSITE: The transcontinental railroad was completed when the Union Pacific met the Central Pacific near Promontory Point, Utah, on May 10, 1869. A golden spike joined the final rails.

LEFT: The Homestead Act offered land to citizens and immigrants alike to complement the western expansion on May 20, 1862. These grants were key to the completion of the transcontinental railroad.

THE POLAR BEAR GARDEN

It might have appeared as if the United States in the nineteenth century possessed sacks of mad money while European superpowers were merely looking, by comparison, to clean out their front closets of dust. First, Napoleon unloaded a vast slab of "unproductive" land—called Louisiana—to finance a war, and then the Russians began shopping an equally huge plot of ice, snow, and woods to shore up their treasury. They called it "Alyeska."

The Russians had claimed the 600,000-square-mile landmass in the early eighteenth century following explorations by Captain Commander Vitus Jonassen Bering to determine if Russia and the North American continent were connected by a land bridge. No bridge was found, but they did discover the far northern coastline that ended at North America's Point Barrow. Bering died from scurvy, but his men landed on an island, where they survived eating whale blubber and sea otters who in turn had been nourished by seaweed, which then cured the men's scurvy. From that time, Russia maintained a presence in Alyeska, fur trapping and fishing. During President James Buchanan's administration, they offered this frozen corner of the continent to the United States, but the Civil War was heating up and the deal captured little interest.

Following the war, the Russian minister to the U.S., Edouard de Stoecki, offered the deal in 1866 to Secretary of State William H. Seward

at two cents an acre, or $7.2 million. Where Seward saw a bargain, Congress and much of the general public burst over "Seward's Folly." Convincing skeptical politicians and the press was a huge challenge.

Massachusetts senator Charles Sumner, chairman of the Foreign Relations Committee, was behind the purchase. During a three-hour speech, he argued that the colony, previously known as "Russian America," should have a republican form of government and its name should come from the land itself. The Aleut Eskimos who lived there called it "Alaska"

GOLD FEVER GROWS ALASKA

Just four years after the purchase of the Alaska Territory, gold was discovered near Sitka in 1872. Another strike came in 1876 near Windham Bay, and the big bonanza of 1880 brought hordes of prospectors into Juneau. A pair of prospectors, guided by a local Native American, found two "large pieces of quartz, black sulfite and galena all spangled over with gold." Their find in what became known as "Gold Creek" was just the first of the thousand pounds of ore they recovered in that initial dig. The miner, Joseph Juneau, gave his name to the town that emerged nearby, and his partner Richard Harris named the area the Harris Mining District.

Gold-seekers flocked to Alaska's Klondike, and struck gold near Nome in the 1890s. By steamship to Skagway and Valdez, fortune-hunters began a long trek on foot with pack mules up the Chilkoot Trail to Chilkoot Pass. More starved and died on the trail than struck it rich. Then, in 1898, a gold strike at Anvil Creek brought thousands more prospectors to Nome—all the way to the beaches, where the shoreline was littered with sluice boxes used to strain water and sand to find nuggets.

Today, gold is just one of the immense resources the United States recouped for a bargain price from the "Polar Bear Garden" that was "Seward's Folly."

ABOVE: The long line of prospectors in the 1890s climbing the Chilkoot Trail toward Chilkoot Pass to enter Alaska and hunt for gold washing down from the mountains into streams and canyons during one of the many gold rushes.

(mainland). He said, "Bestow such a government, and you will give what is better than all you can receive, whether quintals of fish, sands of gold, choicest fur or most beautiful ivory," and, eventually, the Senate approved the treaty by a 37-2 vote on April 9, 1867.

Paying Russia the money presented another challenge. The House of Representatives didn't like anything about President Johnson (he would face impeachment proceedings), and Seward was regarded as Johnson's man, tarred with the same brush. Nonetheless, a year later, on July 14, 1868, the House finally approved the appropriation and the United States took possession of the Territory of Alaska. President Dwight Eisenhower admitted Alaska into the Union on January 3, 1959, as the forty-ninth state.

OPPOSITE TOP: Signing the Alaska Treaty of Cessation are (left to right) Robert S. Chew (chief clerk), William H. Seward (Secretary of State), William Hunter (second assistant Secretary of State), Mr. Bodisco, Russian ambassador Baron Edward de Stoeckl, Charles Sumner (senator), and Fredrick W. Seward (assistant Secretary of State).

OPPOSITE BOTTOM: The check made out to Russia for $7.2 million for the purchase of Alaska on March 30, 1867, the result of an uphill battle with Congress, which disparaged the frozen wasteland.

RIGHT: Cartoon showing a politician searching for voters in uninhabited Alaska, finding nobody home but the polar bears.

The NASA Act

In the modern era, "growing the country" takes on a new meaning. The last time the flag of the United States was unfurled over an unexplored landscape and saluted by representatives of the government was July 20, 1969. Neil Armstrong and Buzz Aldrin spent about eight total hours on the moon, not to claim it as a possession but to announce that humankind had made their first explorer's steps into space beyond Earth. At the conclusion of their walk on the surface, they returned to their space vehicle, piloted by Michael Collins, and navigated back to their home planet. This was the first major act of the United States' space program spreading the work and concepts of the world's best and brightest back into the cosmos from which we first came.

In 1958, President Dwight D. Eisenhower established the National Aeronautics and Space Administration (NASA) in the signing of the National Aeronautics and Space Act. If "growth" is considered a geographic expansion of borders, or an extension of a people's culture into another dominion, then NASA has given us the ability to reach beyond our planet, sending our people to our nearest organic satellite and beyond, through the creation of electronic surrogates. NASA, as facilitated through our constitutional process, has also provided a model for our global community to share in the explorations, pooling resources as we reach past our physical limits to create artificial orbiting worlds like SkyLab, where we work in the vacuum of space.

Explorer spacecraft such as the nuclear-powered *Voyager* have extended our powers of curiosity far beyond our own universe, each armed with hints about our values, cultures, and the extent of our grasp of science and mathematics. Each is like the sailing ships that cast off from ports in Italy, Greece, Norway, and the Pacific Islands, carrying great dreams and big expectations.

NASA's discoveries reach across limitless space through the lenses of the orbiting Hubble Telescope. They allow our robotic rovers to crisscross the surface of Mars, sampling, drilling, and sending back clues that inform us about our own future. Not unlike the ships that returned to Europe from Far East ports, carrying unfamiliar spices, new species of mammals and birds, leaves of tobacco, stalks of sugarcane, gold, scents, and lapis lazuli, surrogate instrumentation draws macro and micro images of distant worlds.

OPPOSITE: Astronaut Edwin E. "Buzz" Aldrin Jr. standing on the lunar surface after arriving on the *Apollo 11* spacecraft following an eight-day flight from Earth. He and Neil Armstrong spent two-and-a-half hours on the Moon and planted the U.S. flag before returning.

ABOVE: NASA's space shuttle program spanned thirty years from 1981 to 2011. In total the shuttle fleet flew on 135 missions.

NASA VISITS THE CIRCUS

Following the creation of the National Aeronautics and Space Agency by the NASA Act, an open competition was initiated to pick the nation's first astronauts to explore space. Much scientific and psychoanalytical work was done to narrow down the supposed requirements for working and traveling in a space environment. Mice, dogs, and apes were tested, but the effect of an airless, gravity-free environment subject to high-speed entry and claustrophobic living conditions for long periods of time offered many challenges requiring human reactions.

Circus performers who were fired from a cannon or whirled on a trapeze were considered, along with deep-sea divers, long-distance swimmers, parachutists, acrobats, and race-car drivers. Finally, President Dwight D. Eisenhower decided the one profession that covered the most situations was the military test pilot. It was 1959, however, and all women were excluded from consideration.

The first U.S. spacecraft, the cramped *Mercury* capsule, allowed a person no taller than five feet, eleven inches and weighing no more than 180 pounds. The candidate had to be no older than forty years, have at least a bachelor's degree, 1,500 hours of flying time, and be qualified to fly jet-fighter aircraft.

More than 500 applications were received and whittled down to sixty-nine candidates. They spent time on treadmills, tilt-tables, centrifuges, and submerged in ice water. They downed doses of castor oil, and endured enemas and constant blood tests in addition to extensive IQ exams. Of the sixty-nine, just seven were chosen, all perfect physical specimens with genius-level IQs.

6 | OUR CONSTITUTION DIVIDED

SECESSION OF THE SOUTHERN STATES AND CIVIL WAR CULMINATES IN THE THIRTEENTH AMENDMENT

Of all the threats to the United States of America, the Civil War came the closest to permanently dividing the country into, at a minimum, two sovereign nations. The conflict that began with the shelling of Fort Sumter off the coast of South Carolina in 1861 had been simmering since the ratification of the Constitution in 1789. The cause was both a moral/cultural divide involving the institution of slavery and an economic one based on agrarian states' rights against industrialized federalism. Slavery was the labor support base of the Southern states. The status quo yielded high revenue for all concerned—except, of course, the slaves themselves. They received no wages, formal education, or citizen's rights; were considered property like horses or cattle; and were subject to severe punishment should they attempt to flee from their owners. The Fugitive Slave Act of 1850 condoned this treatment of runaways. After decades of abolitionist free-state advocates damning the slaveholding southerners, the election of "Free-Stater" Abraham Lincoln to the presidency in 1860 virtually guaranteed the secession of the slave states from the Union and the creation of the Confederate States of America.

South Carolina was the first state to formally leave the Union. Their statement declaring secession was typical of those that ratified the Confederate states' constitution. They claimed:

> The ends for which the Constitution was framed are declared by itself to be "to form a more perfect union, establish justice, insure domestic tranquility, provide for the common defence, promote the general welfare, and secure the blessings of liberty to ourselves and our posterity."

> These ends it endeavored to accomplish by a Federal Government, in which each State was recognized as an equal, and had separate control over its own institutions. The right of property in slaves was recognized by giving to free persons distinct political rights, by giving them the right to represent, and burthening them with direct taxes for three-fifths of their slaves; by authorizing the importation of slaves for twenty years; and by stipulating for the rendition of fugitives from labor.

> We affirm that these ends for which this Government was instituted have been defeated, and the Government itself has been made destructive of them by the action of the non-slaveholding States. Those States have assumed the right of deciding upon the propriety of our domestic institutions; and have denied the rights of property established in fifteen of the States and recognized by the Constitution;

> they have denounced as sinful the institution of slavery; they have permitted open establishment among them of societies, whose avowed object is to disturb the peace and to eloign [to take beyond the jurisdiction of a law court] the property of the citizens of other States. They have encouraged and assisted thousands of our slaves to leave their homes; and those who remain, have been incited by emissaries, books and pictures to servile insurrection.

> For twenty-five years this agitation has been steadily increasing, until it has now secured to its aid the power of the common Government. Observing the forms of the Constitution, a sectional party has found within that Article establishing the Executive Department, the means of subverting the Constitution itself.

The "Article" referred to in this declaration was the Fourth Article, which states:

> No person held to service or labor in one State, under the laws thereof, escaping into another, shall, in consequence of any law or regulation

$150 REWARD

RANAWAY from the subscriber, the night of the 2d instant, a negro m: who calls himself *Henry May*, about years old, 5 feet 6 or 8 inches high, dinary color, rather chunky built, bus head, and has it divided mostly on o side, and keeps it very nicely comb: has been raised in the house, and is a fi rate dining-room servant, and was i tavern in Louisville for 18 months. expect he is now in Louisville trying make his escape to a free state, (in all probability to Cincinnati, Ohio.) haps he may try to get employment on a steamboat. He is a good cook, is handy in any capacity as a house servant. Had on when he left, a d cassinett coatee, and dark striped cassinett pantaloons, new—he had o clothing. I will give $50 reward if taken in Louisvill; 100 dollars if ta one hundred miles from Louisville in this State, and 150 dollars if taken of this State, and delivered to me, or secured in any jail so that I can get again. WILLIAM BURKE. *Bardstown, Ky., September 3d, 1838.*

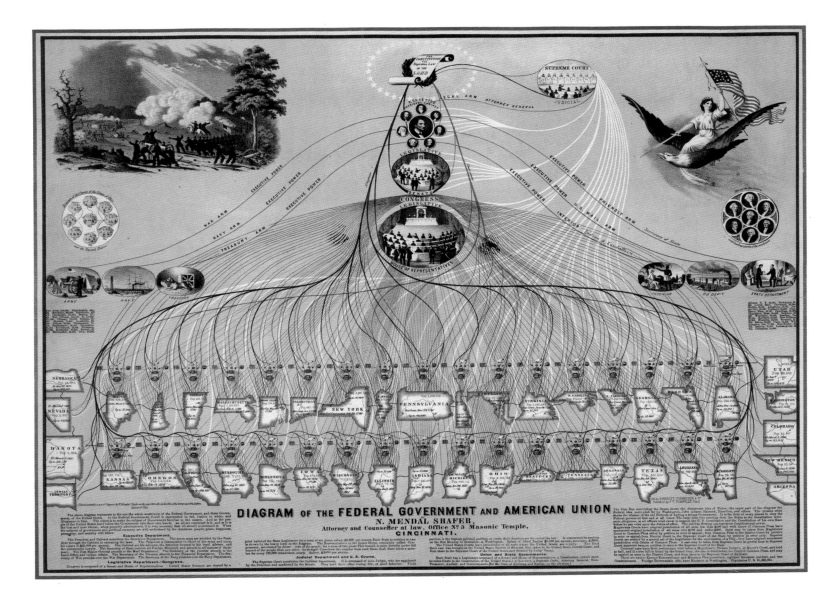

DIAGRAM OF THE FEDERAL GOVERNMENT AND AMERICAN UNION
N. MENDAL SHAFER,
Attorney and Counsellor at law, Office Nº 5 Masonic Temple.
CINCINNATI.

therein, be discharged from such service or labor, but shall be delivered up, on claim of the party to whom such service or labor may be due.... (Northern free-states) have enacted laws which either nullify the Acts of Congress or render useless any attempt to execute them. In many of these States the fugitive is discharged from service or labor claimed, and in none of them has the State Government complied with the stipulation made in the Constitution.

Using this and other provocations, the Confederate States drew up their own constitution; it copied much of the original document with the exception of inclusions such as:

SECTION 2, ARTICLE 3, STATE CITIZENS—EXTRADITION
3. No slave or other person held to service or labor in any State or Territory of the Confederate States, under the laws thereof, escaping

or lawfully carried into another, shall, in consequence of any law or regulation therein, be discharged from such service or labor; but shall be delivered up on claim of the party to whom such slave belongs; or to whom such service or labor may be due.

The new Constitution also allowed the Confederate States to acquire new territory in North America and defend and protect that territory's right to own slaves. Thus armored, the Confederate States of America

---

OPPOSITE: An 1838 newspaper advertisement offering a reward for a runaway slave, Henry May. In free states, former slaves had to carry their freedom papers at all times for inspection.
ABOVE: Elaborate illustrated diagram of the U.S. government in the 1860s showing the three branches of federal power and the individual state legislatures.

LEFT: "Old Abe's Uncomfortable Position." An American cartoon drawn in 1860 depicting President-elect—and still beardless—Lincoln's discomfort at the idea of using military force to preserve the Union.

ABOVE : Mills House on Meeting Street in Charleston, where South Carolina decided to be the first state to secede from the Union in 1860.

accepted Lincoln's bait when he chose to resupply Fort Sumter instead of evacuate the troops. Confederate artillery fired on the offshore Union possession, thereby becoming the aggressor. The Union made strides to defend itself, but was sadly unprepared. President Lincoln called up the loyal free-state militias to federal duty under the Constitutional Act of 1795, which permitted:

> ...whenever the United States shall be invaded, or be in imminent danger of invasion from any foreign nation or Indian tribe...the laws of the United States shall be opposed or the execution thereof obstructed, in any state, by combinations too powerful to be suppressed by the ordinary course of judicial proceedings, or by the powers vested in the marshals by this act.

There was also the matter of geography. Washington, D.C., the Union capital, bordered Virginia—a slave state—and Maryland, which teetered between free and slave loyalty. Riot and rampage threatened in Baltimore, Maryland's capital. To secure Maryland in the Union, Lincoln signed an

executive order dissolving the writ of habeas corpus. This Latin term means "you have the body" and points to the right of any prisoner to challenge the terms of his or her imprisonment. Lincoln's opponents argued his action was unconstitutional, and the Supreme Court agreed that Congress alone could suspend the writ. The court avoided mentioning the context of the suspension—national emergency. Two years later, in March 1863, Congress would pass the Habeas Corpus Act, endorsing Lincoln's bold stroke. Following Lincoln's lead, in 1862 Secretary of War Edward Stanton also suspended the writ of habeas corpus when the first draft of troops was ordered. Anyone protesting or interfering with the draft measures was jailed on the spot.

The year 1862 was the pivotal turning point of the war. Having faced defeats and humiliations at the hands of inept military leaders and name-calling by both political rivals and the press, Lincoln had to face the core slavery issue and the fear of foreign intervention. Lord Henry John Temple Palmerston, the British prime minister, stated publicly, "It is the highest degree likely that the North will not be able to subdue the South." This was the common opinion among the European powers. In Liverpool,

the British were building armored rams for the Confederate navy. Crates of rifles and cannons aboard English ships braved Lincoln's blockade of Southern ports. European nobility shrugged at a jumped-up, backwoods Kentucky farmer trying to lead a country at war with itself.

But while the ink was still damp on the United States Constitution, slavery hung like a shadow over the new country. Now blood was being spilled in its name. Unable to untangle a conflicted Congress, Lincoln searched for any way he could initiate the end of this inhumane institution. He drew from the writings of legal scholar William Whiting (author of the Constitution's Preamble), allowing the president to take all necessary steps to save the country—including the bypassing of state slavery laws. Slave masters had broken up the Union, overthrown justice, and destroyed domestic tranquility. Taking away their slaves was a justifiable act of war. Lincoln embraced this concept, but the timing was critical. General George McClellan's "case of the slows" had allowed the rebel Army of Northern Virginia to dominate the battlefield. Emancipating the slaves at this time would signal weakness to the Confederates and the hovering European powers. After much prodding,

the fearful McClellan finally moved against General Robert E. Lee at Sharpsburg, Maryland, near Antietam Creek on September 17, 1862.

What followed was the bloodiest single day in American history. The two armies crashed together, battling across fields, roads, and what came to be called "Burnside Bridge" after the Union general who sacrificed his army trying to cross it against enfilading rebel fire. At the exhausting conclusion, both armies were savaged. The bodies of 23,000 soldiers littered the battlefield. Lee managed to retrieve his broken army while McClellan failed to follow up with his larger force. Telegraph messages back to Washington announced Lee's retreat and the Union holding its ground. For Lincoln, this virtual draw was the "victory" he needed.

ABOVE: "The Grave of the Union, or Major Jack Downing's Dream." An 1864 cartoon that depicts the burying of the United States Constitution, habeas corpus, speech and press freedoms, and the Union by the Lincoln administration, its supporters in Congress, journalist Horace Greeley (center), and clergyman Henry Ward Beecher.

THE BLACK LIST.

Total vote from free States in favor of the Fugitive Slave bill.

DEMOCRATS.—*Maine*--Messrs. Fuller, Gerry, Littlefield—3.

New Hampshire.—Messrs. **HIBBARD** and **PEASLEE**—2.

New York—Mr Walden—1.

New Jersey—Mr Wildrick—1.

Pennsylvania—Messrs Dimmick, Job Mann, McLanahan, Robbins, Ross and James Thompson—6.

Ohio—Messrs. Hayland and Miller—2.

Indiana—Messrs, Alberston. William J. Brown, Dunham, Gorman, McDonald—5.

Illinois—Messrs. Bissel, T. L. Harris, McClernand, Richardson, Young—5.

Michigan—Mr A. W. Buel—1.

Iowa—Mr Leffler—1.

California—Mr Gilbert—1.   Total 27.

WHIGS.—Messrs. Elliot, of *Mass.*; McGaughey, of *Ind.*; John L. Taylor, of *Ohio*—Total, 3.

Total Ayes from free states, 30.

"THE BLACK LIST" BROADSIDE ATTACKING CONGRESSMEN WHO VOTED FOR THE FUGITIVE SLAVE ACT OF 1850

A list condemning those free-state congressmen who voted in favor of returning runaway slaves captured in the North to their Southern owners.

Thirty-Eighth Congress of the United States of America;

At the _Second_ Session,

Begun and held at the City of Washington, on Monday, the _fifth_ day of December, one thousand eight hundred and sixty-four.

A RESOLUTION

Submitting to the legislatures of the several States a proposition to amend the Constitution of the United States.

Resolved by the Senate and House of Representatives of the United States of America in Congress assembled, (two-thirds of both houses concurring), That the following article be proposed to the legislatures of the several States as an amendment to the Constitution of the United States, which, when ratified by three-fourths of said legislatures shall be valid, to all intents and purposes, as a part of the said Constitution, namely: Article XIII. Section 1. Neither slavery nor involuntary servitude, except as a punishment for crime whereof the party shall have been duly convicted, shall exist within the United States, or any place subject to their jurisdiction. Section 2. Congress shall have power to enforce this article by appropriate legislation.

Schuyler Colfax
Speaker of the House of Representatives.

H. Hamlin
Vice President of the United States
and President of the Senate

Approved February 1. 1865.

Abraham Lincoln

JOINT RESOLUTION PROPOSING THE THIRTEENTH AMENDMENT TO THE CONSTITUTION

Abraham Lincoln's final legacy, the Thirteenth Amendment, abolished slavery in the United States. The president personally signed it on February 1, 1865.

THE THIRTEENTH AMENDMENT

On September 22, 1862, Lincoln signed a preliminary Emancipation Proclamation with the final version signed on January 1, 1863, which declared, "…all persons held as slaves…shall be then, thenceforward, and forever free"—but it applied only to states designated as being in rebellion, not to the loyal slave-holding border states of Delaware, Kentucky, Maryland, and Missouri, or to areas of the Confederacy that had already come under Union control. This executive order, permitted by the Constitution in time of war, also allowed freed slaves to enlist in the Union army, swelling its ranks by 20,000 volunteers. When word of the proclamation reached Prime Minister Lord Palmerston, he reversed his earlier opinion on the Union's chances of winning, as did the British public, even as they were starved for Southern cotton in their mills. The Confederate states would be alone in their fight for the next three years.

As the war wound down, with Union generals Grant, Sherman, and Sheridan routing starved and barefoot rebel forces, Abraham Lincoln, though worn and exhausted, needed one last act to seal a real victory. In 1864, he mounted a campaign to insert a Thirteenth Amendment into the Constitution, freeing all slaves everywhere in the United States.

Worried that the Emancipation Act was only a "war powers" act, Lincoln recognized the Proclamation freed slaves in only ten Confederate states, but did not free any slaves in the border states. This was not the instrument he needed to abolish slavery for all time. Lincoln wanted to amend the Consitution—the first amendment in sixty years—to complete what he had begun in 1862. Dragging his cabinet with him, casting for votes in the Senate like a fisherman, Lincoln demonstrated his skills as a politician, learned in the hustings of state elections, and wheedling compromises in local disputes. Now, he used cajoling, promises of jobs, and granting of favors to snare votes for the final tally. On April 8, 1864, the Thirteenth Amendment was passed by the Senate. The House passed it on January 31, 1865, and final adoption came on December 6, 1865.

But some state legislatures still dragged their feet. Texas waited until 1870, Delaware until 1901, and Kentucky ratified in 1976. The state of Mississippi approved the amendment in 1995, but did not ratify it due to a "clerical oversight" until February 5, 2013. Abraham Lincoln's work in this matter was done.

RIGHT: Tolman Carlton's painting *Watch Meeting—Dec. 31, 1862—Waiting for the Hour:* a group of African American slaves wait for the moment, on January 1, 1863, when the Emancipation Proclamation takes effect.

OPPOSITE: An 1863 copy in Lincoln's handwriting of a page from his Emancipation Proclamation issued on September 22, 1862, freeing the slaves still owned as "property" in the Confederate states in January 1863.

FINANCING A CIVIL WAR

At the outset of the Civil War, neither government had any notion of how they were going to fund the conflict. The Confederate government required all the states to contribute hard money, troops, and supplies. The Union had the bigger army, more railroads, and a larger taxable population. Both governments quickly realized that war devoured budgets, so both heated up their printing presses and began churning out paper money backed not by gold but by promises. It was an immediate solution with grave long-term risks. The U.S. government spewed out $432,000,000 in "greenbacks," so called because of the bright green ink used on the reverse of each bill. Eventually, gold-backed currency was worth only 85 cents more than the devalued greenback dollar. The Confederacy's runaway inflation resulted in Southern families paying $1,000 for every barrel of flour sought.

By the President of the United States of America:

A Proclamation.

Whereas, on the twenty-second day of September, in the year of our Lord one thousand eight hundred and sixty-two, a proclamation was issued by the President of the United States, containing, among other things, the following, to wit:

"That on the first day of January, in the
"year of our Lord one thousand eight hundred
"and sixty-three, all persons held as slaves within
"any State or designated part of a State, the people
"whereof shall then be in rebellion against the
"United States, shall be then, thenceforward, and
"forever free; and the Executive Government of the
"United States, including the military and naval
"authority thereof, will recognize and maintain
"the freedom of such persons, and will do no act
"or acts to repress such persons, or any of them,
"in any efforts they may make for their actual
"freedom.

"That the Executive will, on the first day
"of January aforesaid, by proclamation, designate
"the States and parts of States, if any, in which the

7 | CHALLENGES TO THE CONSTITUTION

THE BALANCE OF POWER GRADUALLY SHIFTS TOWARD THE EXECUTIVE BRANCH

"We the people" is there for a reason. Those who lead the country must continually interpret and reframe the Constitution as they take on the challenge of guaranteeing justice and freedom for all who live under it. Over the past two centuries, presidents, houses of Congress, and the Supreme Court have studied constitutional rhetoric and examined ways to add amendments that address current needs and agendas. The Constitution's basic tenets have not changed; Americans still look to this document for guidance in providing a secure future for generations to come.

Andrew Jackson embodied the image of a forceful, often opinionated, demanding, and intractable leader of the country. He was the first president to use federal troops to break a strike when, during a violent labor dispute near the Chesapeake and Ohio Canal, the Maryland governor appealed to the president to intervene. His deep-seated animosity toward the Second National Bank in Philadelphia led to a bitter battle with Senator Henry Clay and the bank's president, Nicholas Biddle, himself a shrewd and highly respected financier. Biddle had transformed the bank from a federally agented institution to a central bank with regulated credit lending procedures for smaller banks. In order to increase interest earnings, these banks lent exceedingly large numbers of banknotes to their borrowers. The notes could be converted to hard cash, but for convenience in the daily workings of commerce, people seldom took the time to obtain hard currency, as long as they believed the banks were sound. By collecting the notes and converting them to gold or silver, Biddle made certain the banks had enough reserves to keep them from overextending their lending procedures. Biddle's actions only angered Jackson that much more. The president had had adverse experiences with paper money in his younger days, and despised that type of currency.

WASHINGTON'S NEUTRALITY ACT

Although George Washington made a conscious effort to keep an appropriate distance between Congress and the presidency, he was not above exercising his chief executive powers in the early days of his administration. When France went to war with Britain and Spain in 1793, the Alliance of 1788 (made by the U.S. with France during the height of the Revolutionary War) now created a problem. The United States had promised to "defend the French West Indies against all powers." If Britain attacked the French island of Martinique, Americans feared they had to make good their pledge. In doing so, this could throw the country into danger of attack by the British in Canada, and by Spain from the west and south. To avoid this kind of exposure, Washington in 1794 declared a neutrality policy. He did so even though, technically, the Constitution dictated that he present it before Congress. Nevertheless, tensions increased, and eventually, Washington sent Chief Justice John Jay to London in an effort to negotiate a settlement.

LEFT: George Washington, first president of the United States. In his farewell address, he warned against sectionalism and involvement in foreign wars.

ABOVE: Jackson's adversary, Henry Clay, shown here offering his California Compromise to the Senate on February 5, 1850. Congressmen argued over whether California should be admitted as a slave or free state.

RIGHT: Cartoon of Andrew Jackson as "King Andrew the First," trampling on the Constitution. The image is meant to portray his habit of using the presidency to force his agenda on the nation.

Biddle obtained Clay's support when he tried to recharter the bank four years before the expiration of its present charter. If Jackson vetoed the act, Clay would challenge him for the presidency in the coming election, knowing Americans were in favor of the bank as it stood. The rechartering passed Congress and, as expected, Jackson, seeing Clay's plan, vetoed it.

This veto was viewed as one of the most important in the history of the Constitution. Jackson went beyond merely listing constitutional reasons for the veto; he incorporated his political, social, and economic rationale. The bank, he maintained, enjoyed monopolistic privileges and threatened the country's democracy while foreign investors in the bank benefited from Americans' taxes. Jackson challenged the Supreme Court, but the court ruled in favor of Congress, stating it had the right to establish a bank, citing implied powers listed in the Constitution.

Jackson went on to assert that before Congress considered any legislation, it must first consult with the president, not wait for a possible veto. He was reelected over Clay in 1832 and immediately sought to withdraw all the government's deposits from the bank. His Secretary of the Treasury refused to follow his orders. Jackson fired him—the first time a president had fired a cabinet member. In fact, Jackson went ahead and took the money out piecemeal, depositing it in smaller institutions called "pet banks." Biddle countered by curtailing loans throughout the banking system and other measures designed to impact Jackson's actions, which led to a serious economic recession. Eventually Congress and the American people realized that Biddle's power-wielding tactics had created an economic disaster, and passed resolutions forbidding rechartering. The delighted Jackson cried that the vote "has put to death that mammoth of corruption and power, the Bank of the United States."

The South Skirts Around the Constitution

The post-Civil War era brought its own set of constitutional issues. Although slavery had been abolished by the Thirteenth Amendment in 1865, black citizens still suffered a virtual slavery in the coming decades and well into the twentieth century. Now that former slaves would receive pay for their labor, southern (and even northern) politicians and businessmen feared their own erosion of political power and job loss.

Lincoln's successor, President Andrew Johnson, sought to carry on Lincoln's policy of "malice toward none" by supporting states' rights for the South. To that end, Johnson agreed with southern officials that blacks needed guidance to more easily acclimate themselves into the free white society and not be granted too much freedom too quickly. He further proclaimed that individual states should decide whether or not blacks should be allowed to vote. (In this respect, even many northern states barred African Americans from the polling booth.)

This gave the former Confederates all they needed to set up what became known as the "Black Code," a near-slavery policy in which blacks were forbidden to vote, serve on juries, possess firearms, or own land. The southern officials labeled a person who did not work in the fields for a white man as a vagrant—an ambiguous judgment, since some blacks did not work for any white man in any capacity. Republicans found themselves divided into two factions. Radicals favored granting the blacks civil rights and the freedom to grow their own economy. Moderates wanted to let the South determine its own future.

In addition, many Confederate rebels (including Alexander H. Stephens of Georgia, imprisoned on charges of treason) were elected to Congress in a special election for the southern states in the fall of 1865. This caused more than a little alarm among the two houses, and on December 4, 1865, a joint committee voted to bar these former secessionists from Congress.

Early in 1866, Congress extended the Freedmen's Bureau (a section of the War Department), which had been established the previous year for refugees. This move was designed to enforce the protection of black rights by providing schools and fair labor practices in order to grow the southern economy. Then Congress passed the Civil Rights Act, which said that states could not prevent blacks from testifying in court, contracting for labor, or owning property. Johnson vetoed these policies, but on April 9, 1866, Congress stood firm and repassed the Civil Rights Act by a two-thirds majority. It was the first time a major piece of legislation passed over a president's veto.

In 1866 Congress proposed the Fourteenth Amendment, granting full citizenship to "all persons born or naturalized in the United States and…of the State wherein they reside." The amendment also forbade states to "make or enforce any law which shall abridge the privileges…of citizens of the United States…nor deprive any person of life, liberty or property, without

ABOVE: Andrew Johnson, the seventeenth president of the United States, succeeded Abraham Lincoln after Lincoln's assassination. In 1875, he was elected to the Senate, the only former president to do so.
OPPOSITE: The Coan School at Norfolk, Virginia. The school was established for freedmen after the Civil War.

due process of law." Another section mentioned that the southern states should allow blacks to vote, and if this right was denied, the state would be given less representation in Congress. Also, officials who had been aligned with the Confederacy were forbidden to hold state or federal office unless pardoned by a two-thirds majority of Congress. The amendment did not appeal to President Johnson, who still believed that individual states should decide black suffrage and other issues. He wanted nothing to stand in the way of reconciliation between the North and South, and campaigned around the country to promote his cause, but gained little support. Northern constituents wanted formal equality for blacks, and in the end Republicans won a majority in the 1866 congressional election.

With the proposed Fourteenth Amendment still in limbo thanks to the southern states' objections, the northern radicals in Congress (those who

COAN SCHOOL, NORFOLK, VIRGINIA.

favored black equality) forged ahead with the Reconstruction Acts. The first Reconstruction Act, passed in March 1867, stated that the former Confederate states would not be readmitted to the Union unless they ratified the Fourteenth Amendment and guaranteed voting rights to all in their state constitutions. Furthermore, these states (with the exception of Tennessee, which had ratified the amendment the previous year) were divided into five military districts, ruled by officers charged with the duty to protect the civil rights of all persons. The states could offset this division by drafting new state constitutions giving blacks voting rights, and in addition the states must ratify the Fourteenth Amendment. If they complied, they would be allowed seats in Congress and avoid military rule. Not surprisingly, Johnson vetoed and Congress overruled. However, the ambiguity of the act presented more problems, since it lacked clear-cut procedures. Southern states decided they would live with military rule rather than give blacks voting rights. Congress then passed another act giving officers the authority to register voters and supervise elections of delegates to constitutional conventions, and still another act containing more definitive guidelines. White southerners fought these measures as well by staying away from the polls. Yet by 1868 enough states in the Union (Arkansas cooperated with the rulings and was readmitted in July) had ratified the Fourteenth Amendment, and it became part of the Constitution.

CARPETBAGGERS AND SCALAWAGS

Toward the end of the Civil War, a number of ambitious northerners headed south, stirred by the prospect of establishing themselves as planters in the soil-rich country. The white southern population, seeing these people as vultures trying to make a quick dollar on land devastated by war, called the entrepreneurs "carpetbaggers," a derisive term referring to travelers who carried bags made of old carpet remnants, a common practice at the time. Yet many of these northerners felt they had a mission to protect and nurture the rights of the newly freed blacks and guide them along the path to a life with good jobs and a decent education. Other white southerners sided with the North after the war when they realized that government subsidies for railroads, banking, and other industries could result in profitable investments. They were called "scalawags" (a term describing a useless horse) by former Confederates who scorned anyone joining forces with the North.

THE ROAD TO BLACK SUFFRAGE

The Fourteenth Amendment granted citizenship to any persons born or naturalized in the United States and, as such, those persons were given all rights of liberty, life, and property. In addition, states were forbidden to make laws denying these rights. The amendment still did not, however, clearly emphasize that all citizens (including blacks) had the right to vote. Congress hoped, with the Fourteenth Amendment, that black suffrage would be assumed by the states. The Fifteenth Amendment, ratified in 1870, clearly spelled out that "the right of citizens of the United States to vote shall not be denied or abridged by… any State on account of race, color, or previous condition of servitude." Yet, it gave states the right to enact their own voting laws, and soon many states pushed through measures designed to keep blacks from the voting booth. These included levying excessive poll taxes and setting up complex literacy tests.

THE FIRST IMPEACHMENT

In 1867, Congress had passed the Tenure of Office Act, which forbade the president from firing officials appointed through the Senate without first getting permission from the Senate. In 1868, Johnson removed Secretary of War Edwin Stanton, a radical sympathizer, who opposed Johnson's post-Civil War policies. The House of Representatives, following the Constitution's guidelines, impeached Johnson, charging him with misconduct in the Stanton affair. (Impeachment means that the House finds the president may have committed a crime and should be brought to trial by the Senate, but at that point, he is not convicted.) Johnson's lawyers contended he had done nothing against the law, and removed Stanton only because he felt the Tenure of Office Act unconstitutional. The lawyers further maintained that Johnson was within his rights to remove Stanton, since he had been appointed by Lincoln, and cabinet members had tenure only "during the term of the president by whom they may have been appointed." Other charges stemmed from Johnson's refusal to go along with the civil rights policies mandated by Congress, and the "inflammatory and scandalous" speeches he made during his campaign to gain support for his policies in dealing with the South. After the House's impeachment vote, Johnson went on trial before the Senate. Johnson's lawyers said he was innocent of the charges of "violating criminal law." The House maintained he had gone beyond the limits of presidential authority. In a very close final call, the Senate decided against convicting the president by a single vote. Bill Clinton is the only other president to have been impeached and tried before the Senate.

LEFT: Senate sergeant-at-arms serving the impeachment summons to President Johnson, 1868. Johnson is rated as one of the worst presidents because of his opposition to federally guaranteed rights for African Americans.

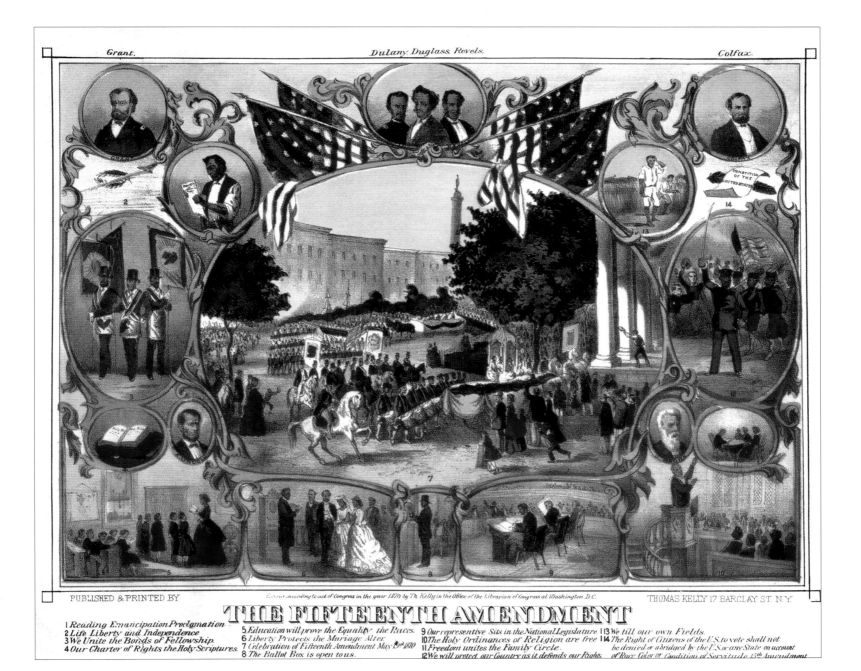

Grant.   Dulany. Duglass. Revels.   Colfax.

PUBLISHED & PRINTED BY   Entered according to act of Congress in the year 1870 by Th. Kelly in the Office of the Librarian of Congress at Washington, D.C.   THOMAS KELLY 17 BARCLAY ST. N.Y.

THE FIFTEENTH AMENDMENT

1 Reading Emancipation Proclamation
2 Life Liberty and Independence
3 We Unite the Bonds of Fellowship
4 Our Charter of Rights the Holy Scriptures.

5 Education will prove the Equality the Races.
6 Liberty Protects the Mariage Alter.
7 Celebration of Fifteenth Amendment May 19th 1870
8 The Ballot Box is open to us.

9 Our representive Sits in the National Legislature
10 The Holy Ordinances of Religion are free
11 Freedom unites the Family Circle.
12 We will protect our Country as it defends our Rights

13 We till our own Fields.
14 The Right of Citizens of the U.S. to vote shall not
be denied or abridged by the U.S. or any State on account
of Race, Color or Condition of Servitude 15th Amendment

The Fourteenth and Fifteenth Amendments were a turning point in American history. Their passage marked the first time newly freed slaves enjoyed the privilege of voting and owning property. (By comparison, for example, after slavery had been abolished in the British Caribbean sugar islands, the freedmen were forced to pay outrageous poll taxes and adhere to strict property ownership laws.) In addition, it signaled the advance of centralized political influence in the country by lowering the power allowed to each of the individual states. Now that blacks and whites were no longer separated by "slave" and "free" designations, the United States and its people became more closely related in a complex social and economic populace, one that many believed needed more oversight than in earlier generations.

OPPOSITE TOP: A cartoon from an 1874 newspaper in the North on the efforts of the White League in Louisiana to intimidate and disenfranchise black voters.

ABOVE: Parade held in Baltimore, May 19, 1870, to celebrate the passing of the Fifteenth Amendment granting universal male suffrage. States were allowed to set their own voting laws, but the amendment declared that all men must be allowed to vote regardless of race.

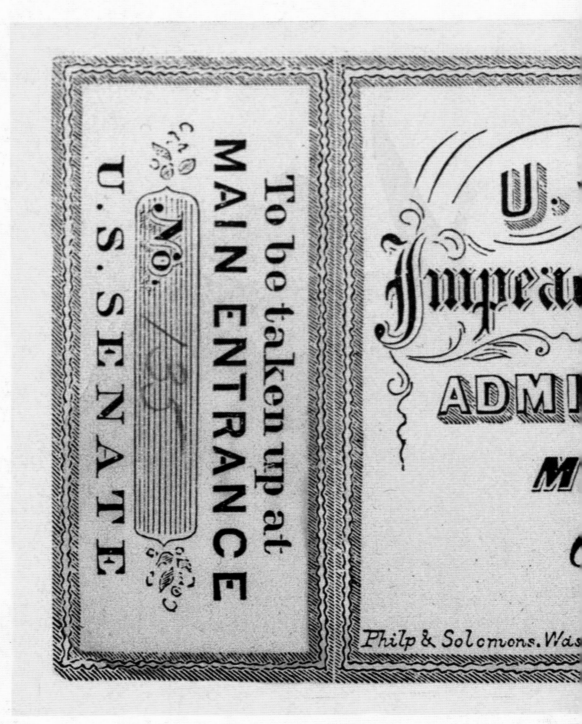

ADMISSION TICKET TO THE IMPEACHMENT TRIAL OF PRESIDENT ANDREW JOHNSON

This ticket admits one to the Senate Gallery to observe the Impeachment of President Andrew Johnson, which began on March 5, 1868, and lasted three months.

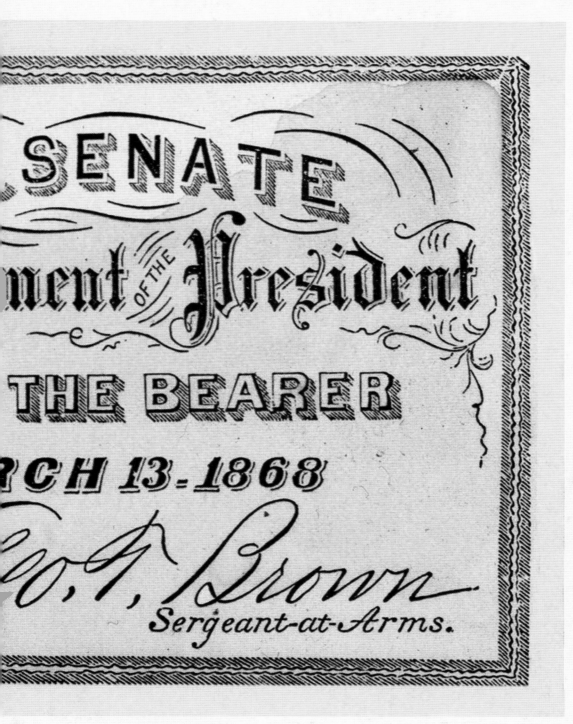

SENATE

ment OF THE President

THE BEARER

RCH 13-1868

Geo. A. Brown
Sergeant-at-Arms.

THE KU KLUX KLAN ACT AND JIM CROW LAWS

Although the Fourteenth and Fifteenth Amendments secured equal rights for blacks, they also created a backlash among middle-class southern whites who saw the rise of blacks in industry and politics as a threat to their own economic status. To counteract the radicals, who used whatever means possible to encourage blacks to exercise their voting rights, defiant whites in the South formed secret societies. The most notorious of these was known as the Ku Klux Klan (KKK). The Klan, established in 1866, started out as a harmless social club, but soon evolved into a vigilante organization designed to terrorize blacks into submission and force them out of politics and the work force. Their tactics included dressing in sheets and passing themselves off as the ghosts of Confederate soldiers come to take revenge on the rebellious blacks. This led to outright force, including whipping black officeholders and, in some cases, Klansmen resorted to murder and lynching.

Republican and Civil War hero General Ulysses S. Grant was elected president in 1868. In 1870 and 1871, Congress initiated three Force Acts in an attempt to stem the tide of the Klan movement by sending troops in to oversee federal elections and arrest any Klansmen engaged in terrorist activities. The last of these, the Ku Klux Klan Act, had the most impact; those who tried to prevent qualified citizens from voting were fined or imprisoned. The president suspended the writ of habeas corpus in nine South Carolina counties and sent federal troops to ensure a fair 1872 election.

This helped weaken the Klan organization, but did not eradicate the KKK, its supporters, or their agenda. By the mid-1870s, whites in the North and South, including those who might have been sympathetic to the African Americans' plight, had grown weary of the situation. Northerners and the federal government, seeing that a threat of slavery no longer existed, left the South to manage its own affairs.

A practice designed to keep African Americans marginalized in a de facto caste social structure, known as the Jim Crow system, rose up in the South in the latter part of the nineteenth century. (Jim Crow was the name of a character in minstrel shows—often a caricature of a black person—performed in the pre-Civil War South.)

The Jim Crow system grew quickly. Blacks were arrested on minor charges, and when they couldn't pay their fines (sometimes as much as

SEGREGATION IN THE WEST

Blacks also suffered racial discrimination in the military following the Civil War, including those sent out west. Two segregated (colored) infantries were assigned white officers, thus limiting their chances to rise through the ranks. Blacks sent out west (known as "Buffalo soldiers") constructed roads and forts, protected wagon trains, and engaged in campaigns to control the Indian tribes. Over time, settlers in western towns developed an antagonistic attitude toward members of the black military. Incidents of whites murdering black soldiers were not uncommon. Yet, once their service ended, many blacks settled out west and encouraged others to leave the South and its brutalities to find a better life in the West.

$500), a judge sentenced them to hard labor in the fields, on railroad gangs, or in factories for as little as five cents a day. Whenever possible, blacks resisted this bigotry by moving to the larger cities in the South, where discrimination still occured but jobs paid better. Eventually an elite community of black doctors, lawyers, and merchants existed to serve the African American clientele. The rise of African American professionals only caused the southern white community to search for other ways to keep this faction "in their place."

No language in the Constitution forbade separate facilities for blacks and whites. With that in mind, local politicians passed laws establishing black drinking fountains, waiting rooms, train and bus seating, and forbade blacks from entering parks, white-owned movie theaters, restaurants, and other public places. Although the practice had existed for years, these laws supported the discrimination by making it legal.

Black public schools caught the brunt of this segregation. State taxes were distributed to local school districts, with all-white schools receiving the bulk of the funds, while all-black systems received very little.

OPPOSITE: An African American using the colored entrance of a movie theater in Mississippi in 1939. This is one example of the Jim Crow laws that established racial segregation for public facilities in the South.

TOP RIGHT: Jim Crow song sheet cover, *c.*1835, of Thomas Dartmouth "Daddy" Rice in his celebrated blackface minstrel performance.

BOTTOM RIGHT: A cartoon published in *Puck* magazine, 1913, ridiculing the Jim Crow laws. The drawing depicts an "Airship for the Sunny South with a segregated 'Jim Crow' trailer."

JIM CROW.
NEW YORK.
Published by North &Hall, No 1 Franklin Sq

TESTING THE ELECTORAL COLLEGE AND ITS POWER

To win the presidential election, a candidate must have the majority of electoral votes, a total of 270. Each state appoints a certain number of electors equal to the number of its senators and representatives in Congress. With the two-party system, a party needs to win the majority of the votes in a state to win the whole state. When voters cast a ballot, they are in effect voting for their state's electors as well. The exceptions are Nebraska and Maine, whose residents still vote for their electors.

Electoral disputes are settled by the states. Congress counts the votes (usually just a formality) on January 6.

Over the years, politicians and the public have objected to the Electoral College because a candidate may win enough electoral votes but not a majority of the popular vote. In other words, if a candidate has less than 50 percent of the popular vote but carries key states with a greater number of electors, that candidate may win according to the Electoral College. For example, in 1968, Richard Nixon won 43 percent of the popular vote and 301 electoral votes. His opponent Hubert Humphrey won 42 percent of the popular vote and only 197 electoral votes, even

though the popular election was close. A third candidate, George Wallace, got 13 percent of the popular votes and 40 electoral votes.

The election of 1876 put the machinery of the Electoral College to the test. Republicans had nominated Rutherford B. Hayes of Ohio; the Democrats put up the wealthy Samuel Tilden of New York. After most votes were counted, it appeared Tilden had carried four northern states and all the southern states, giving him 184 electoral votes against Hayes' 165, with an additional twenty votes disputed. Of these twenty, nineteen were from Florida, South Carolina, and Louisiana, enough to swing the election. In the South, Republicans moved quickly, and telegraphed their political workers in those states, ordering them to declare Democratic ballots invalid, which would give the election to Hayes.

Democrats protested, and when it was time to add up the ballots, the Democratic House and the Republican Senate couldn't agree on who should do the counting. After Congress created an electoral commission to settle the matter, all sorts of corruptive practices came to light: the Louisiana governor sold electoral votes; blacks had been forced away from the polls; and the Florida election board had offered its votes to Tilden. Controversy and accusations wore on until the commission finally awarded the election to Hayes, but that didn't end it. Democrats threatened to filibuster (an extremely long speech used to keep

congressional members from acting on a measure) to prevent recording the vote. Finally the Compromise of 1877 settled the conflict. Southern Democrats cut a deal with Hayes: if he promised to remove troops from their states and let them handle their own affairs, they would agree to the election results. Hayes gave his consent and thus the Reconstruction period was brought to an end.

Democrats, for the most part, held forth in the South for about the next hundred years. Blacks had been freed, but southern manipulation of their rights (poll taxes, literacy tests, and rampant discrimination in schools, restaurants, and other public places) was a practice largely ignored by the whites throughout other parts of the nation. This climate existed until the 1960s, when the black community, sensing that civil rights was an idea whose time had come, rose up and demanded true equality, long overdue.

SEPARATE BUT EQUAL

The Supreme Court put its endorsement on forced segregation when, in 1896, it ruled that states could decree that public places be separated into black and white sections in the *Plessy vs. Ferguson* case. In 1892, a black man, Homer Plessy, refused to be placed in a segregated railroad car. The Supreme Court, voting 7-1 in favor of Ferguson, said that the states were within their rights to establish separate accommodations and educational facilities, because this did "not necessarily imply the inferiority of either race." Justice John Marshall Harlan, who submitted the one dissenting vote, stated, "Our Constitution is color blind. The arbitrary separation of citizens on the basis of race…is a badge of servitude…inconsistent with civil freedom."

OPPOSITE TOP: Rutherford B. Hayes, nineteenth president of the United States. In his inaugural address, Hayes promised to support wise, honest, and peaceful government in the South.

OPPOSITE BOTTOM: The Electoral Commission of 1877 holds a secret session by candlelight in Washington. The commission was set up to decide the result of the controversial presidential election.

RIGHT, TOP AND BOTTOM: Segregation continued into the 1960s in public places.

THEODORE ROOSEVELT TAKES OVER

Few, if any, presidents ignored the Constitution's presidential limits of power as much as Theodore Roosevelt. He had served as vice president under William McKinley and took office in 1901 after McKinley's assassination. The new president barely had his large family settled into the White House before he imprinted his own brand of imperial rule on the executive branch. In 1902, he mediated in a strike brought by the United Mine Workers against the anthracite coal companies, which were owned by the railroads. The strike had gone on for several months with no end in sight. The miners demanded a 19–20 percent raise and shorter hours, plus fringe benefits, but the owners said no. Roosevelt brought the parties together and asked for concessions on both sides. This served only to anger the coal operators and gain public support for the miners. In the end, Roosevelt threatened to send in federal troops to take over the mines. That worked. Both sides agreed to have the

president appoint a commission to resolve the issue and the miners returned to work. In 1903 they received a 10 percent raise in pay (the cost of which the coal companies, in turn, passed on to the public by increasing the price of coal). This also made the coal companies happy, since they were not required to recognize the UMW.

Roosevelt garnered high praise from the American people for his leadership strength and take-charge strategy, especially since he had moved forward without first asking for a backing from Congress. It was also the first time government had arbitrated a dispute between management and labor as well as the first time both parties met at the White House on equal footing. By widening the parameters for what was considered rightful presidential action, this resolution by government intervention marked a new era in the American presidency.

Roosevelt's ultimate dream, building a canal through the isthmus of Panama, was also realized without involvement from Congress. Panama, a province of Colombia, declared itself a republic (with U.S. support) after Colombia refused to grant Roosevelt permission to build the canal. Roosevelt ordered gunboats sent down as protection, and the digging began in earnest. "I took Panama," Roosevelt said, "without the help of the cabinet." He also went around the House of Representatives, the Senate, and the Constitution, later saying, "The Panama Canal would not have been started if I had not taken hold of it," implying that a prolonged congressional debate with numerous hearings might have resulted in the project's defeat.

Big business was not beyond Roosevelt's aim, either. He was known as a trustbuster, yet believed in acting prudently. In 1905 he focused on the railroads and asked for an increase in power for the Interstate Commerce Commission, so that the ICC could fix rates, not merely dispute unreasonable ones. He also insisted on gaining the right to inspect the railroads' private records—the only way to determine if rates were fair. Congress objected, saying that private records should stay private. Yet Roosevelt continued to push and in 1907 the Hepburn Bill was passed, granting the commission the authority to inspect the railroad companies' finances, in the event that a shipper filed a complaint against the railroad.

Roosevelt managed all this and more, and one may wonder how he was able to accomplish these unprecedented measures and why Congress didn't protest his independent actions more frequently. Perhaps it was because the people and the press lauded his initiative so completely that opposition from Congress might serve only to invite criticism.

OPPOSITE: President Theodore Roosevelt, twenty-sixth president of the United States, with his family in 1903. From left: youngest son Quentin, Theodore, Theodore Jr., Archibald, Alice, Kermit, wife Edith, and Ethel.
TOP RIGHT: Shovels at work at the Culebra Cut, an artificial valley which forms part of the Panama Canal. This view is from the west bank. The photograph appeared in the book *The Panama Canal*, by J. Saxon Mills, published in the early 1900s.

WILSON'S RAILROAD

In April 1917, the United States entered World War I, and President Woodrow Wilson, seeing that the country's railroad industry had suffered financial setbacks due to rising taxes and operating costs, decided to nationalize the railroads for the duration of the war. The United States Railroad Association (USRA) trimmed costs by eliminating nonessential routes. At the same time, the USRA ordered 100,000 new railroad cars and 1,930 steam engines. Later, Wilson told Congress he enacted the measure "because there were some things which the government can do and private management cannot."

ABOVE: Woodrow Wilson, twenty-eighth president of the United States. After World War I, Wilson advocated for the United States to join the League of Nations, but Congress refused to support the measure.

PRESIDENTS, CONGRESS, SUPREME COURT, AND CIVIL RIGHTS

In the 1950s, during the Eisenhower administration, the issue of civil rights gained a foothold. Other countries had begun to take notice that nearly 100 years after the Emancipation Proclamation, blacks still did not enjoy the same privileges as whites. Separate schools and facilities for blacks were common throughout the South and resentment and anger were rising within black communities across the country. Eisenhower did little to force legislation granting equal rights, but after he appointed Earl Warren as Chief Justice of the Supreme Court, things slowly began to change. Warren felt it was time to help advance the cause, and in 1954 the court took on the case of *Brown vs. Board of Education of Topeka,* in which the "separate but equal" decision by the court in the 1896 *Plessy vs. Ferguson* case came under dispute. In *Brown vs. Board of Education,* Oliver Brown, a welder from Topeka, Kansas, sued the Topeka board, stating that his daughter was forced to take a bus to the black school rather than attend the nearby neighborhood school with her white friends.

It was argued that there was no "equal" where segregation was concerned and its existence was harmful for both blacks and whites. The very fact of segregation implied that blacks were inferior to whites. Chief Justice Earl Warren convinced the other eight justices to rule for Brown against the "separate but equal" decision made in 1896, thus reversing *Plessy vs. Ferguson.*

During the next few years, the southern states made no efforts toward desegregation and, although Eisenhower gave lip service to the Supreme Court decision, he did little to support it, fearing that forced integration could only lead to mob rule by whites, and it appeared he was right. Often

ABOVE: Rosa Parks, American civil rights advocate, sits at the front of a public bus in Montgomery, Alabama, on December 21, 1956, the day buses were integrated in the city. Reporter Nicholas C. Criss is seated behind her.

"I HAVE A DREAM"

In August 1963, 200,000 people, mostly black, led by Dr. Martin Luther King Jr., descended on Washington, demanding the passage of the Civil Rights Act. Dr. King's "I Have a Dream" speech, in which he proclaimed there would be a time when his children would be judged "not by the color of their skin but by the content of their character," became an iconic event in the nation's history.

RIGHT: The Reverend Martin Luther King Jr. (third from right) leads the march from Selma, Alabama, to the state capitol at Montgomery in 1965. Altogether there were three marches protesting the extreme restrictions that Alabama had enacted for black voters.

if a southern white school allowed integration, crowds gathered in protest and shouted offensive epithets to blacks as they tried to enter. In 1957, when Central High School in Little Rock, Arkansas, opened the institution to a few blacks, Governor Orval Faubus called out the National Guard to keep the black students from entering. Eisenhower, realizing that the governor had broken federal law, sent troops and ordered 10,000 National Guardsmen to federal duty, taking control from Faubus. The black students entered school and a small contingent of the National Guard remained there for the rest of the year.

The civil rights movement, only a tiny seedling at first, was spread all across the country by the late 1950s. In 1955, Rosa Parks, a black seamstress for a Montgomery, Alabama, department store, refused to give up her bus seat to a white man after the seats designated to whites had been filled. The bus driver didn't specifically have the authority to demand that she stand, but it was customary for a driver to call the police if a black passenger refused. She was arrested. In explaining her actions, she later said, "I would have to know once and for all what rights I had as a human being and a citizen." On the day of her trial and for several days after, protesters staged a major boycott of the bus company. The boycott, led by a young minister, Dr. Martin Luther King Jr., gained national prominence, which in turn led to the formation of the Southern Christian Leadership Conference (SCLC) and the Congress of Racial Equality. Blacks organized "sit-ins" at whites-only lunch counters, forcing the restaurants to serve them. In 1961, a group of blacks, along with sympathetic whites, set up a series of "freedom rides" to test the federal laws forbidding segregated transportation. One Alabama bus was set on fire, and mob violence ensued. That year, the nation had a new president, John F. Kennedy. He was the son of a Boston millionaire and a man who understood that the country could no longer ignore racial inequalities and still keep the peace. He put forth a civil rights bill in 1963, which included a ban on discrimination in public places and protection of voting rights for all citizens.

Kennedy's civil rights proposal lingered in Congress. On the day of his assassination, November 22, 1963, Lyndon Baines Johnson was sworn in as president aboard *Air Force One*. Johnson had served eleven years in the Senate and knew how to manipulate legislators to force bills through committee and ensure their passage. The Civil Rights Act, passed in 1964, forbade racial and gender discrimination by employers and outlawed segregation in public places. The Twenty-fourth Amendment to the Constitution, also passed in 1964, made certain that nothing prevented qualified blacks from voting in national elections. The Voting Rights Act of 1965 and a Supreme Court ruling in 1966 banned poll taxes from state elections as well.

This shows how much can be accomplished when a president knows how to handle the congressional dynamic. However, by 1968, Johnson was seen as a failure when, during the later years of his administration, he allowed the Vietnam War to escalate, causing widespread protests by young people opposed to being drafted into a war they felt was

ABOVE: Lyndon Baines Johnson is sworn in as the thirty-sixth president of the United States by Judge Sarah T. Hughes aboard *Air Force One* at Love Field, Dallas, following the assassination of President John F. Kennedy in 1963. Mrs. Kennedy is on the far right. Johnson was the only president to be given the oath of office by a woman.

unwinnable and unnecessary. Seeing his popularity quickly declining, he declared that he would not run again for the presidency.

During the past two centuries, presidents have been allowed to seize power during a "state of emergency." According to the Special Committee on the Termination of the National Emergency, over 400 provisions give the president authority to enact such measures as the ability to seize property and commodities, send troops abroad, institute martial law, seize and control all transportation and communication, regulate the operation of private enterprise, and restrict travel—all without the need to follow constitutional guidelines.

In 1973, the committee met to discuss whether or not the country actually existed in a state of emergency and what would be considered one in the future. That year the Senate passed the War Powers Act over President Richard Nixon's veto. Congress was concerned about how both the Johnson and Nixon administrations had handled the Vietnam War (fraught with illegalities and deceptions), and felt that it was time to reassert its authority. In fact, the wars in North Korea and Vietnam had never been declared by Congress, although the Constitution states that the power is given to the legislative branch. The War Powers Act now requires the president to request authority from Congress before troops are deployed, and also limits the length of deployment to sixty days with a thirty-day withdrawal period unless an extension is approved. Presidents have deployed troops several times without consulting Congress, yet no president has been censured or otherwise called to task. All presidents since 1973 have said they believe the War Powers Act is unconstitutional.

8 | LEGISLATING HUMAN BONDAGE

THE TRAIL OF TEARS—THE INDIAN REMOVAL ACT OF 1830

They were called the five "Civilized Tribes," proposed in 1790 by George Washington and Secretary of War Henry Knox as models for the "cultural transformation." Washington and Knox suggested that when indigenous people (such as these) learned American customs and values, they would be able to merge those customs with their own tribal traditions and join society. They viewed this as the best possible future for Native Americans and the Anglo-European settlers of North America. While living alongside one another, these five—the Cherokee, Choctaw, Chickasaw, Creek, and Seminole—also simultaneously maintained their status as autonomous nations. As "civilized" peoples, many lived in houses, educated their children in U.S. schools, and wore the same clothes as their white neighbors. The Cherokee, for example, had even developed a written language and alphabet. In the 1820s, several tribally run farm communities were located throughout the "Deep South." Some even owned black slaves. Though these natives had been virtually assimilated into white society, it was argued that the lands they farmed were, all in all, too valuable to remain in their hands. This seemingly peaceful cohabitation was never meant to last.

After angry debate and over the objections of legislators Daniel Webster and Davy Crockett, President Andrew Jackson urged passage of the Indian Removal Act in 1830. Crockett stormed out of the House of Representatives, yelling all the while, "I would rather be honestly damned than hypocritically immortalized! You can go to hell, I'm going to Texas!"

The Supreme Court overturned the act, claiming the Cherokee as a sovereign nation, but President Jackson challenged: "Well, (Chief Justice) John Marshall has made his decision. Now let him enforce it," suggesting the impossibility of upholding such an unpopular ruling. The Indian Removal Act was finally passed in 1831 and the "Civilized Tribes" were pried off their land, allowed to take what they could carry in wagons and on their backs, and were escorted from Georgia and other southern states toward the Indian Territory in Oklahoma and the Texas panhandle.

ABOVE RIGHT: Cherokee Chief Sequoya (1770–1843) holding a copy of the Cherokee alphabet used for books and news materials that circulated throughout the "Civilized Tribe" that was driven off their land.

OPPOSITE: The removal of the Cherokee along with five other tribes in 1838 from their lands in the East to reservations in the West by an act of Congress. Thousands died during the long trek to the Indian Territory.

TEXANS' SECOND TRAIL OF TEARS— CHEROKEE WAR OF 1839

The influx of so many tribes into Texas threatened to explode into racial warfare at any time. In December 1838, Governor Sam Houston left office to be replaced by Mirabeau Lamar, who referred to the Indians—all Indians—as "Wild Cannibals of the Woods." With the spirit of eradication in mind, Lamar's Texas troops conducted a two-day slaughter on July 15 and 16, called the Cherokee War of 1839. They burned villages and killed every Native American they could find, including women and children: Cherokees, Delawares, Shawnees, Cados, Kickapoos, Creeks, Seminoles, and Comanches. No prisoners were taken. The fleeing survivors escaped north into Oklahoma.

Of the 13,000 Cherokee herded west, 4,000 died of starvation, disease, and exposure. Black freedmen and European Americans who had married into the tribes also made the trek. Now dependent on the government for their subsistence, the Native Americans found their new homes in Oklahoma to be scrubland, a far cry from the rich farmsteads they had left in the southeast. The white settlers already living in Oklahoma did not welcome their new neighbors with open arms, and soon raids and depredations by both whites and Indians began. Food, blankets, and shelter were provided by a politically motivated Indian Bureau, who short-weighted scales, sold cheap trade goods, and stocked their stores with watered whiskey. They filled their pockets with the unspent government funds and ignored the tribes' pleas for seed corn, cattle, horses, and farm implements.

By the end of the forced migration, 46,000 Native Americans had been transplanted, throwing open twenty-five million acres of Georgia plantation land to new white settlement. The movement ended around 1838. In Texas, Governor Sam Houston managed to pacify most of the tribes and yet the segregation and isolation of the Native Americans would continue well into the twentieth century. By this time, the tribes had discovered the oil reserve riches beneath their scrubland and found entertainment and income in the glitz and glitter of legal, tribe-owned gambling casinos.

"OLD HICKORY" JACKSON AND THE INDIANS

Hickory is a hard wood, and Andrew Jackson was a hard man of action, quick to take offense, to exact punishment, and to intimidate anyone who opposed him. As the seventh president of the United States (1829–1837), he carried with him his victories against the British in the Battle of New Orleans in 1815 and the bloody swath he cut through central Florida in pursuit of the Seminole Indians who were allied with British interests at the time. His aggressive brush with these "savages" motivated his endorsement of the Indian Removal Act of 1830. He came into politics—virtually creating the modern Democratic Party—as a wealthy southern slave holder. He was a populist who used the spoils system—throwing open former Indian lands to his voter base of white settlers and speculators—to buy the loyalty of his cronies.

THE FUGITIVE SLAVE ACT

S lavery dominated politics, the economy, and was an eroding force in American society from the colonial era to the late nineteenth century. It continued to taint much of the United States' identity through the twentieth as well. But the friction between free and slave interests began striking sparks in the mid-nineteenth century. Ever-increasing awareness of the entrenched cruelty and inherent contradiction of legal, commercialized human bondage in a country founded upon lofty ideals concerning basic, individual human rights fostered an aggressive and growing force for abolition. Though northern industries made profits off the products harvested and processed by unpaid slaves, religious and social organizations sought freedom for the millions bound to the southern plantations, fields, and mills. Their objections, however, ran counter to the U.S. Constitution as it was originally conceived—in an atmosphere of political compromise. At the time of its drafting, southern ratification was necessary and so the Fugitive Slave Clause of 1793 was written into the Constitution to enforce Article 4, Section 2 as Clause 3, which stated:

> That when a person held to labor in any of the United States, or in either of the Territories on the Northwest or South of the river Ohio, under the laws thereof, shall escape into any other part of the said States or Territory, the person to whom such labor or service may be due, his agent or attorney, is hereby empowered to seize or arrest such fugitive from labor, and to take him or her before any Judge of the Circuit or District Courts of the United States...that the person so seized or arrested, doth, under the laws of the State or Territory from which he or she fled, owe service or labor to the person claiming him or her, it shall be the duty of such Judge or magistrate to give a certificate thereof to such claimant, his agent, or attorney, which shall be sufficient warrant for removing the said fugitive from labor to the State or Territory from which he or she fled.

Many of the northern states passed local "personal liberty" laws that circumvented this federal legislation, refused the use of state-owned jail facilities to hold suspected runaways, and/or juries simply failed to indict any black brought before them in state-mandated trials. The U.S. Supreme Court ruled in 1842 that "states did not have to aid in hunting or recapture of slaves." "Free Staters" sent operatives into the South to encourage runaways and created the renowned Underground Railroad of hidden trails and safe houses designed to elude slave-catchers and their bloodhound dogs. Slave-catching became a lucrative business for the bounties of significant cash offered for each slave returned. Recaptured slaves were often beaten, had their Achilles tendon slashed, or were forced

DRED SCOTT DECISION IGNITES SHAME

Dred Scott was a freed slave who had lived in Illinois and Wisconsin. He moved to Missouri, a divided slave "free soil" state. In 1857, he was arrested as a runaway slave and held without trial, in accordance with the Fugitive Slave Act, on the grounds that, given his former slave master was dead, he could not prove he was free. His case was appealed to the U.S. Supreme Court, where Chief Justice Roger Taney declared that "all blacks—slaves as well as free—were not and could never become citizens of the United States." He went on to declare the Missouri Compromise unconstitutional, thereby permitting slavery in all the United States territories. Since Scott was black, he was not a citizen and therefore had no right to sue. Taney further claimed, "the framers of the Constitution believed that blacks 'had no rights which the white man was bound to respect.' [Blacks could be] bought and sold and treated as an ordinary article of merchandise and traffic, whenever profit could be made by it."

After the case was closed, the sons of Scott's former master bought him as well as his wife and set them free. He died nine months later.

ABOVE: Dred Scott (1799–1858) filed suit for his freedom in 1857 after he was transported to a free state. The Supreme Court ruled he could not sue since he had "no rights which any white man was bound to respect." Scott was purchased by a free-state family and freed.

to wear an iron collar by their owners both as punishment and to discourage any future attempts to escape.

To greater fortify this system of slave retrieval, the Missouri Compromise of 1850 had, based on the 1793 clause, a definitive Fugitive Slave Act written in. Besides strengthening the original clause, the Fugitive Slave Act of 1850 demanded any federal law officer who did *not* arrest an alleged runaway be liable to a $1,000 fine (equivalent to approximately $26,000 in today's currency). Suspected slaves were not permitted to request a jury trial or allowed to testify on their own behalf, and any person who aided a runaway slave was subject to six months in prison and a $1,000 fine. These penalties were openly flaunted. An example occurred in Oberlin, Ohio, in 1858, when thirty-seven people helped an escaped slave and were indicted. Only two served any jail time.

BELOW: Following the war, a flood of freed slaves crossed through Union army lines from their southern states looking for work, homes, and education in the North without fear of being captured and dragged back to their masters' plantations.

UNCLE TOM'S CABIN

Harriet Beecher Stowe was a Connecticut teacher who had attended the Hartford Female Academy. She was also an ardent abolitionist and deeply affected by the passage of the Fugitive Slave Act. In 1852, she wrote a book based on the reminiscences of an ex-slave living in Canada. *Uncle Tom's Cabin* was about this old slave who was loyal to his owners and the trials and tribulations of the people around him. Stereotypes abide and sentimentality soaks through the pages, but in the vernacular of the day her writing forced an examination of slavery at a human level. It first ran as a magazine serial, and then the book's first edition sold 300,000 copies. *Uncle Tom's Cabin* became a runaway best-seller and ultimately one of the most widely read publications of the century. Abraham Lincoln met Stowe near the beginning of the Civil War and the story goes that, when the two were introduced, he said, "So this is the little lady who started this great war."

The Chinese Exclusion Act and Japanese Internment

Unlike the out-and-out slavery of the Deep South, the Chinese Exclusion Act of 1882 was its own version of extreme racial discrimination. At a time in U.S. history when the country's growth and opportunities were outstripping the population's ability to extract the available bounty, three solutions arrived. Each provided a massive influx of the cheap labor power needed to grow the country's infrastructure. In the South, up to the year 1820, slaves had been kidnapped from Africa and sold like cattle to plantation owners. In the East, thousands of Irish were fleeing the potato famine and those who survived the ocean crossing arrived poor but eager to work. On the West Coast, the 1849 gold rush brought an explosion of commerce; strong hands and strong backs were much in demand. Thousands of Chinese emigrated to the coasts of California and the Northwest. As the gold rush petered out circa 1869, construction began on the transcontinental railroad. Its eastern leg, contracted to the Union Pacific Railroad, was worked by Irish, African American, and Eastern European laborers. They were to be met at some point by the Central Pacific Railway coming from the west, built mostly by the burgeoning California Chinese population, which had become the predominant immigrant population in the region.

At the conclusion of the post-Civil War period, construction began to wane and many mines were closed. As labor demand shrank, the Chinese became viewed as a burden on the labor market. Although they worked for very low wages, were conscientious, plentiful, and cheap to house (most were males recruited from China exclusively to work, not to settle in with families), Congress closed immigration to the Chinese by 1878. President Hayes vetoed that attempted legislation, but the Chinese Exclusion Act finally passed in 1882. Now, this huge labor pool faced the choice of remaining and enduring racial mistreatment by competing white workers who claimed the "coolies" caused depressed wages, or returning to impoverished China. The Chinese who remained settled into enclaves in major West Coast cities (Chinatowns), frequently establishing restaurant and laundry businesses.

For Chinese immigrants, creating families was challenging given that the exclusion was primarily aimed at women. At that time, Chinese women were considered quite exotic, and many new arrivals were presumed by white society to be prostitutes. Chinese custom also kept married women at home to serve their parents until sent for by their husbands. Ironically, smuggling actual Chinese prostitutes into California and West Coast cities for long-suffering Chinese males in the U.S. became a thriving business.

The hardest blow for existing immigrants was the Exclusion Act of 1882, which proclaimed a ten-year limit on the suspension of Chinese immigration. Even if they wished to, they were now unable to unite families, and those in the States had little hope of returning to mainland China in their lifetime. In reality, this act remained in force much longer; it was not repealed until the Magnuson Act on December 17, 1943.

On December 7, 1941, Japan attacked the U.S. naval base at Pearl Harbor, Hawaii, with an aircraft carrier strike force of torpedo planes, dive bombers, and fighter aircraft. Surprise was complete, as was the almost total devastation of the U.S. Navy battleship fleet. At the same time the attack force was closing in on the Hawaiian Island naval base,

Japanese diplomats were conducting peace talks with Cordell Hull, the Secretary of State in Washington. No declaration of war by the Japanese was made prior to the attack due to a clerical translation error. When told of the error in timing, the architect of the attack, Admiral Isoroku Yamamoto, is reported to have said, "We have awakened a sleeping giant."

Awakened, the Depression-weary Americans shook off their exhausted torpor and headed for military recruiting depots, for industrial plants switching over to war production, and to the task of civil defense in case the attacks approached their homeland. They also began to look quite differently into the faces of the 112,000 Japanese-Americans who were living alongside them as neighbors and fellow citizens. The military generals were unnerved. They had seen both the Pearl Harbor navy and army commanders stripped of their commands prior to court martial. These weren't like the Germans or the Italians the U.S. was now committed to fight in Europe, enemies who looked "just like us." These were "Japs" who were ready to betray Americans just as their spies did at Pearl Harbor. These were the "Mongolians" who already infested the West Coast with their truck farms and businesses, taking away jobs from natural-born Americans since the turn of the century. Panic mixed with racial prejudice, and a need to retaliate was in the air.

Two months after the attack, with Japanese forces sweeping over bases in the Pacific, sinking ships and crushing U.S. allies, Franklin Delano Roosevelt signed Executive Order 9066—under Constitution-provided emergency powers—on February 19, 1942, allowing local military commanders to designate "exclusion zones" from which any person could be expelled, and all people of Japanese ancestry were instantly "excluded" from the entire California, Oregon, and Washington coast and from the state of Arizona. The constitutionality of this order was upheld by the Supreme Court two years later (1944), and the United States Census Bureau secretly turned over its records to pinpoint the homes of Japanese residents to military and police "Jap hunters." (This was denied but later proved in a 2007 investigation.)

Japanese-Americans of all generations were swept up into internment camps guarded by troops and barbed wire, losing their homes, businesses, and civil rights for the duration of the war. The camps were all located in most of the states east of the Rocky Mountains and west of the Mississippi River and provided with minimum necessities, running water, sanitation facilities, and education for children.

In 1980, an investigation into the wartime relocation and internment was called for by President Jimmy Carter. A presidential commission recommended reparation payments of $20,000 to each camp survivor. In 1988, Congress passed legislation which apologized and claimed government actions were based on "race prejudice, war hysteria, and failure of political leadership." Altogether, $1.6 billion was paid out to internees and their heirs.

OPPOSITE: A Chinese family waits on a street corner in San Francisco's Chinatown. Throughout California and the West Coast, Chinese immigrants gathered together in enclaves for economic and social survival and to avoid racial friction with white citizens. ABOVE: On April 4, 1942, Japanese citizens of the United States line up to board a train to their internment camp at the Santa Anita Racetrack in California. All Japanese Americans were "excluded" from West Coast homes and businesses, to be interned under guard for the war's duration.

RACIAL EXCLUSION CONTINUES— IMMIGRATION ACT OF 1924

As if the Exclusion Act of 1882 wasn't tough enough for Chinese working hard to make a place for themselves and their culture in the United States, the Immigration Act of 1924 doubled down by excluding all classes of Chinese immigrants, and then extending even more restrictions to additional Asian groups. Nowhere in these draconian acts did Congress address the true underlying conflicts: labor competition that white workers were experiencing due to the influx of cheap, immigrant laborers. In the wake of the shunned Chinese, immigrant Japanese quickly filled in the cheap labor gap. Through dint of hard work, they had greater good fortune assimilating than their Asian neighbors. The Japanese avoided isolationist enclaves, reaching into American society through education and long work hours, learning to adapt and integrate into the established white society.

9 | LEGISLATING MORALITY

CONGRESS PASSES THE FIRST LAWS REGARDING PROTEST, IMMIGRATION, SEDITION, AND COMPETITION

War with France, our former ally, seemed imminent. The Federalist Congress and their champion, President John Adams, feared internal conflicts within our new government as minority congressmen rose to speak against his policies and his "imperial" style that stifled freedom of dissent. Specifically, the Federalists considered any civilian protest which ran counter to holding the Union together in a time of potential war to be treasonous. In response to this internal threat, a series of four laws—the Alien and Sedition Acts—were speedily pushed through Congress and signed by Adams.

To halt the rush of immigrants, particularly "hordes of Wild Irishmen, nor the turbulent and disorderly of all the world, to come here with a basic view to distract our tranquility," the Naturalization Act was passed on June 18, 1798. The required time of residence in the U.S. was extended from five to fourteen years before becoming eligible for citizenship. Not surprisingly, this core of non-English naturalized citizens had been staunch supporters of the Federalist opposition, Jefferson's Democratic Republicans, in the election of 1796. This influx of foreign-born citizens helped establish the fledgling two-party system of government.

Following the Naturalization Act, on June 25, the Alien Act gave the president power to deport undesirable aliens during peacetime. The government began drawing up lists of these aliens and a number of aliens fled the country, but President Adams never signed an official deportation order.

The Alien Enemies Act was third to pass on July 6 and covered the arrest, imprisonment, or deportation of any alien during wartime who owed allegiance to a foreign power.

The fourth law, passed on July 14, was the Sedition Act, which collided head-on with the Constitution's Bill of Rights. It declared that "any treasonable activity, including those who 'write, print, utter, or publish... any false, scandalous and malicious writing' against the government were guilty of high misdemeanor, punishable by fine and imprisonment." The ink was barely dry when Democratic Republican newspapers were shut down and twenty-five lawbreakers, mostly editors, were jailed.

The public outcry was so great and prolonged that Thomas Jefferson, John Adams' adversary in his run for a second term, was readily swept into office in 1800 and an era of retraction ensued. Everyone convicted under the Sedition Act was pardoned and all fines were returned with interest.

A law to regulate competition was enacted in response to the Standard Oil Trust. A financial trust exists when stockholders in several companies

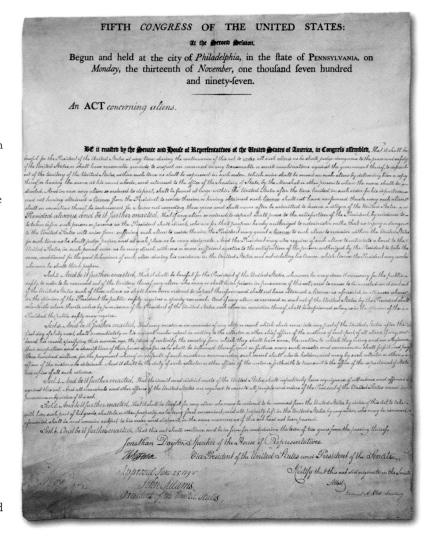

in the same industry transfer their shares to a single set of trustees. The stockholders then receive certificates entitling them to shares of the combined holdings of the jointly managed companies. The trustees apportion out the dividends to the shareholders from the profits sent to the trust from the collective of companies. In that industry, prices and costs are fixed to maximize profits and kill competition.

The Standard Oil Trust was established by John D. Rockefeller in 1882 and every stockholder received twenty trust certificates for each share of Standard Oil Stock. The trust had selected all the directors and officers of the participating companies, thereby creating an oil monopoly with which no single oil company could compete. The Sherman Anti-Trust Act of 1890—named after Senator John Sherman of Ohio, a chairman of the Senate Finance Committee and the Secretary of the Treasury under President Hayes—was designed to dissolve these trusts. In Standard Oil's case: Sonoco, Esso, Chevron, and many "Standard Oil of (Name the State)" companies spun away from the parent.

By the time President Theodore Roosevelt came along at the turn of the twentieth century, the Supreme Court had weakened the loosely worded Sherman Act. Specifically, in the case of *United States vs. E. C. Knight Company* it was shown that even though Knight controlled 98 percent of sugar refining in the U.S., it had violated no law. Despite this setback, Roosevelt became feared for his "trustbusting," and the act was used a number of times against companies such as Northern Securities, American Tobacco, and, 100 years after its passage, against the modern-day giant Microsoft Corporation.

OPPOSITE: A copy of the Aliens Act, one of four Alien and Sedition Acts passed by Congress in rapid succession in 1798, when war with France was imminent and President John Adams feared internal strife might cause a breakdown in society.
RIGHT: A cartoon published in the *New York American* on March 30, 1912, titled "Everybody's Doing It" (after an Irving Berlin song) and depicting several elements dealing with lawbreakers battling for their trusts and lawmakers fighting against the monopolies.

FEDERAL PANIC—FAR-REACHING CONSEQUENCES

James Madison, an early champion, along with John Adams, of a strong central government, had a change of heart over the power of national authoritarian rule. He helped Kentucky legislators justify the ascendancy of states' rights over federal law. Along with Thomas Jefferson, he secretly wrote the Kentucky and Virginia resolutions supporting states' rights. They declared the federal union to be a "voluntary association of states," and if the federal government went too far, each state had the right to nullify that law. This argument appeared to give constitutional standing to the secession of the southern states from the Union, so much so that in 1830–31 they quoted Madison in their justifications. In fear that his nullification support would undermine the Union, Madison publicly declared that all the states had transferred their sovereignty to the federal government at the time the Constitution was ratified.

Nothing, however, could sway the southern states' resolve, and in 1861 South Carolina became the first state to officially secede from the Union. So began the Civil War.

PROHIBITION

When our soldiers returned in 1919 from World War I in France, they came off the troop ships to a country where, by the end of that year, it would be illegal to buy a mug of beer at their neighborhood saloon. First appearing in the 1820s, a campaign of religious revivalism proclaiming that alcohol addiction was "destroying American lives and values" had been gathering steam and political support. The voting power of the Anti-Saloon League and crowds of rural Protestants saw to the passage of the Eighteenth Amendment to the Constitution on January 29, 1919, which "prohibited the manufacturing, transportation and sale of alcohol within the United States." Twenty-three of the forty-eight states had already passed "dry" laws by 1916 and their representatives had won a two-thirds majority in Congress. To aid the enforcement of the amendment, a new "enabling" law, the Volstead Act—named after its sponsor, Representative Andrew J. Volstead of Minnesota—was passed.

President Woodrow Wilson immediately vetoed the act, but the veto was then overridden by Congress that same day. The day after Prohibition took effect, portable home-size stills went on sale around the country, reproductions of George Washington's recipe for beer in his own handwriting went up on kitchen walls, and people who had never taken a drink scrubbed their bathtubs clean to make gin.

A police officer in a rural Chicago suburb claimed that "just driving down a block of houses in some neighborhoods with your car windows open could make you dizzy from the smell of cooking whiskey mash." Anyone wanting a drink frequented saloons called "speakeasies" opened "for members only", while less particular establishments called "blind pigs" catered to the working man drinking dubious alcoholic beverages from coffee cups.

Criminals who had been content with extortion, hold-ups, smash-and-grab thefts, prostitution, and gambling for income embraced beer and whiskey manufacturing, sales, and distribution. They carved up big cities

TOP RIGHT: Whiskey barrels are lined up at the curb in a publicity photograph of 1925 showing a local politician dumping alcohol from busted barrels into the sewer, enforcing the Prohibition law.

BOTTOM RIGHT: The repeal of Prohibition by President Roosevelt in 1933 with the Twenty-first Amendment brought smiles to the faces of these drinkers who line up for a photograph touting the return of the alcohol industries and the freedom to take a drink without breaking the law.

OPPOSITE: Page 1 of a joint resolution proposed for consideration of Congress on December 5, 1932, that the Eighteenth Amendment (Prohibition) be repealed by the Twenty-first Amendment—the only example of this constitutional rectification.

Seventy-second Congress of the United States of America;

At the Second Session,

Begun and held at the City of Washington on Monday, the fifth
day of December, one thousand nine hundred and thirty-two.

JOINT RESOLUTION

Proposing an amendment to the Constitution of the United States.

*Resolved by the Senate and House of Representatives of the United
States of America in Congress assembled (two-thirds of each House
concurring therein),* That the following article is hereby proposed
as an amendment to the Constitution of the United States, which
shall be valid to all intents and purposes as part of the Constitution
when ratified by conventions in three-fourths of the several States:

"ARTICLE —

"SECTION 1. The eighteenth article of amendment to the Constitution of the United States is hereby repealed.

"SEC. 2. The transportation or importation into any State, Territory, or possession of the United States for delivery or use therein
of intoxicating liquors, in violation of the laws thereof, is hereby
prohibited.

"SEC. 3. This article shall be inoperative unless it shall have been
ratified as an amendment to the Constitution by conventions in the
several States, as provided in the Constitution, within seven years
from the date of the submission hereof to the States by the Congress."

Speaker of the House of Representatives.

*Vice President of the United States and
President of the Senate.*

INTERPRETING THE VOLSTEAD ACT—*NEW YORK DAILY NEWS*

The actual length of the Eighteenth Amendment was only 111
words. By comparison, the Volstead Act, which in fact explained
the amendment, consumed twenty-five pages. As a public service,
the *New York Daily News* interpreted the act for their readers
as follows:

- You may drink intoxicating liquor in your own home or in the
  home of a friend when you are a bona fide guest.
- You may buy intoxicating liquor on a bona fide medical
  prescription of a doctor. A pint can be bought every ten days.
- You may consider any place you live permanently as your home.
  If you have more than one home, you may keep a stock of
  liquor in each.
- You may keep liquor in any storage room or club locker,
  provided the storage place is for the exclusive use of yourself,
  family or bona fide guests.
- You may get a permit to move liquor when you change your
  residence.
- You may manufacture, sell or transport liquor for non-beverage
  or sacramental purposes provided you obtain a government
  permit.
- You cannot carry a hip flask.
- You cannot give away or receive a bottle of liquor as a gift.
- You cannot take liquor to hotels or restaurants and drink it in
  the public dining room.
- You cannot buy or sell formulas or recipes for homemade
  liquors.
- You cannot ship liquor for beverage use.
- You cannot store liquor in any place except your own home.
- You cannot manufacture anything above one half of one
  percent (liquor strength) in your home.
- You cannot display liquor signs or advertisements on your premises.
- You cannot remove reserve stocks from storage.

and rural counties into "territories," maintaining customer-buying
motivation with Thompson submachine guns and black powder bombs.
Criminal elements that had been scattered and entrepreneurial were now
acquiring business skills and becoming organized, reaping huge profits
amid short life spans.

Breaking the Prohibition law became a commonplace if not
grassroots culture. Even President Warren Harding had a full-time
White House "bootlegger" to supply the offices and Executive
Mansion with illegal alcohol for guests and weekly poker parties.

Enforcement was impossible and the health effects of poorly distilled
alcohol were disastrous. Citizens were being blinded, internal organs
were rotting out, and by 1932 the country was worn down by a
gripping depression that had not only destroyed the economy but
littered the streets with nefarious dead gangsters. Franklin Delano
Roosevelt promised a "New Deal" and was elected president. One of
his first acts as chief executive was to set the gears in motion to repeal
the Eighteenth Amendment with the Twenty-first Amendment, which
came to pass on December 5, 1933.

DESEGREGATION OF THE MILITARY

Ever since the 54th Massachusetts Infantry fixed their bayonets and charged across the open sands of Morris Island, South Carolina, into the blazing guns of Confederate Fort Wagner on July 18, 1863, the African American soldier's ability and desire to fight bravely has never been in question. The combat glory won by those freshly minted Union troops was passed on to the Buffalo soldiers of the 10th Cavalry who patrolled the West in the 1870s and 1880s, battling Apaches, Comanche, Sioux, and other great Native American tribes. Black army regulars followed Teddy Roosevelt and his Rough Riders up San Juan Hill in the 1898 Spanish–American War. In World War II, the Tuskegee Airmen of the 332nd Fighter Group escorted B-17 bombers over Europe. They never lost a Flying Fortress to enemy aircraft. The red-painted tails of their P-51 Mustang fighters became "Red-Tailed Angels" to the bomber pilots.

Time and again, African American soldiers had proved themselves worthy, but the military remained segregated. Black units drove trucks, worked at maintenance jobs, unloaded supplies, cooked mess hall meals, and made sure the officers' shirts were pressed. In combat, black units were mostly led by white officers. Advancement into the officer ranks was extremely difficult for black enlisted men.

REVISITING MILITARY RACE RELATIONS

On January 12, 1949, President Truman called together members of his Committee on Equality of Treatment and Opportunity in the Armed Forces, chaired by Charles H. Fahy. The committee was tasked with determining the concerns of the military leaders in regards to his executive order. Leaders from the army and Marine Corps supported their policies of segregation. Black soldiers went to all-black units. The navy, which had used blacks primarily as cabin stewards and mess deck sailors, said they would follow the order. The United States Air Force also announced their willingness to comply. The Marine Corps roster noted that of their 8,200 officers, only one was black.

LEFT: On July 26, 1948, President Harry S. Truman wrote the Executive Order desegregating the military, giving all races an equal chance for training, promotion and benefits.

It took a man from Missouri to "emancipate" the military. President Harry S. Truman, who rose to the office as thirty-third president from the office of vice president following the death of Franklin Delano Roosevelt, turned to his constitutional powers on July 26, 1948, and signed Executive Order 9981, which established equal treatment and opportunity in all the armed forces regardless of race.

From the Pentagon's point of view, the 1950s and early 1960s represented a calm period in race relations. Truman's executive order had brought blacks into the military mainstream and the cultural upheavals of the mid- and late 1960s provided the impetus for some measure of real equality. Increasing activism of the civil rights movement, and the widening of the Vietnam War, led to more wrenching change.

Decades would pass before the armed forces became completely color-blind, but the door had been opened and the question that never should have been asked was now answered. All men truly are created equal.

OPPOSITE TOP: Part of a racially integrated squad of U.S. Marines running to defend Tan Son Nhut air base on April 25, 1975, during evacuation of Americans from Vietnam.

ABOVE: Tuskegee Airmen in August 1944 next to one of their P-51 fighter planes. Escorting bombers to targets over Italy, they never lost a Flying Fortress to enemy fighter aircraft, winning the confidence of the white pilots with which they flew.

RIGHT: A 1943 poster of African American pilot Lieutenant Robert W. Dietz, encouraging civilians to buy war bonds to help finance World War II. Various races were depicted on these posters by the Department of the Treasury to reach as many Americans as possible.

Keep us flying!

BUY WAR BONDS

10 | CORRECTIONS AND CLARIFICATIONS

AFTER DECADES OF CAMPAIGNING, WOMEN FINALLY GAIN THE RIGHT TO VOTE

Ironically, the fight for women's rights in the United States began during the London Anti-Slavery Convention in 1840. Elizabeth Cady Stanton and Lucretia Mott joined forces after being ousted from the conference, which had ruled against women's participation. This set the stage for the Seneca Falls Women's Rights Convention of 1848. Cady crafted the Declaration of Sentiments, using the Declaration of Independence as her guide, but changed the phrase to "all men and women are created equal." The Sentiments document included eleven resolutions indicating the rights that women should enjoy as well as men. The ninth, the right to vote in all elections, proved to be the most shocking—even for some of the women in attendance. "Thee will make us ridiculous," Lucretia Mott told Stanton. It took the eloquence of former slave Frederick Douglass to persuade the group to pass the resolution, although the whole concept of women's rights was the subject of widespread ridicule in the press during the next several months. Stanton was thrilled. What could spread the word wider and faster than a sizable amount of ink in the press?

In 1851, Stanton and Susan B. Anthony crossed paths, but it wasn't until 1866 that they formed the American Equal Rights Association to secure the vote for all men and women, black or white. During the second half of the nineteenth century, Stanton and Anthony split from other suffragettes and formed the National Women's Rights Association when the vote was secured for black men with the Fourteenth Amendment, but the language did not include women's suffrage. In 1878, six years after Susan B. Anthony was arrested for attempting to vote in the 1872 presidential election, the Women's Suffrage Bill was introduced in

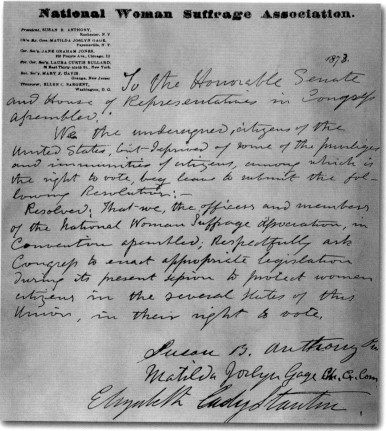

A "GOOD BOY"

Women's suffrage might have been delayed further were it not for Harry Burns, a twenty-four-year-old congressman from Tennessee, who cast the deciding vote in favor of the Nineteenth Amendment. Burns apparently chose to heed his mother's advice contained in a letter telling him to "be a good boy" and "vote for suffrage."

Congress. An idea somewhat before its time, it lingered there with little being done, although women continued to campaign for better working conditions and suffrage. Gradually, women's right to vote in local elections was granted in many western states, including Wyoming, Utah, Colorado, and Idaho, and later in Michigan, Kansas, Oregon, and Arizona. Then, in 1912, Theodore Roosevelt's Bull Moose Party initiated a women's suffrage plank in its convention platform.

Just when it appeared the movement had really taken hold (Jeanette Rankin became the first woman elected to the House of Representatives in 1916), the United States entered World War I and the women's campaign took a back seat. In the long term, this strengthened their cause, as it gave women the opportunity to show their worth and ability by carrying on men's work during wartime.

Finally, on August 16, 1920, Tennessee ratified the Nineteenth Amendment, giving the two-thirds majority needed for passage—eighty years after Susan B. Anthony and Elizabeth Cady Stanton had first crossed paths.

OPPOSITE TOP: "What a Woman may be and yet not have the Vote": English postcard, c.1910. British women over the age of thirty were granted voting rights in 1918 and in 1928 suffrage was extended to women over twenty-one.

OPPOSITE BOTTOM: Petition, signed by Susan B. Anthony and Elizabeth Cady Stanton of the National Women's Suffrage Association, to Congress, 1873, requesting that legislation be enacted granting women the right to vote.

ABOVE: Suffragette picketers outside the White House in Washington, D.C., c.1917. Sixteen suffragette picketers were arrested that year. A court later declared the arrests invalid.

ONE LIVED TO SEE IT

Only one signer of the 1848 Seneca Falls Declaration of Sentiments lived to see ratification of the Nineteenth Amendment seventy-two years later. Charlotte Woodward, who had been a worker in a glove factory in 1848, voted in the 1920 election.

FDR Attacks the Depression

Determined to bring the country out of the worst depression in its history, President Franklin Roosevelt, like his distant cousin Theodore, used his presidential powers to skirt around the Constitution's edicts.

During the unbridled optimism of the 1920s, middle-class investors, anxious for instant wealth, dipped into their savings to get in on the stock-buying frenzy sweeping the nation. In October 1929, stock values tumbled and shareholders, seeing their stock certificates turn into worthless paper, rushed to sell. Manufacturing declined as companies across the nation declared bankruptcy, sending hundreds of thousands to the unemployment lines. Banks failed when jobless homeowners could no longer pay on loans and mortgages, and unemployment reached 25 percent. Farmers lost their land to foreclosure.

In an effort to contain the damage and get the country back on track, President Herbert Hoover, in 1929 and 1930, initiated farm subsidy programs, established tariffs to prevent competition from foreign trade, and negotiated with labor and business leaders. While this helped for a time, overall these tactics did little to prevent the domino effect of failure upon failure as the economy sunk further.

On the platform of a "New Deal," Franklin Delano Roosevelt easily won the 1932 election. At his inauguration on March 4, 1933, he promised to "ask the Congress for the one remaining instrument to meet the crisis— broad Executive power to wage a war against the emergency."

Roosevelt met with nearly zero opposition. The country was in serious trouble and the President said he had plans to fix it. Republicans and Democrats in both houses of Congress rallied to support him.

His first directive, the Economy Act, lowered the salary of federal employees and reduced some veterans' benefits. On March 5, the day after he took office, he created the Emergency Banking Act, in effect a bank holiday, to give the Federal government time to shore up the banks' declining funds, and permitted the Federal Reserve to issue more currency. To avoid a lowering of currency values, the act also forbade private hoarding and deportation of gold. In April he took the country off the gold standard, hoping that this would cause prices to rise. Congress created the Federal Deposit Insurance Corporation, designed to protect bank deposits. The legislators put through the Civilian Conservation Corps (CCC)m providing jobs in forestry, farming, and land reclamation for men aged eighteen to twenty-five.

His most far-reaching measure was a series of proposals designed to stimulate the overall economy, create jobs, and assist farmers, collectively known as the New Deal.

The Agricultural Adjustment Act (which created the Agricultural Adjustment Administration) forced farmers to limit the production of

wheat, cotton, tobacco, and some other staples and offer the growers subsidies in return. In other words, the farmers were paid to not grow crops on a certain number of acres. Agricultural prices rose, which benefited most growers, but not dairy, cattle, and tenant farmers.

The Tennessee Valley Authority (TVA), passed in 1933, established a board to build power plants, dams, and transmission lines. In particular, TVA projects provided cheap electrical power to underdeveloped areas in the Tennessee Valley area. Not without downsides, the TVA project also forced hundreds from their homes and did little to offset the poverty in the region.

The National Industrial Recovery Act (NIRA) was conceived to create organizations of capitalists and workers—under government supervision—to solve labor/management issues using fair business practice "codes" as well as stimulate economic recovery. The act provided for the National Recovery Administration agency, which permitted manufacturers to raise prices and limit production, while guaranteeing workers minimum wages and maximum hours, as well as bargaining rights and the opportunity to unionize. The NRA handled the drafting of the business codes, but ran into roadblocks from the manufacturers, who insisted on revising codes to accommodate their specific issues and who were also wary of workers' attempts to form unions. While the NRA met with some success (providing more than one million jobs, ending some deflation, and setting the basis for minimum wages and child labor laws), the agency did not end the Depression as was hoped. By 1934, business activity improved, then quickly fell, and manufacturing once again declined.

Roosevelt's charisma and pragmatic approach to problem solving, coupled with the country's demand for action in getting the nation back on its feet, helped push these and many other programs through Congress. Then, in 1935, the Supreme Court flexed its muscles in the *Schecter vs. the United States* case and virtually killed the NRA.

The case concerned the Schecter brothers, poultry dealers in Brooklyn, New York, who had been convicted of selling sick poultry and violating the NRA wage and hours laws. The Supreme Court overturned two of their convictions on the grounds that the Schecters operated only in New York State and weren't subject to interstate commerce laws as outlined in Article I of the Constitution. The court also stated that Roosevelt had legislated beyond the limits of his authority in regulating commerce through NRA directives. In effect, this invalidated the NRA given that everything ruled by the court fell under guidelines specified in the *Schecter* case.

By 1935, like an annoying houseguest, the Depression refused to leave. Roosevelt introduced what is called "the Second New Deal." This included Social Security, the legislation with the greatest enduring impact, guaranting those over sixty-five income for their retirement years. Employees would have a small percentage of their pay (starting at one percent for incomes under $3,000) deducted for Social Security taxes, and that amount would be matched by the employer. When a worker reached age sixty-five, he would be given a monthly amount based upon his wages during the previous years worked. Percentages have been adjusted and

OPPOSITE: Unemployed men in San Francisco, California, 1934. That year, the jobless rate had reached approximately 21.7 percent.

TOP RIGHT: Front page of the *New York Times*, March 6, 1933, announcing FDR's proclamation declaring a four-day bank closing and an embargo on gold.

BOTTOM RIGHT: Symbol for the Work Progress Administration (WPA), 1935, which attempted to provide jobs to the long-term unemployed during the Depression. The WPA was eliminated in 1943 due to a worker shortage in World War II.

increased since Social Security was first introduced, but it is still in effect today. Social Security provides funds (but not necessarily enough for all expenses) for seniors and the disabled.

Another program, the Works Progress Administration, provided jobs to over a million unemployed workers beginning in 1935. Construction projects included hospitals, schools, airports, parks, bridges, roads, buildings, and nearly any other project its agents could imagine, including the arts. Muralists added their artistic touch to walls in government buildings and writers used their journalistic talents to author travel guidebooks.

By 1937, it appeared that a number of measures Roosevelt had initiated in his first term in office were doomed. Lawyers told employers not to bother adding Social Security procedures to their bookkeeping. They felt certain that the conservatives on the Supreme Court would influence the liberals and moderates to rule it unconstitutional. The Wagner Act, passed in 1935, encouraged collective bargaining and allowed workers to take part in strikes to support their demands. Some groups saw this as a socialist measure and predicted its demise if the Supreme Court ruled against it.

Roosevelt saw a way out. He petitioned Congress to increase the number of Supreme Court justices, a thinly veiled plan to "pack" the court with judges sympathetic to his policies. He couched it in terms that made it appear as though elderly justices would have less pressure to perform their duties if additional judges could take over from time to time. FDR assumed there would be no opposition in the largely Democratic Congress, but his optimism was short-lived. The press and most of Congress opposed the Supreme Court packing, fearing that it would set a precedent for future manipulations by the executive branch. Roosevelt eventually gave in, but in the meantime, two of the moderate judges shifted their positions and joined the other, more liberal justices. This saved Social Security.

From then on, Roosevelt had little to fear from the Supreme Court and any potential rulings against his policies. Still, the New Deal policies faded as the 1930s wore on. To counteract a recession in 1937, which undid most of the advances made since 1933, Roosevelt put forth several plans, many of which were defeated by conservatives in both political parties. A few proposals made their way through Congress, including one that extended financial aid to farmers (the second Agricultural Adjustment Act) and establishment of both a national minimum wage and a forty-four-hour workweek. Programs such as the CCC and WPA were shut down by the early 1940s.

TOP RIGHT: "The Supreme Court under Pressure" cartoon depicts Roosevelt telling the old men on the Supreme Court to get in step with his New Deal legislative efforts.
BOTTOM RIGHT: Workers weighing bushels of peas in a field near Calipatria, California, 1939. Most migrant workers were paid $5 a day for a twelve-hour day.

WHAT SORT OF MAN LED THE COUNTRY OUT OF THE DEPRESSION?

Franklin Delano Roosevelt was a charmer, a leader at a time when the country needed not only a problem-solver but a source of inspiration and optimism. It's fair to say he redefined the presidency and he set the nation toward a new consciousness by enacting legislation designed to address the basic needs of America's jobless, poverty-stricken, and depressed citizens. History has shown, however, that in spite of all the massive legislation put forth and passed, he lacked an in-depth knowledge of economic principles. Strictly speaking, the New Deal did not end the Depression, but Roosevelt's actions most likely helped to offset a far worse scenario of increased poverty, homelessness, and despair. In his take-charge manner, he redefined the presidency, believing that the government should provide not only personal rights as outlined in the Constitution, but citizens were also entitled to enjoy a sense of well-being, earn a living wage, be guaranteed fair treatment in the workplace, and have security in their old age. Many policies that exist today came out of programs he initiated, such as Social Security, the Agricultural Adjustment Act, and the Federal Deposit Insurance Corporation, all of which required bureaus, agencies, and consultants. Thus the role of the federal government was expanded in a way the Founding Fathers could never have imagined.

Roosevelt's administration had affected the Constitution and the three branches of government in other ways. He tried to add or "pack" the Supreme Court with twelve justices, and this effort failed. While there is nothing in the Constitution stipulating the number of justices, no president since then has attempted to meddle with Congress to alter the Supreme Court system. In addition, Roosevelt served an unprecedented three-plus terms in office, which eventually led to the Twenty-second Amendment limiting the president to just two terms.

RIGHT: President Roosevelt smiles during the opening baseball game of the 1934 season in Washington, D.C.

THE LEND-LEASE ACT AND WORLD WAR II

As Roosevelt's New Deal struggled, he turned his attention to foreign policy. The threat of war in Europe turned to reality when German soldiers stormed into Austria, Czechoslovakia, and later Poland in 1938–39. Denmark, Norway, Belgium, the Netherlands, and France fell to Adolf Hitler's armies by mid-1940. On the one hand, Roosevelt declared a neutrality policy, yet, because his sympathies lay with Britain, which now was threatened with an invasion by German forces, he ignored Congress and gave the British old American destroyers in exchange for British bases in the Western Hemisphere. Roosevelt knew that a British victory was essential to American security and commercial interests, but above all, Germany simply needed to be stopped.

Americans, however, were sharply divided on whether to get involved in any conflict. In the 1930s, Congress had passed several Neutrality Acts, but that didn't stop Roosevelt from loaning funds to China after Japan's invasion of that country in 1937. The president insisted that China and Japan were not at war, so no neutrality policy was violated.

Roosevelt was easily reelected in 1940 for an unprecedented third term. Voters thought America would be forced into the war in Europe, and they preferred to retain the president they knew rather than "change horses in midstream." After the election, Roosevelt approached Congress and requested that Britain be given additional war material to be paid for "in goods and services at the end of the war," a program known as "Lend Lease." In 1941, after Germany invaded the Soviet Union, Roosevelt again went before Congress and asked to extend the draft. (The Selective Service Act, passed in 1940, was valid for only one year.)

America did enter the war, not due to Germany's aggressive policies, but rather the United States' issues with Japan and that country's invasion of China and Manchuria. After months of meetings between Roosevelt and the Japanese envoys, negotiations broke down. On December 7, 1941, the Japanese attacked the naval base at Pearl Harbor in Honolulu, Hawaii. The president appeared before Congress on December 8 and asked for a declaration of war against Japan, calling December 7 a "date which will live in infamy." Congress declared war and on December 11, Germany and its ally Italy honored their treaty with Japan and declared war on the United States, which led to the beginning of American involvement in World War II

During the next three years, under Roosevelt's leadership, the U.S. fought on two fronts—Europe and the South Pacific. In 1944, voters still held their president in high regard, and few wished to change administrations in the middle of a war. Although it was obvious his health had deteriorated, Roosevelt campaigned vigorously for another chance at office, with Missouri senator Harry Truman as his running mate. The Democrats easily won the election.

THE G.I. BILL

The Servicemen's Readjustment Act, passed in 1944, was initiated in lieu of a military bonus to soldiers returning from the war. Known as the G.I. Bill of Rights, it offered subsidies to the veterans so they could obtain a college education, purchase homes or start new businesses with low-interest loans. The bill helped stimulate the economy, and nearly eight million veterans enrolled in institutes of higher education. The bill was enacted in an effort to stem any possible issues arising from veterans' entitlements once the war ended. (In 1932, World War I veterans had marched on Washington demanding bonuses promised to them by Congress, although according to the policy, they weren't entitled to those funds until 1945.) President Roosevelt favored a postwar assistance program for the poor as well as veterans, but veterans' organizations sought congressional support for a veterans-only bill.

On April 12, 1945, President Roosevelt, in the first year of his fourth term, died of a cerebral hemorrhage. Truman was sworn in as the thirty-third president of the United States. As commander in chief of the armed forces, it was his duty to make what could easily be regarded as the most far-reaching presidential decision in the nation's history to date.

Under Roosevelt's directive, scientists had been researching and developing the most powerful weapon ever devised—the atomic bomb. The weapon, now in its final stages, was scheduled to be deployed that summer. Truman had a difficult decision: by its very destructiveness, the bomb could end the war and save thousands of soldiers' lives (avoiding an invasion of Japan), but it would kill thousands of civilians. Truman issued the order to proceed and the bomb was dropped on Hiroshima on August 6, 1945, and another on Nagasaki a few days later. The Japanese surrendered on August 15.

OPPOSITE TOP: British prime minister Winston Churchill (far left), President Roosevelt, and Joseph Stalin, premier of the Soviet Union, meet in February 1945 in Yalta, Ukraine, to determine post–World War II organization. Roosevelt's declining health is now evident as he starts his fourth term in office. He died two months later.

PRESIDENTIAL TERM LIMITS

There had been no provision in the Constitution limiting presidential terms of office, but after Roosevelt's unprecedented twelve years in office, Congress approved the Twenty-second Amendment, limiting the president to two terms. Essentially, the amendment stipulated that no one could be elected more than twice and a vice president who becomes president due to a vacancy could not be elected more than once if the partial term was more than two years. The amendment has been disputed and proposals to repeal it continue to come up in Congress occasionally, especially by legislators who are content with the president's administration and want him to stay on. Some feel that a president in his second term is a lame duck and may not work as hard to bring about necessary changes needed in difficult situations, whereas a third term would extend his authority and accountability. Others say that if a president is not concerned about being reelected in his second term he is allowed more time to work on his objectives in order to leave behind a creditable list of achievements.

RIGHT: President Roosevelt and Vice President Harry S. Truman at the inaugural ceremonies, January 20, 1945, for Roosevelt's unprecedented fourth term.

VOTING AT EIGHTEEN AND THE RIGHT TO BEAR ARMS

Although eighteen was the age designated for military service, those men who were drafted to fight for their country were not allowed to vote until they reached twenty-one. During the Vietnam War in the late 1960s and early 1970s, young men and women protested that if they were old enough to die for their country, they were old enough to vote. As an extension of the Voting Act of 1965, Congress passed the Twenty-sixth Amendment, lowering the voting age to eighteen. Oregon appealed and the Supreme Court upheld the appeal, saying that Congress could establish the voting age only in federal elections, not local ones. This ruling meant that eighteen-year-olds were allowed to vote for president but had to reach twenty-one before casting ballots for governor, state representatives, or any other official in their district.

This created a new set of problems: Different voting ages meant two different elections and two sets of voting lists. Eventually most states agreed to establish eighteen as the age for signing legal contracts as well as voting.

The issue of gun control has been at the forefront of American consciousness since the shootings at Columbine High School in Colorado, Virginia Tech University in Virginia, and Sandy Hook Elementary School in Newtown, Connecticut.

Guns have always had a place in America's history. Early settlers used firearms for hunting, self-defense, and later in the fight for independence. When the framers of the Constitution added the Second Amendment, memories of being subject to British military rule were still fresh in their minds and they felt that the "right to bear arms" was essential to the safety and protection of the nation's citizens.

Today, the right to bear firearms, as outlined in the Constitution and put forward by the National Rifle Association, contrasts with those who insist that the need for every citizen to possess any type of firearm is not only unnecessary but dangerous and puts firearms in the hands of people ill-equipped to operate them safely.

TOP RIGHT: A soldier serving in Da Nang, South Vietnam, in 1967, seems to send a message with a takeoff of the hippie slogan "make love not war" written on his helmet. The Vietnam War was the subject of intense controversy and protest during the 1960s and early 1970s, and one of the issues leading to passage of the Twenty-sixth Amendment giving eighteen-year-olds the vote.

BOTTOM RIGHT: An eighteen-year-old from Chicago votes in the 1972 Illinois presidential primary, the first year that eighteen-year-olds could vote, after passage of the Twenty-sixth Amendment to the Constitution.

OPPOSITE TOP: Men gather for a turkey shoot in the countryside, 1874.

OPPOSITE BOTTOM: American frontiersman, explorer, and soldier Daniel Boone forged his Wilderness Road through the Appalachian Mountains to Kentucky in the mid-1770s and later served in the Revolutionary War.

In 2008, the Supreme Court ruled that handguns are "arms" and in the case of *Heller vs. the District of Columbia* upheld an individual's right to possess guns for self-defense, a right protected under the Second Amendment. The court added that the ruling did not allow felons or the mentally ill to own firearms, and statutes forbidding the carrying of firearms inside areas such as schools or government buildings were still in effect. This was the first case in which the Supreme Court clarified that the Second Amendment permits a private citizen to keep and bear arms.

In 2010, in the *McDonald vs. Chicago* case, a private citizen disputed the Chicago law forbidding ownership of handguns for its residents. Otis McDonald claimed he needed a handgun due to increased crime in his neighborhood. The Supreme Court ruled in favor of McDonald, reversing a decision by a lower court and further declared that the Second Amendment was incorporated in the wording of the Fourteenth Amendment, which stated that "No State shall make or enforce any law which shall abridge the privileges of citizens of the United States."

The current firearms ownership debate centers around keeping firearms out of criminals' hands as well as better enforcement of existing gun rules rather than increasing restrictions to law-abiding citizens.

Most citizens agree that arms kept for protection or sporting events should be allowed, but assault weapons and those capable of firing more than ten rounds of ammunition at a time should be outlawed for private citizens. The National Rifle Association and many other gun owners agree that background checks for gun purchasers are necessary, yet they feel registration of any kind can potentially lead to eventual gun confiscation.

This is a complex issue, and one which will cause numerous debates in the years to come.

11 | AND YET SHE STANDS

HOW THE CONSTITUTION IS INTERPRETED TODAY

After the Constitution was approved in 1789, Congress still had twelve amendments to consider. Of these, Amendments Three through Twelve were ratified. One and Two were tabled, and, as a result, Amendment Three became One, Four became Two, and so on. As previously mentioned, these ten became the Bill of Rights. The tabled Second Amendment (specifying that Congressional pay raises go into effect after the start of the next congressional session) was ratified in 1992. It is now the Twenty-seventh Amendment.

Other amendments still technically open to consideration, proposed prior to the seven-year limit for an amendment to remain viable, are:

THE CONGRESSIONAL REPRESENTATION AMENDMENT: This would have been Amendment One in the Bill of Rights. It stipulated that the House of Representatives would never have less than 200 members. Today, the House has over 400 members, so the chances of debate over that amendment are slim.

THE NOBLE TITLE AMENDMENT: Initiated by Congress in 1810, there is, again, little indication that this amendment will surface anytime soon. It declared that if an American citizen accepted a title, such as a knighthood or title of nobility without the consent of Congress, he or she would no longer be a citizen of the United States.

THE SLAVERY AMENDMENT: In 1861, Congress proposed this amendment permitting states to keep their slave-holding status without interference by the federal government. Many felt it was a final effort to prevent the southern states from seceding. To avoid war, President Lincoln signed it—the only proposed amendment with a presidential signature.

CHILD LABOR AMENDMENT: This is the only amendment put forth in the twentieth century that is still outstanding, having been ratified by twenty-eight states. Congress wanted to ensure that children under the age of eighteen would have freedom from exploitation in the workforce in every state in the union. Since a number of federal and state regulations are in place to safeguard young people who work, another amendment appears unnecessary.

As it stands there are still several amendments pending and many more proposed which have failed or expired. Two-thirds of both houses of Congress must approve an amendment. If approved, it is sent to all fifty states for ratification. Thirty-eight states are required to ratify before it becomes law. All amendments are subject to debate and lengthy discussion among the legislators, not only in Congress but in the states' houses of government as well. The framers of the Constitution wanted to be certain that Congress would have limited power in making any changes to the Constitution; too many changes and the citizens would lose respect for it and their legislative bodies. Out of more than 9,000 proposed amendments, only thirty-three have passed through the House of Representatives and the U. S. Senate and then sent on to the states. Of these, twenty-seven have been ratified.

As the American people take on sensitive matters, such as same-sex marriage, abortion, or invasion of privacy brought on by new technology, lawmakers work with the other two branches of government—often the courts—for interpretation of the Constitution, rather than draft new amendments.

STEPS IN THE ESTABLISHMENT OF A MORE STABLE GOVERNMENT

The FEDERAL CONSTITUTION

PHILADELPHIA CONVENTION 1787

ANNAPOLIS CONVENTION 1786

MT. VERNON CONVENTION 1785

ARTICLES OF CONFEDERATION

AMENDMENTS THAT FAILED

THE EQUAL RIGHTS AMENDMENT: This amendment first appeared in 1923, shortly after the ratification of the Women's Suffrage Amendment. It failed at that time because some feared that the amendment would override laws protecting working women. Essentially, it states that equal rights under the law shall not be denied on account of sex. In 1972, during the era of civil rights fever, Congress sent another ERA proposal to the states but an upturn in the conservative philosophy—which feared the loss of protections enjoyed by women—prevented many states from ratifying it. Congress moved to extend the ratification deadline to ten years—flying in the face of the Constitution's seven-year limit. The ERA expired in June 1982.

THE DISTRICT OF COLUMBIA REPRESENTATION AMENDMENT: This amendment proposed that the district be considered a state, with the number of representatives proportionate to its population, plus two senators. The seven-year time limit expired in 1985 without ratification.

THE SCHOOL PRAYER AMENDMENT: Brought before Congress in 2003, this amendment proposes that "the people retain the right to pray and to recognize their religious beliefs…on public property, including schools."

TERM LIMITS FOR THE U.S. CONGRESS: This amendment, introduced in 2011, would set a limit of two terms for senators (totaling twelve years) and three years for representatives (totaling six years).

REPEAL OF THE TWENTY-SECOND AMENDMENT: Introduced January 2013, this amendment would remove the term limitations for presidents.

POLITICALLY SENSITIVE ISSUES

ABORTION: In 1973, the Supreme Court struck down a Texas law forbidding a woman to have an abortion during the first trimester of pregnancy (unless it endangered the health of the mother). The court ruled that abortion is permissible until the end of the first trimester of a pregnancy without intervention by the state. The court added guidelines for the states' drafting of abortion legislation.

The case came about when Texas resident Norma McCovey, pregnant at the time, filed a suit in the federal district court protesting the Texas law. She claimed it infringed on her First, Fourth, Fifth, Ninth, and Fourteenth Amendment rights of privacy and requested permission for an abortion. The court agreed that the Texas law was unconstitutional, but refused to grant the abortion.

The Supreme Court did also rule that following the end of the first trimester, the state may enact abortion legislation "related to maternal health," require abortions to be performed by a licensed physician, and determine where they may be performed. The issue continues to elicit controversy; antiabortion advocates conduct campaigns to have the decision overturned, and pro-choice groups feel a woman should have control over her pregnancy during the entire nine months.

OPPOSITE: A mid-twentieth-century American cartoon showing the steps from the Articles of Confederation to the Federal Constitution.

SAME-SEX MARRIAGE: The Federal Marriage Amendment (FMA) would limit marriage to unions of one man and one woman and deny marriage rights to same-sex couples. In 2006 both houses of Congress failed to gain a majority vote on the measure. States dictate their own marriage laws according to their constitutions, but if a state law forbids same-sex marriage, that state can refuse to recognize a same-sex marriage performed legally in another state. At present, the federal government does not recognize a union between homosexual couples even if it is allowed by the state in which they were united. For example, the couple may not file a joint federal income tax return, but may file a state return. Several states, including Massachusetts, Vermont, New Hampshire, Connecticut, New York, and Iowa, as well as the District of Columbia, permit same-sex marriage. Opponents of the amendment argue that this would be the second constitutional amendment restricting a right; the other was the Eighteenth Amendment forbidding the sale or consumption of alcohol. Religious groups, such as the United Church of Christ, maintain that marriage is religion-oriented and should not be under government control. Other opponents of the FMA say that marriage comes under the right of pursuit of happiness as guaranteed by the Constitution. They further maintain that the amendment is unnecessary, because the Constitution's Full Faith and Credit Clause stipulates that states must respect the "public acts, records, and judicial proceedings of every other state," and states have always enacted their own family laws (including those related to marriage), without any resulting conflict.

COMBATING TERRORISM AND THE RIGHTS OF THE INDIVIDUAL: The tragic events of 9/11 profoundly affected the nation's consciousness. The destruction of the Twin Towers and portions of the Pentagon, and the loss of thousands of lives gave rise to acts usually reserved for wartime. While the nation tried to absorb the shock of those unprecedented attacks, President George W. Bush and Congress established tighter security systems at airports with the Transportation Security Administration, and pushed the Patriot Act through Congress. In October 2001, a secret executive order by the president permitted warrantless searches, and allowed the seizure of e-mail and telephone records belonging to anyone suspected of terrorist activities. A federal court declared these actions illegal and the administration backed off, stating it would follow the guidelines in the Federal Surveillance Act of 1978, which had set procedures for obtaining secret warrants. The Patriot Act gave the Secretary of the Treasury the power to oversee financial transactions, especially those conducted by foreign groups. It gave law enforcers greater authority to detain immigrants suspected of terrorism.

The Eighth Amendment to the Constitution forbids the infliction of cruel and unusual punishments, and the Supreme Court has ruled that torture falls under that mandate. After 9/11, President Bush's efforts to prevent further attacks included setting up a prison at Guantanamo Bay, Cuba, for suspected terrorists. A military tribunal was formed to conduct trials. The Supreme Court declared that suspects could not be held indefinitely, but Congress enacted legislation to permit imprisonment of enemy combatants and denied them the right of habeas corpus. Hearsay evidence was also allowed, usually not accepted in normal trials. In 2006 a revision of the War Crimes Act allowed torture (such as waterboarding, beatings, and electrical shocks) by government agents and military personnel. In 2009, President Obama struck down that policy and ordered that prisoners "shall be treated humanely and shall not be subjected to violence…nor to outrages upon personal dignity."

IMMIGRATION REFORM: In the past, the word "immigrant" usually meant people arriving from Europe or Asia. Most of today's immigrants, numbering in the millions, arrive from Mexico or parts of Central America. The Constitution stipulates that anyone born in the United States is a citizen, so those who come into the country unlawfully do so, hoping their children born in the U.S. will have greater opportunities as natural-born citizens.

In 1986, Congress granted amnesty only to undocumented aliens currently living in the United States. The influx of immigrants continued, although in the mid-2000s the number of those entering illegally declined. Recently, thousands have come to the border each day seeking asylum from oppressive governments—a legal option to enter the United States. These people hope that the authorities will allow them to be processed so they can become citizens. This has resulted in overcrowding of the immigration facilities. Measures being discussed on ways to strengthen border protection, including the addition of technology tools, such as drones and cargo scanners, or extending the walls currently in place.

The proposed DREAM Act would offer a conditional road to U.S. citizenship for illegal aliens who arrived in the country as minors. If they graduate from American high schools and complete two years in the military or at an institute of higher learning, they would gain temporary residency for six years. Although most DREAMERS have temporary status, this proposal is still unresolved, due to federal cases pending. In 2018 the Senate had submitted several options, all of which failed to gain the required 60 votes needed to proceed.

PATIENT PROTECTION AND AFFORDABLE CARE ACT: This act, signed into law by President Obama in 2010, has generated heated debates ever since it was first proposed. While most Americans favored the section forbidding insurance companies to deny coverage due to preexisting conditions, others objected to a section mandating that all citizens purchase health insurance. Some have said the legislation did not address the central health-care problems as much as it could; others felt too much attention was given to the issue and the president should address other, more important issues concerning the nation. Several states have challenged the constitutionality of the law—in particular the item requiring individuals to buy insurance or face a fine, saying it violated the

ABOVE: President George W. Bush is interrupted by his chief of staff, Andrew Card, on September 11, 2001, in Sarasota, Florida, with the news of the terrorist attack on the Twin Towers in New York City.
OPPOSITE LEFT: A U.S. military guard checks on detainees inside maximum lock-up at Camp V, styled after state-of-the-art maximum security U.S. federal prisons on the U.S. Naval base at Guantanamo Bay, Cuba, in 2006. Approximately 445 enemy combatants from terrorist organizations are imprisoned here.
OPPOSITE RIGHT: Obamacare supporters outside the U.S. Supreme Court on the third day of arguments over the constitutionality of the Patient Protection and Affordable Care Act, March 28, 2012.

Constitution's Commerce Clause (Congress' power to regulate commerce), since not purchasing insurance could not be defined as "commerce" and was not within Congress' authority to tax. Eventually certain cases collectively reached the Supreme Court, which ruled that although the insurance purchase requirement was unconstitutional according to the Commerce Clause, the penalty was permitted as a tax. The law is in effect, but opponents continue to dispute it and many cases are still pending.

BALANCED BUDGET: At first glance, it appears an amendment requiring a balanced budget would sail through the ratification process, because it simply makes sense. Balanced-budget proposals have come before Congress often in

the past hundred years but have never garnered enough votes to make it to the states for ratification. Opponents have argued that deficit spending keeps the economy strong, but in recent years, Republicans have stood firm against using nonexistent funds to add to the government's expenditures, while Democrats balk at canceling much-needed federal programs. Both want to pay down the national debt, which continues to mount with each passing second. They continue to argue about the best way to do it.

ELECTORAL COLLEGE: The Electoral College ensures each state, regardless of population, has a fair say in the presidential election. Every state gets at least three electoral votes, usually based on the popular vote. A state's number of electors is identical to the total number of its senators and representatives in Congress. It takes 270 Electoral votes to win the presidency. However, many Americans feel the Electoral College should be eliminated.

This feeling prevailed during the election dispute of 2000. On election night, Democratic candidate Al Gore apparently had the lead with 51 million popular votes and 267 electoral votes. Republican George W. Bush garnered 50.5 million popular and 246 electoral. Florida's twenty-five electoral votes were still in dispute due to problems with the validity of the punch-card ballots. Bush was leading in Florida by 1,700 popular votes but a later machine recount lowered the lead to a few hundred. After a month-long battle, the Supreme Court settled the dispute and in a 5-4 vote declared George Bush the winner in Florida.

In 2016, the Electoral College again determined the winner of the presidential election. Republican candidate Donald Trump secured 304 electoral votes to Democrat Hillary Clinton's 227. Clinton had received nearly 2.9 million more popular votes than Trump but Trump had carried several large states, gaining all their electoral votes.

PROTECTING CHILDREN IN THE ELECTRONIC AGE: Once children began to have access to pornography and sexual predators could reach young people through websites and chat rooms, laws such as the Communications Decency Act and the Child Online Protection Act made their way through Congress. Later, the Supreme Court and lower courts felt these laws impinged on First Amendment rights. So far, the issue is back in the hands of parents, who can use filtering software to block inappropriate material.

The words of the United States Constitution themselves are quaint in their expression, but the force behind the ideas carries the weight of combat—mortal and intellectual—that wrenched a people free and thrust them into a world for which they were unprepared. The final document is a massive compromise composed of smaller compromises. It is far from perfect, but its imperfection provided a framework within which an incredibly diverse stew of people set to work. The result is this republic, stitched together by a skein of laws, values, economics, transportation and communications networks, all bound by this contract signed by a small group of eighteenth-century founders. The deal was sealed on July 4, 1788, with a grand parade down Philadelphia's main street. "'Tis done! We have become a nation!" cheered American citizen Dr. Benjamin Rush.

As the first reprints were read in coffee houses, grog shops, and on village greens, the test began. More than 200 years later, the American people continue to test their Constitution every single day.

APPENDIX

THE CONSTITUTION OF THE UNITED STATES AND BILL OF RIGHTS

A TRANSCRIPT

ARTICLE. I.

SECTION. 1.

All legislative Powers herein granted shall be vested in a Congress of the United States, which shall consist of a Senate and House of Representatives.

SECTION. 2.

The House of Representatives shall be composed of Members chosen every second Year by the People of the several States, and the Electors in each State shall have the Qualifications requisite for Electors of the most numerous Branch of the State Legislature.

No Person shall be a Representative who shall not have attained to the Age of twenty five Years, and been seven Years a Citizen of the United States, and who shall not, when elected, be an Inhabitant of that State in which he shall be chosen.

Representatives and direct Taxes shall be apportioned among the several States which may be included within this Union, according to their respective Numbers, which shall be determined by adding to the whole Number of free Persons, including those bound to Service for a Term of Years, and excluding Indians not taxed, three fifths of all other Persons. The actual Enumeration shall be made within three Years after the first Meeting of the Congress of the United States, and within every subsequent Term of ten Years, in such Manner as they shall by Law direct. The Number of Representatives shall not exceed one for every thirty Thousand, but each State shall have at Least one Representative; and until such enumeration shall be made, the State of New Hampshire shall be entitled to chuse three, Massachusetts eight, Rhode-Island and Providence Plantations one, Connecticut five, New-York six, New Jersey four, Pennsylvania eight, Delaware one, Maryland six, Virginia ten, North Carolina five, South Carolina five, and Georgia three.

ABOVE: A late eighteenth-century
American print reflecting confidence in the
Constitution.

When vacancies happen in the Representation from any State, the Executive Authority thereof shall issue Writs of Election to fill such Vacancies.

The House of Representatives shall chuse their Speaker and other Officers; and shall have the sole Power of Impeachment.

Section. 3.

The Senate of the United States shall be composed of two Senators from each State, chosen by the Legislature thereof, for six Years; and each Senator shall have one Vote.

Immediately after they shall be assembled in Consequence of the first Election, they shall be divided as equally as may be into three Classes. The Seats of the Senators of the first Class shall be vacated at the Expiration of the second Year, of the second Class at the Expiration of the fourth Year, and of the third Class at the Expiration of the sixth Year, so that one third may be chosen every second Year; and if Vacancies happen by Resignation, or otherwise, during the Recess of the Legislature of any State, the Executive thereof may make temporary Appointments until the next Meeting of the Legislature, which shall then fill such Vacancies.

No Person shall be a Senator who shall not have attained to the Age of thirty Years, and been nine Years a Citizen of the United States, and who shall not, when elected, be an Inhabitant of that State for which he shall be chosen.

The Vice President of the United States shall be President of the Senate, but shall have no Vote, unless they be equally divided.

The Senate shall chuse their other Officers, and also a President pro tempore, in the Absence of the Vice President, or when he shall exercise the Office of President of the United States.

The Senate shall have the sole Power to try all Impeachments. When sitting for that Purpose, they shall be on Oath or Affirmation. When the President of the United States is tried, the Chief Justice shall preside: And no Person shall be convicted without the Concurrence of two thirds of the Members present.

Judgment in Cases of Impeachment shall not extend further than to removal from Office, and disqualification to hold and enjoy any Office of honor, Trust or Profit under the United States: but the Party convicted shall nevertheless be liable and subject to Indictment, Trial, Judgment and Punishment, according to Law.

Section. 4.

The Times, Places and Manner of holding Elections for Senators and Representatives, shall be prescribed in each State by the Legislature thereof; but the Congress may at any time by Law make or alter such Regulations, except as to the Places of chusing Senators.

The Congress shall assemble at least once in every Year, and such Meeting shall be on the first Monday in December, unless they shall by Law appoint a different Day.

Section. 5.

Each House shall be the Judge of the Elections, Returns and Qualifications of its own Members, and a Majority of each shall constitute a Quorum to do Business; but a smaller Number may adjourn from day to day, and may be authorized to compel the Attendance of absent Members, in such Manner, and under such Penalties as each House may provide.

Each House may determine the Rules of its Proceedings, punish its Members for disorderly Behaviour, and, with the Concurrence of two thirds, expel a Member.

Each House shall keep a Journal of its Proceedings, and from time to time publish the same, excepting such Parts as may in their Judgment require Secrecy; and the Yeas and Nays of the Members of either House on any question shall, at the Desire of one fifth of those Present, be entered on the Journal.

Neither House, during the Session of Congress, shall, without the Consent of the other, adjourn for more than three days, nor to any other Place than that in which the two Houses shall be sitting.

Section. 6.

The Senators and Representatives shall receive a Compensation for their Services, to be ascertained by Law, and paid out of the Treasury of the United States. They shall in all Cases, except Treason, Felony and Breach of the Peace, be privileged from Arrest during their Attendance at the Session of their respective Houses, and in going to and returning from the same; and for any Speech or Debate in either House, they shall not be questioned in any other Place.

No Senator or Representative shall, during the Time for which he was elected, be appointed to any civil Office under the Authority of the United States, which shall have been created, or the Emoluments whereof shall have been encreased during such time; and no Person holding any Office under the United States, shall be a Member of either House during his Continuance in Office.

Section. 7.

All Bills for raising Revenue shall originate in the House of Representatives; but the Senate may propose or concur with Amendments as on other Bills.

Every Bill which shall have passed the House of Representatives and the Senate, shall, before it become a Law, be presented to the President of the United States; If he approve he shall sign it, but if not he shall return it, with his Objections to that House in which it shall have originated, who shall enter the Objections at large on their Journal, and proceed to reconsider it. If after such Reconsideration two thirds of that House shall agree to pass the Bill, it shall be sent, together with the Objections, to the other House, by which it shall likewise be reconsidered, and if approved by two thirds of that House, it shall become a Law. But in all such Cases the Votes of both Houses shall be determined by yeas and Nays, and the Names of the Persons voting for and against the Bill shall be entered on the Journal of each House respectively. If any Bill shall not be returned by the President within ten Days (Sundays excepted) after it shall have been presented to him, the Same shall be a Law, in like Manner as if he had signed it, unless the Congress by their Adjournment prevent its Return, in which Case it shall not be a Law.

Every Order, Resolution, or Vote to which the Concurrence of the Senate and House of Representatives may be necessary (except on a question of Adjournment) shall be presented to the President of the United States; and before the Same shall take Effect, shall be approved by him, or being disapproved by him, shall be repassed by two thirds of the Senate and House of Representatives, according to the Rules and Limitations prescribed in the Case of a Bill.

Section. 8.

The Congress shall have Power To lay and collect Taxes, Duties, Imposts and Excises, to pay the Debts and provide for the common Defence and general Welfare of the United States; but all Duties, Imposts and Excises shall be uniform throughout the United States;

To borrow Money on the credit of the United States;

To regulate Commerce with foreign Nations, and among the several States, and with the Indian Tribes;

To establish an uniform Rule of Naturalization, and uniform Laws on the subject of Bankruptcies throughout the United States;

To coin Money, regulate the Value thereof, and of foreign Coin, and fix the Standard of Weights and Measures;

To provide for the Punishment of counterfeiting the Securities and current Coin of the United States;

To establish Post Offices and post Roads;

To promote the Progress of Science and useful Arts, by securing for limited Times to Authors and Inventors the exclusive Right to their respective Writings and Discoveries;

To constitute Tribunals inferior to the supreme Court;

To define and punish Piracies and Felonies committed on the high Seas, and Offences against the Law of Nations;

To declare War, grant Letters of Marque and Reprisal, and make Rules concerning Captures on Land and Water;

To raise and support Armies, but no Appropriation of Money to that Use shall be for a longer Term than two Years;

To provide and maintain a Navy;

To make Rules for the Government and Regulation of the land and naval Forces;

To provide for calling forth the Militia to execute the Laws of the Union, suppress Insurrections and repel Invasions;

To provide for organizing, arming, and disciplining, the Militia, and for governing such Part of them as may be employed in the Service of the United States, reserving to the States respectively, the Appointment of the Officers, and the Authority of training the Militia according to the discipline prescribed by Congress;

To exercise exclusive Legislation in all Cases whatsoever, over such District (not exceeding ten Miles square) as may, by Cession of particular States, and the Acceptance of Congress, become the Seat of the Government of the United States, and to exercise like Authority over all Places purchased by the Consent of the Legislature of the State in which the Same shall be, for the Erection of Forts, Magazines, Arsenals, dock-Yards, and other needful Buildings;—And

To make all Laws which shall be necessary and proper for carrying into Execution the foregoing Powers, and all other Powers vested by this Constitution in the Government of the United States, or in any Department or Officer thereof.

Section. 9.

The Migration or Importation of such Persons as any of the States now existing shall think proper to admit, shall not be prohibited by the Congress prior to the Year one thousand eight hundred and eight, but a Tax or duty may be imposed on such Importation, not exceeding ten dollars for each Person.

The Privilege of the Writ of Habeas Corpus shall not be suspended, unless when in Cases of Rebellion or Invasion the public Safety may require it.

No Bill of Attainder or ex post facto Law shall be passed.

No Capitation, or other direct, Tax shall be laid, unless in Proportion to the Census or enumeration herein before directed to be taken.

No Tax or Duty shall be laid on Articles exported from any State.

No Preference shall be given by any Regulation of Commerce or Revenue to the Ports of one State over those of another: nor shall Vessels bound to, or from, one State, be obliged to enter, clear, or pay Duties in another.

No Money shall be drawn from the Treasury, but in Consequence of Appropriations made by Law; and a regular Statement and Account of the Receipts and Expenditures of all public Money shall be published from time to time.

No Title of Nobility shall be granted by the United States: And no Person holding any Office of Profit or Trust under them, shall, without the Consent of the Congress, accept of any present, Emolument, Office, or Title, of any kind whatever, from any King, Prince, or foreign State.

SECTION. 10.

No State shall enter into any Treaty, Alliance, or Confederation; grant Letters of Marque and Reprisal; coin Money; emit Bills of Credit; make any Thing but gold and silver Coin a Tender in Payment of Debts; pass any Bill of Attainder, ex post facto Law, or Law impairing the Obligation of Contracts, or grant any Title of Nobility.

No State shall, without the Consent of the Congress, lay any Imposts or Duties on Imports or Exports, except what may be absolutely necessary for executing it's inspection Laws: and the net Produce of all Duties and Imposts, laid by any State on Imports or Exports, shall be for the Use of the Treasury of the United States; and all such Laws shall be subject to the Revision and Controul of the Congress.

No State shall, without the Consent of Congress, lay any Duty of Tonnage, keep Troops, or Ships of War in time of Peace, enter into any Agreement or Compact with another State, or with a foreign Power, or engage in War, unless actually invaded, or in such imminent Danger as will not admit of delay.

ARTICLE. II.

SECTION. 1.

The executive Power shall be vested in a President of the United States of America. He shall hold his Office during the Term of four Years, and, together with the Vice President, chosen for the same Term, be elected, as follows

Each State shall appoint, in such Manner as the Legislature thereof may direct, a Number of Electors, equal to the whole Number of Senators and Representatives to which the State may be entitled in the Congress: but no Senator or Representative, or Person holding an Office of Trust or Profit under the United States, shall be appointed an Elector.

The Electors shall meet in their respective States, and vote by Ballot for two Persons, of whom one at least shall not be an Inhabitant of the same State with themselves. And they shall make a List of all the Persons voted for, and of the Number of Votes for each; which List they shall sign and certify, and transmit sealed to the Seat of the Government of the United States, directed to the President of the Senate. The President of the Senate shall, in the Presence of the Senate and House of Representatives, open all the Certificates, and the Votes shall then be counted. The Person having the greatest Number of Votes shall be the President, if such Number be a Majority of the whole Number of Electors appointed; and if there be more than one who have such Majority, and have an equal Number of Votes, then the House of Representatives shall immediately chuse by Ballot one of them for President; and if no Person have a Majority, then from the five highest on the List the said House shall in like Manner chuse the President. But in chusing the President, the Votes shall be taken by States, the Representation from each State having one Vote; A quorum for this Purpose shall consist of a Member or Members from two thirds of the States, and a Majority of all the States shall be necessary to a Choice. In every Case, after the Choice of the President, the Person having the greatest Number of Votes of the Electors shall be the Vice President. But if there should remain two or more who have equal Votes, the Senate shall chuse from them by Ballot the Vice President.

The Congress may determine the Time of chusing the Electors, and the Day on which they shall give their Votes; which Day shall be the same throughout the United States.

No Person except a natural born Citizen, or a Citizen of the United States, at the time of the Adoption of this Constitution, shall be eligible to the Office of President; neither shall any Person be eligible to that Office who shall not have attained to the Age of thirty five Years, and been fourteen Years a Resident within the United States.

In Case of the Removal of the President from Office, or of his Death, Resignation, or Inability to discharge the Powers and Duties of the said Office, the Same shall devolve on the Vice President, and the Congress may by Law provide for the Case of Removal, Death, Resignation or Inability, both of the President and Vice President, declaring what Officer shall then act as President, and such Officer shall act accordingly, until the Disability be removed, or a President shall be elected.

The President shall, at stated Times, receive for his Services, a Compensation, which shall neither be encreased nor diminished during the Period for which he shall have been elected, and he shall not receive within that Period any other Emolument from the United States, or any of them.

Before he enter on the Execution of his Office, he shall take the following Oath or Affirmation:—"I do solemnly swear (or affirm) that I will faithfully execute the Office of President of the United States, and will to the best of my Ability, preserve, protect and defend the Constitution of the United States."

Section. 2.

The President shall be Commander in Chief of the Army and Navy of the United States, and of the Militia of the several States, when called into the actual Service of the United States; he may require the Opinion, in writing, of the principal Officer in each of the executive Departments, upon any Subject relating to the Duties of their respective Offices, and he shall have Power to grant Reprieves and Pardons for Offences against the United States, except in Cases of Impeachment.

He shall have Power, by and with the Advice and Consent of the Senate, to make Treaties, provided two thirds of the Senators present concur; and he shall nominate, and by and with the Advice and Consent of the Senate, shall appoint Ambassadors, other public Ministers and Consuls, Judges of the supreme Court, and all other Officers of the United States, whose Appointments are not herein otherwise provided for, and which shall be established by Law: but the Congress may by Law vest the Appointment of such inferior Officers, as they think proper, in the President alone, in the Courts of Law, or in the Heads of Departments.

The President shall have Power to fill up all Vacancies that may happen during the Recess of the Senate, by granting Commissions which shall expire at the End of their next Session.

Section. 3.

He shall from time to time give to the Congress Information of the State of the Union, and recommend to their Consideration such Measures as he shall judge necessary and expedient; he may, on extraordinary Occasions, convene both Houses, or either of them, and in Case of Disagreement between them, with Respect to the Time of Adjournment, he may adjourn them to such Time as he shall think proper; he shall receive Ambassadors and other public Ministers; he shall take Care that the Laws be faithfully executed, and shall Commission all the Officers of the United States.

Section. 4.

The President, Vice President and all civil Officers of the United States, shall be removed from Office on Impeachment for, and Conviction of, Treason, Bribery, or other high Crimes and Misdemeanors.

Article III.

Section. 1.

The judicial Power of the United States, shall be vested in one supreme Court, and in such inferior Courts as the Congress may from time to time ordain and establish. The Judges, both of the supreme and inferior Courts, shall hold their Offices during good Behaviour, and shall, at stated Times, receive for their Services, a Compensation, which shall not be diminished during their Continuance in Office.

Section. 2.

The judicial Power shall extend to all Cases, in Law and Equity, arising under this Constitution, the Laws of the United States, and Treaties made, or which shall be made, under their Authority;—to all Cases affecting Ambassadors, other public Ministers and Consuls;—to all Cases of admiralty and maritime Jurisdiction;—to Controversies to which the United States shall be a Party;—to Controversies between two or more States;— between a State and Citizens of another State,—between Citizens of different States,—between Citizens of the same State claiming Lands under Grants of different States, and between a State, or the Citizens thereof, and foreign States, Citizens or Subjects.

In all Cases affecting Ambassadors, other public Ministers and Consuls, and those in which a State shall be Party, the supreme Court shall have original Jurisdiction. In all the other Cases before mentioned, the supreme Court shall have appellate Jurisdiction, both as to Law and Fact, with such Exceptions, and under such Regulations as the Congress shall make.

The Trial of all Crimes, except in Cases of Impeachment, shall be by Jury; and such Trial shall be held in the State where the said Crimes shall have been committed; but when not committed within any State, the Trial shall be at such Place or Places as the Congress may by Law have directed.

Section. 3.

Treason against the United States, shall consist only in levying War against them, or in adhering to their Enemies, giving them Aid and Comfort. No Person shall be convicted of Treason unless on the Testimony of two Witnesses to the same overt Act, or on Confession in open Court.

The Congress shall have Power to declare the Punishment of Treason, but no Attainder of Treason shall work Corruption of Blood, or Forfeiture except during the Life of the Person attainted.

Article. IV.

Section. 1.

Full Faith and Credit shall be given in each State to the public Acts, Records, and judicial Proceedings of every other State. And the Congress may by general Laws prescribe the Manner in which such Acts, Records and Proceedings shall be proved, and the Effect thereof.

Section. 2.

The Citizens of each State shall be entitled to all Privileges and Immunities of Citizens in the several States.

A Person charged in any State with Treason, Felony, or other Crime, who shall flee from Justice, and be found in another State, shall on Demand of the executive Authority of the State from which he fled, be delivered up, to be removed to the State having Jurisdiction of the Crime.

No Person held to Service or Labour in one State, under the Laws thereof, escaping into another, shall, in Consequence of any Law or Regulation therein, be discharged from such Service or Labour, but shall be delivered up on Claim of the Party to whom such Service or Labour may be due.

Section. 3.

New States may be admitted by the Congress into this Union; but no new State shall be formed or erected within the Jurisdiction of any other State; nor any State be formed by the Junction of two or more States, or Parts of States, without the Consent of the Legislatures of the States concerned as well as of the Congress.

The Congress shall have Power to dispose of and make all needful Rules and Regulations respecting the Territory or other Property belonging to the United States; and nothing in this Constitution shall be so construed as to Prejudice any Claims of the United States, or of any particular State.

Section. 4.

The United States shall guarantee to every State in this Union a Republican Form of Government, and shall protect each of them against Invasion; and on Application of the Legislature, or of the Executive (when the Legislature cannot be convened), against domestic Violence.

Article. V.

The Congress, whenever two thirds of both Houses shall deem it necessary, shall propose Amendments to this Constitution, or, on the Application of the Legislatures of two thirds of the several States, shall call a Convention for proposing Amendments, which, in either Case, shall be valid to all Intents and Purposes, as Part of this Constitution, when ratified by the Legislatures of three fourths of the several States, or by Conventions in three fourths thereof, as the one or the other Mode of Ratification may be proposed by the Congress; Provided that no Amendment which may be made prior to the Year One thousand eight hundred and eight shall in any Manner affect the first and fourth Clauses in the Ninth Section of the first Article; and that no State, without its Consent, shall be deprived of its equal Suffrage in the Senate.

Article. VI.

All Debts contracted and Engagements entered into, before the Adoption of this Constitution, shall be as valid against the United States under this Constitution, as under the Confederation.

This Constitution, and the Laws of the United States which shall be made in Pursuance thereof; and all Treaties made, or which shall be made, under the Authority of the United States, shall be the supreme Law of the Land; and the Judges in every State shall be bound thereby, any Thing in the Constitution or Laws of any State to the Contrary notwithstanding.

The Senators and Representatives before mentioned, and the Members of the several State Legislatures, and all executive and judicial Officers, both of the United States and of the several States, shall be bound by Oath or Affirmation, to support this Constitution; but no religious Test shall ever be required as a Qualification to any Office or public Trust under the United States.

Article. VII.

The Ratification of the Conventions of nine States, shall be sufficient for the Establishment of this Constitution between the States so ratifying the Same.

The Word, "the," being interlined between the seventh and eighth Lines of the first Page, The Word "Thirty" being partly written on an Erazure in the fifteenth Line of the first Page, The Words "is tried" being interlined between the thirty second and thirty third Lines of the first Page and the Word "the" being interlined between the forty third and forty fourth Lines of the second Page.

Attest William Jackson Secretary

done in Convention by the Unanimous Consent of the States present the Seventeenth Day of September in the Year of our Lord one thousand seven hundred and Eighty seven and of the Independance of the United States of America the Twelfth In witness whereof We have hereunto subscribed our Names,

G°. Washington
Presidt and deputy from Virginia

THE U.S. BILL OF RIGHTS
THE PREAMBLE TO THE BILL OF RIGHTS

Congress of the United States
begun and held at the City of New-York, on
Wednesday the fourth of March, one thousand seven hundred and
eighty nine.

THE Conventions of a number of the States, having at the time of
their adopting the Constitution, expressed a desire, in order to prevent
misconstruction or abuse of its powers, that further declaratory and
restrictive clauses should be added: And as extending the ground of
public confidence in the Government, will best ensure the beneficent
ends of its institution.

RESOLVED by the Senate and House of Representatives of the United
States of America, in Congress assembled, two thirds of both Houses
concurring, that the following Articles be proposed to the Legislatures
of the several States, as amendments to the Constitution of the United
States, all, or any of which Articles, when ratified by three fourths of
the said Legislatures, to be valid to all intents and purposes, as part of
the said Constitution; viz.

ARTICLES in addition to, and Amendment of the Constitution of the
United States of America, proposed by Congress, and ratified by the
Legislatures of the several States, pursuant to the fifth Article of the
original Constitution.

Note: The following text is a transcription of the first ten amendments
to the Constitution in their original form. These amendments were
ratified December 15, 1791, and form what is known as the «Bill of
Rights.»

AMENDMENT I

Congress shall make no law respecting an establishment of religion,
or prohibiting the free exercise thereof; or abridging the freedom
of speech, or of the press; or the right of the people peaceably to
assemble, and to petition the Government for a redress of grievances.

AMENDMENT II

A well regulated Militia, being necessary to the security of a free State,
the right of the people to keep and bear Arms, shall not be infringed.

AMENDMENT III

No Soldier shall, in time of peace be quartered in any house, without
the consent of the Owner, nor in time of war, but in a manner to be
prescribed by law.

Amendment IV

The right of the people to be secure in their persons, houses, papers, and effects, against unreasonable searches and seizures, shall not be violated, and no Warrants shall issue, but upon probable cause, supported by Oath or affirmation, and particularly describing the place to be searched, and the persons or things to be seized.

Amendment V

No person shall be held to answer for a capital, or otherwise infamous crime, unless on a presentment or indictment of a Grand Jury, except in cases arising in the land or naval forces, or in the Militia, when in actual service in time of War or public danger; nor shall any person be subject for the same offence to be twice put in jeopardy of life or limb; nor shall be compelled in any criminal case to be a witness against himself, nor be deprived of life, liberty, or property, without due process of law; nor shall private property be taken for public use, without just compensation.

Amendment VI

In all criminal prosecutions, the accused shall enjoy the right to a speedy and public trial, by an impartial jury of the State and district wherein the crime shall have been committed, which district shall have been previously ascertained by law, and to be informed of the nature and cause of the accusation; to be confronted with the witnesses against him; to have compulsory process for obtaining witnesses in his favor, and to have the Assistance of Counsel for his defence.

Amendment VII

In Suits at common law, where the value in controversy shall exceed twenty dollars, the right of trial by jury shall be preserved, and no fact tried by a jury, shall be otherwise re-examined in any Court of the United States, than according to the rules of the common law.

Amendment VIII

Excessive bail shall not be required, nor excessive fines imposed, nor cruel and unusual punishments inflicted.

Amendment IX

The enumeration in the Constitution, of certain rights, shall not be construed to deny or disparage others retained by the people.

Amendment X

The powers not delegated to the United States by the Constitution, nor prohibited by it to the States, are reserved to the States respectively, or to the people.

INDEX

Figures in italics indicate captions.

CREDITS

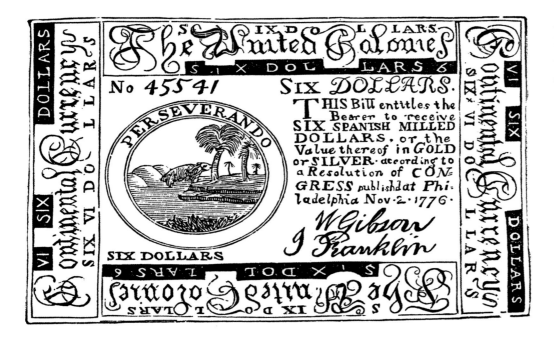

LEFT: At the beginning of the Revolutionary War in 1775 the Continental Congress asked Benjamin Franklin to create a paper money design representing hard cash. The Continentals were distributed in dollars (after the Spanish dollar), ranging from a sixth of a dollar to an $80 bill.

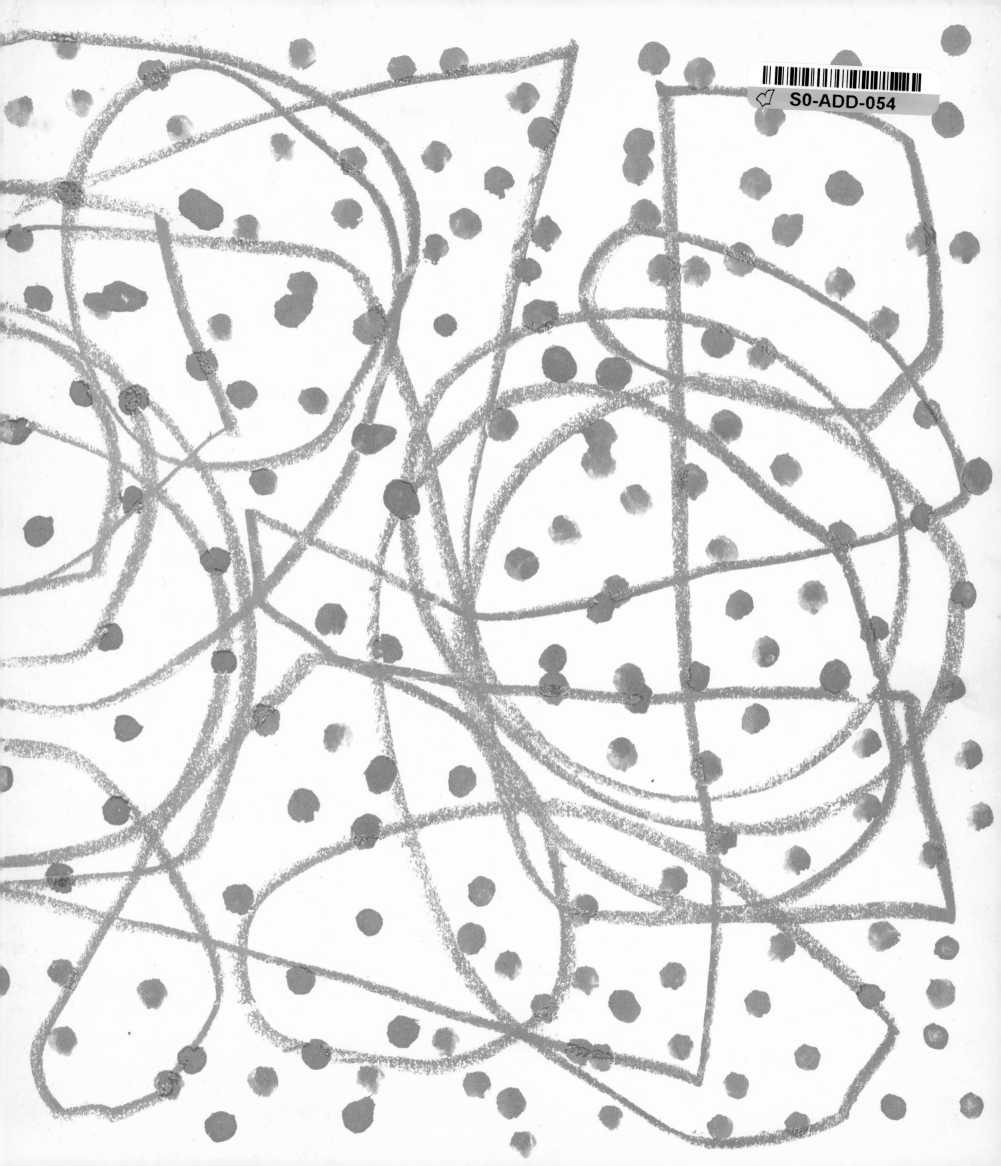

JOAN MIRÓ · HIS GRAPHIC WORK

INTRODUCTION SAM HUNTER

HARRY N. ABRAMS INC. NEW YORK

For Jane and Andrew Ritchie

Library of Congress Catalog Number 58-13486

Published in the United States of America, 1958,
by Harry N. Abrams, Inc., New York
No part of the contents of this book may be reproduced
without the written permission of the publishers
Copyright 1958 in Germany, by Verlag Gerd Hatje, Stuttgart
Printed in Germany

For richness, variety, and invention, Miró's print production is equalled or surpassed in our century only by Picasso. It has been suggested that the calligraphic bias of his style quite naturally led him into graphic work, yet the actual evidence does not support such an assumption. Miró's first prints, a group of four etchings illustrating Tristan Tzara's poem, *L'Arbre des voyageurs*, did not appear until 1930, more than a decade after he had begun to paint seriously and at least five years after he had developed his mature style. Nor did his print-making activity gather full momentum until the close of the war, in 1944, when he produced in a single year of concentrated application the magnificent *Barcelona Series* of fifty lithographs in black, which can be said to rival Rouault's *Miserere* for sustained intensity and power, although they are ironic rather than tragic in mood. Since that date—that is, in the short space of a decade and a half — Miró has produced nearly four-hundred etchings, lithographs, and woodcuts, divided almost equally between independent prints appearing either singly or in suites, and book or "souvenir" illustrations.

Miró's interest of recent years in the graphic and ceramic media, at times it would seem at the expense of his easel painting, has been part of a curious post-war phenomenon among the older generation of modern innovators. We have been confronted by the spectacle of Picasso, Léger, Matisse, and Braque as well, all earnestly investing their best energies in the "applied arts," in projects of architectural decoration, in tapestry design, in ceramics and prints. Without in any way discounting the creative opportunities which the reproducible media provide, one must note that they had played more of an occasional role for these artists in the past, and that the extraordinary emphasis on prints and ceramics particularly, stems at least in part from an enterprising commercialism. Frequently, the dealer, the publisher of special editions, or the director of ceramics manufacture competes with the artist for our attention and seems to be the driving force behind the astonishing new flow of artistic reproductions. And, again, the most rudimentary signs, marks, the merest evidence of recognizable authorship, have been welcomed as vital creations and allowed to enter the market place as "significant" examples.

An approving and fascinated public now receives an altogether more agreeable and acceptable image of the old revolutionary heroes of modernism, Picasso and Miró, surrounded by their ceramics and vases at Vallauris or Gallifa, or supervising print production at the Paris studios of Lacourière or Mourlot. These artists have, in effect, become one-man workshops; their tireless efforts and apparently unlimited virtuosity in a variety of media seem scarcely able to meet the clamorous demand for anything from their hands.

However, while Joan Miró's remarkable output of prints in the past decade and a half very likely has some relationship to commercial pressures, and may also represent a cunning stratagem, calculated to conserve and revive, from the stimuli of new media, a slackening pictorial invention, it also has its own inner necessity and historical logic, as will appear directly. Here, the artist's own clearly expressed views are a useful guide, and in the end supply perhaps the most compelling explanation for his revived interest in the graphic arts.

One must go back in time to Gauguin, to the Nabis, and to the Brücke community of artists in the early years of our own century for the origins of this activity. In their profoundest sense, Miró's prints represent an extension of a fervent ideal of "communal" art, and propose a challenge to the dominance of the easel picture formulated some sixty years ago. With the breakdown of a traditional patronage system, under the pressures of industrial life and a rising middle class with little or no taste for the fine arts, the artist turned, often nostalgically, to the great communal epochs of the past for spiritual support. The revival of such primitive art forms as the early Christian woodcut, whose pertinence to modern sensibility Gauguin first recognized, may be understood in part as a desperate attempt to close the widening gap between the individual creative spirit and a fast diminishing audience for his product. The effort to recover some rudimentary basis for communication between the artist and society, and the rediscovery of less sophisticated art forms, however, only succeeded in further alienating the public. The prints of Gauguin, the Nabis, and of Munch lend themselves to a variety of historical and æsthetic interpretations, but on one level they all represent a desire to find a new communal ideal, related in some ways to the medieval workshop. As a corollary, they break down an old hierarchy of artistic values and, by their vitality and expressive power, challenge the privileged status of the easel painting.

At the same time, the radical flatness of modern painting, beginning with the Post-Impressionist period, and the emphasis on decorative values, gave the print a further expressive potential. It became allied, æsthetically as well as socially, with the mural in the assault on easel painting. In support of the new æsthetic, Albert Aurier, the Symbolist critic and a champion of Gauguin, wrote that a work of art should be *"decorative:* for decorative painting, properly speaking, as the Egyptians and probably the Greeks and the Primitives conceived it, is nothing but a manifestation of an art at once subjective, synthetist, symbolist . . . . Painting can only have been created to decorate with thoughts, dreams and ideas the blank walls of human buildings. The easel picture is nothing but an illogical refinement invented to satisfy the fancy or commercial spirit of decadent civilizations."[1] And another spokesman for the Symbolists declared: "In the early part of 1890 the war cry went up from studio to studio: 'No more easel pictures! Painting must not usurp a freedom which cuts it off from the other arts! The painter's work begins where the architect decides that his work is finished! Give us walls and more walls to decorate! Down with perspective! The wall must be kept as a surface, and must not be pierced by the representation of distant horizons. There are no such things as pictures, there is only decoration!"[2]

The attack on the integrity of the easel picture, with its connotations of a servile "illusionism" and a discredited individualism, took the form of a vigorous renascence of the graphic arts as well as a renewed interest in mural painting. Around the Symbolist magazines *Mercure de France* and *La revue blanche* gathered such artists as Lautrec, Bonnard, Vuillard, Denis, and other members of the Nabis, some of whose most significant contributions were made in the graphic arts. The dealer Vollard began to commission fine book illustration in the early years of the new century, and we are directly indebted to his enlightened sponsorship for some of the most exquisite examples of modern graphic art.

Certain contradictions within this intensive revival in the graphic arts and minor media have emerged more clearly in our own time. Advanced art has increasingly assumed a strongly individualistic character, in its quest for freedom, and seems to move restlessly in ever-changing directions; yet the ideal of a stable, anonymous, collective art persists. An excellent case in point is the twentieth-century artist who perhaps most obviously foreshadows Miró: Hans Arp.

Attacking the vanity and egotism of modern man, Arp wrote of his first "concrete art," his collages of 1915 (which were soon followed by a large and fertile production of woodcuts and "automatic" drawings): "We rejected everything that was copy or description, and allowed the elementary and spontaneous to react in full freedom. Since the disposition of planes, and the proportions and colors of these planes seemed to depend purely on chance, I declared that these works, like nature, were ordered 'according to the law of chance,' chance being for me merely a limited part of an unfathomable *raison d'être*, of an order inaccessible in its totality."[3] And again, "the works of concrete art should not be signed by their creators. These paintings, these sculptures, these objects, should remain anonymous in the great studio of

nature like clouds, mountains, seas, animals, men, yes, men should return to nature, artists should work in community like the artists of the Middle Ages."[4] One may appropriately extend these words to the fine woodcuts which Arp has produced regularly and in great numbers throughout his career.

Miró, similarly, has identified art and nature, by giving free reign to spontaneous impulse, and by emphasizing the elementary potencies of his media, which often supply the major hints for, where they do not actually dictate, the form of his creations. In his prints of recent years, he has taken advantage of a wide range of textural possibilities — the richness or thinness of the lithographic *tusche;* varied periods of biting of his metal plates; and so forth — to express the independence and fertility of the act of creation itself, apart from any representational or symbolizing intent. The inspiration of materials, a source of power and invention for so many of the Surrealists, had been a direct force in Miró's painting during his period of collage construction from 1928 to 1932, and then again in 1935, when he made a series of rather macabre paintings in which coils of hemp competed with painted forms, in a condensed, modern rendering of a medieval gallows theme. In an interview with James Johnson Sweeney, Miró has, significantly, also pointed to a somewhat later date in his painting, just preceding his intensive graphic production, when the materials of his art began to exert a greater influence, and suggest new creative alternatives. Referring to the period of late thirties, he declared:

"Also the material of my painting began to take on a new importance. In watercolors I would roughen the surface of the paper by rubbing it. Painting over this roughened surface produced curious chance shapes. Perhaps my self-imposed isolation from my colleagues led me to turn for suggestions to the materials of my art. First to the rough surfaces of the heavy burlap series of 1939; then to ceramics...."[5] And one might, with justice, add prints, beginning with the magnificent *Barcelona Series* of lithographs completed just a few years later.

Finally, for Miró print-making has a polemical and ideal import, none the less compelling for the absence of those social conditions which would give it full reality. He has said in an interview:

"I am not dreaming of the millenium, but I have a profound faith in a better world than the one we occupy and which holds us prisoner. I have faith in a collective culture of the future, vast as the seas and lands of our globe, where the sensibility of each individual will be expanded. The studios of the Middle Ages will be revived, and students will participate fully, each bringing his own contribution.

"As for me, my hope has always been to work fraternally, as part of a team. In America the craftsman has been killed. In Europe we must save him. I believe he will live again with power and beauty. These last years have, in fact, witnessed the re-evaluation of the craftsman's expressive means: ceramics, lithographs, engravings, etchings, silkscreen paintings, etc.... All these forms of art, less expensive than paintings and often as authentic in their plastic statement, will more and more take the place of painting. The supply will soon be unable to keep up with the demand, and artistic education and understanding will no longer be reserved for the few, but will be for all."[6]

IX

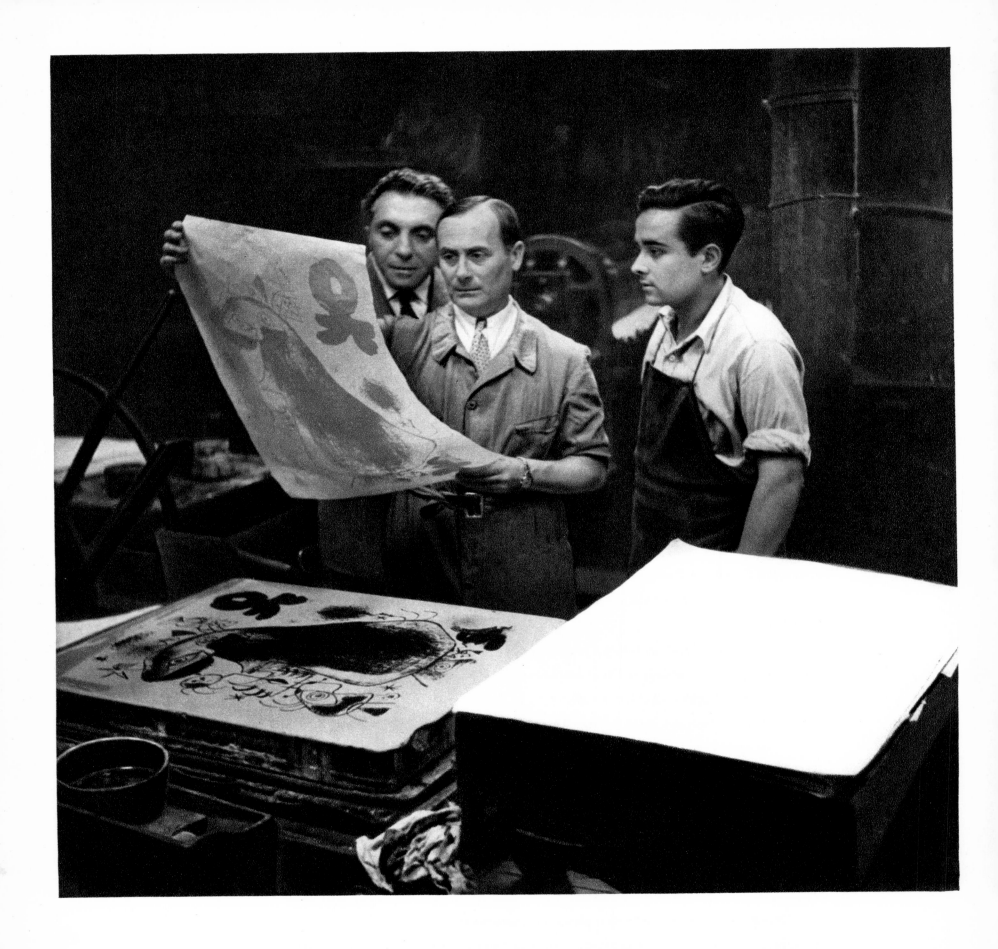

Any account of Miró's graphic work must begin with his paintings, for until the close of the war, they directly determined the formal characteristics and the thematic material of his prints. Since that date, however, Miró has shown a more vivid awareness of the independent powers of the graphic media, and of ceramics as well. While his painting has not been usurped by any means, it now seems less capable of generating fresh ideas and no longer leads the way. Curiously, those qualities of immediacy and spontaneity which have always been the hallmark of Miró's art are today more evident in the graphic and ceramic media.

Joan Miró was born at Montroig, near Barcelona, on April 20, 1893. Like his fellow countrymen, Picasso and Gris, he has shown an equally stubborn atavism in his art and a more pronounced attachment to his native soil. Even after 1920, when he began to play an increasingly active role in the absorbing Paris art scene, he continued to divide his residence between the family farm at Montroig or a town house in Barcelona, and Paris. Since 1940, he has spent greater portions of each year in Spain, either in Barcelona or Palma de Mallorca, the largest of the Balearic Islands off the Mediterranean coast of Spain which culturally and linguistically belongs to Catalonia. Miró's Catalan heritage is a significant factor in his art to which the artist points with pride. He had spoken with warmth of his early interest in the bold colors and vigorous stylization of "the primitive Catalan church paintings and the Gothic retables."[7] Miró has also expressed his admiration for the genius of Antonio Gaudi, perhaps the most extreme and fantastic architectural exponent of the style of *Art nouveau* in his remarkable buildings in the city of Barcelona. Gaudi's nervosity of line, his organic imagery in detail and ornament, and his grotesque invention, generally, left a profound impression on the young Miró.

The gay decoration of Catalan folk art has also been a fruitful source of artistic ideas for Miró, contributing significantly to the atmosphere of his style. In "popular" art forms, and in the simplified ideograms of children's paintings, he found a fresh basis for that innocence of vision which has been one of the primary affirmations of so much modern painting. Robert Desnos' description of Miró's Paris studio in the rue Blomet, when the artist had just completed *The Farm* (page X, top), in 1922, suggests the importance of the popular imagination and Catalonian folk art in his evolution:

"In one corner of the studio was a table covered with Balearic toys, little gnomes, strange animals in plaster illuminated in lively colors. These little creatures seemed to have come out of *The Farm*. They gave the studio a holiday, fairy-tale air, and I tried in vain to wrack my brains for a memory of which I was only able to call back the ghosts, the savor, so to speak – a childhood tale in which mushrooms played the principal role."[8]

This important painting, which represented a turning point for Miró, was, indeed, directly inspired by the artist's affectionate longing for his native countryside. He has described *The Farm* as a painting "made in Paris to keep me in touch with Montroig".[9] Miró even went to the lengths of bringing dried grasses from his farm to France while the painting was in progress, as much out of nostalgic sentiment, one suspects, as a passion for exact fidelity of detail. More than two decades later, commenting on the ceramics which he executed with Artigas at Gallifa, near Barcelona, Miró paid a further tribute to the inspiration of his native province: "The vigorous Catalan landscape, without any trace of anecdotal description, has been a capital element in my plastic and poetic conception."[10] Catalonia, and Spain, have not only supplied Miró with specific impressions and directly affected his imagery and forms, but also provided a necessary refuge from the shifting currents and counter-currents of artistic influence agitating the life of Paris, the vantage point from which he could calmly survey the painting of his time and firmly fix the outlines of his personal identity as an artist.

Miró began the study of painting at the age of fourteen when he entered the School of Fine Arts in Barcelona. Three years later his parents prevailed upon him briefly to abandon painting and enter a business office, but he resumed his studies at Barcelona's Academy Gali in 1912 and has devoted himself to art ever since. During this early period in Spain two teachers played a significant part in his development, Modesto Urgell, a Böcklin follower at the School of Fine Arts, whose romantic realism was later to influence another young Catalan artist, Salvador Dali, and Pasco. Christian Zervos indicates that Urgell's painting left a "lasting poetic impression"[11] on his young student, and that his introspective habits of mind confirmed in Miró an already marked taste for solitude and reflection. In contact with the Surrealists Miró later revived an inward "poetry" as the central aim of his art, and became a voracious reader of the Symbolist poets, finding their counsel of revolt, and flight from the world of everyday reality a bulwark against the mechanism and shallow materialism of modern life. Miró himself has placed his debt to Urgell more explicitly, attributing to his teacher's mournful night pictures the origin of many of his own obsessive signs—the circle, the moon, the star—and the ubiquitous horizon line that bisects his paintings of the middle twenties. In Pasco, Miró found a liberal instructor who encouraged his highly individual bent for color, and invited him to take such experimental liberties as drawing from a sense of touch alone. "Even today," Miró said in 1948, "thirty years after, the effect of this touch drawing experience returns in my interest in sculpture: the need to mold with my hands—to pick up a ball of wet clay like a child and squeeze it."[12] Miró also credits Pasco with awakening his interest in music by introducing him to Bach and Mozart, who, in the artists's words, "sharpened my sense of lines, of form."[13] In Miró's mature style, many musical parallels suggest themselves: a melodic quality of line, with its inventive variations, the "acoustical" quality of his spatial backgrounds, which are both echo and motion, and, of course, the introduction of fragments of musical notation. Such parallels, however, can also easily be found in the work of other artists of the period, notably Klee and Picasso, and may be ascribed to a general campaign to break down the confinement of the separate sensory perceptions as much as to the personal idiosyncracy of the individual artist. The interrelationship of the arts, and of aural-visual experience, has been very much on the minds of modern poets and painters from the time of Poe, Baudelaire, Rimbaud, and Gauguin.

The earliest work by Joan Miró which the author has seen is a soft, amorphous landscape (the collection of the Pierre Matisse Gallery, New York) executed in the glowing colors, and with the free brushwork of Renoir's late manner. It was painted around 1916, and grew, one may guess, out of Miró's visit during the war to a large exhibition of Impressionist paintings held in Barcelona. The following two years were important for the artist, and in the work of this period he showed the first unmistakable signs of a personal style. By 1917, Miró's landscapes betrayed a new Fauve exuberance in color and brush stroke, disciplined somewhat by the influence of Cézanne, and by Van Gogh's emphatic, parallel outlines. Characteristic of his early style is a flat, linear elaboration of surface, broken up into small units of design. (The somewhat stylized landscapes of this period are curiously reminiscent, too, of Dufy's Marseilles harbor scenes of 1908; painted under the mixed influence of Cézanne and Fauvism, Dufy's paintings also remained essentially decorative and 'miniaturist' in spirit.) At the end of the year, Miró made the acquaintance of José Dalmau, the Barcelona dealer who was a friend of Picasso and showed the work of the rising Cubist generation. And, in 1918, Dalmau gave Miró his first one-man show in Barcelona, just as, three years later, he was to sponsor his first Paris one-man show.

Miró made his initial trip to Paris in March of 1919, returning to Spain the following spring, in the first of those annual shifts of residence which has ever since been the pattern of his life. One of the first persons he called on was Picasso, who bought a *Self-Portrait* (page IX) from his younger countryman and befriended him, cheerfully assuming the role of protector and sponsor. That *Self-Portrait* of 1919 demonstrates a new refinement of means, in Miró's characteristic but increasingly flat and mannered stylization of form. Its incisive outlines, shallow relief modeling and biaxial symmetry point to the Byzantine icon, or those Catalan Romanesque frescoes of which Miró was so enamored, as well as to the competing influence of Cubist geometry.[14] The artist's meticulous elaboration of decorative pattern in his shirt front, with its impression of stiff brocade, however, suggest that he was not prepared to sacrifice surface detail to the Cubists' passion for uniform structural accents.

By 1920, at its moment of supreme tension, Miró's painstaking descriptive realism began to disintegrate from within, as the more emphatically decorative areas isolated themselves more and more, and assumed an abstract importance. The process of cleavage is even clearer in the paintings of the following two years, where costume ornament and accessories, individual details of hair, of facial feature, take on a striking nervous life of their own. Miró's virginal and studied grace, cursive energy, and mannered idiom give a curiously mixed atmosphere to these paintings, both of preciosity and naïveté.

It is interesting to note that another outsider to the School of Paris, and a Spaniard, Juan Gris, reacted similarly to the advanced art of his time in his early style. Both artists in the beginning showed a certain provincial timidity; even while working under the influence of Cubism, they held tenaciously to a simplified decorative naturalism of native inspiration, and clung a'so to the more sophisticated flourishes of *Art nouveau*. Each in his own way, however, profited from his early resistance to Cubism, and to the potent influence of his countryman, Picasso. In the end, both Gris and Miró fashioned impressive personal styles, one by applying Cubist æsthetic principles with a fanatical strictness; and the other by irreverently animating, and finally undermining, its sober architectural façade and regimented forms. In doing so, each revealed a striking side of Spanish artistic temperament, its cold, aristocratic refinement, and its gaiety, its feeling for contrast and color.

The Farm, on which Miró worked for a full year, represented the culmination of his early style of flat, fragmentary realism, expressed by purposely disconnected, and heightened, decorative details. But a geometric compartmentalization of form and a "constructivist" spirit were also evident in the painting. Miró was later to comment on his art of this transitional period thus: "I understood quite soon that it was necessary to go beyond this spirit of the miniature, to go much further. To expand the detail until it fused with the ensemble. To make one aware that it existed, even without seeing it."[15]

A more radical process of formal elision and evocative association began to take place in his painting with *The Tilled Field*, completed in 1924. Here, for the first time, descriptive detail is merely indicatory, and poetic fancy has begun to function freely. The stiffness of Miró's

linear perspective scheme has given way to a greater fluency of design, and to a less rationalized space. Many of the images originate still in the flora and fauna, and the general topography, of *The Farm*, but they now signify rather than describe objects and incident, inviting us to participate in a fascinating guessing game of association. His forms derive more from fantasy, from childhood memory than from visible nature. And the way his shapes fit into, and control, the rhythmic life of the composition becomes an equally important factor; they function both as symbols and purely plastic signs, within that ingenious system of coordinated ambiguities which so strikingly characterizes Miró's mature expression.

Miró carried the symbolic condensation of his imagery even further in the *Catalan Landscape* of the same year, using thinner color and replacing the large geometric silhouettes and the regularized flat forms of *The Tilled Field* with a freely moving, cursive calligraphy, and the barest ideographs. He still managed to suggest, in remote, abstract transposition, a barnyard iconography and recognizable motifs from Montroig. Then, his metamorphic invention reached a climax of dramatic enrichment in the dense, brilliant detail of the *Harlequin's Carnival* (page X, bottom) of 1925, an agitated colorful dance of insectile phantasmagoria, animated toys, and gaudy baubles, as if the nursery had sprung into life. Much of the imagery, and the varieties of motion and locomotion, of the contemporary animated cartoon stem directly from Miró's inventions of this period.

If Miró's child-like images were gay in color, they also revealed elements of a sardonic humor, and a taste for the grotesque. Pierre Guéguen later catalogued the characteristics of Miró's repertory of shape and silhouette, a world consisting of "hooks, thorns, darts, needles,

barbed wire, curved triangles, mallets, spits, concave lenses, and distorting lenses, a world of multicolored horns."[16] And Georges Hugnet has noted the resemblance of his forms to "instruments of torture."[17] The words of this Surrealist poet, and early friend of the artist, do little to encourage the popular and more facile appreciations of Miró's paintings, which have so often been praised for their innocence and appealing vivacity alone. Writing in 1931, Hugnet found a "Spanish heritage of cruelty, insolence, and pride" in Miró's "cult of blood, and brutal symbolic realism." In connection with the artist's collages, he notes: "There is a desperate summons to murder in those instruments of torture of the new Inquisition. This art in the service of the fetish, of taboo, comes attired in the rope, sharp spikes, the plastic expression of the garrotte, and the crucifixion. Dali's sadism rules its torture chamber."[18]

One suspects, however, that the convulsive aspects of Miró's art in 1925 were even more related to the Surrealist uprising, that eloquent barometer of international anxiety, than to a native "Spanish heritage of cruelty." Indeed, the influence of Surrealism, which was officially proclaimed by André Breton in his first manifesto of 1924, may have been the decisive factor in freeing Miró's sense of the "marvelous," his already marked instinct for fantasy; and the "automatic" methods of such painters as Masson, who occupied the studio directly next door in the rue Blomet, gave him a viable pictorial means for expressing that fantasy. The feverish Dada demonstrations, exhibitions, and publications in Paris from 1920 onward evidently made a profound impression on the young artist, now ready and eager to come forward and claim his liberation with the "advanced" generation. In 1925, Miró was invited to participate in the first collective Surrealist exhibition at the Galerie Pierre, with Picasso, Klee, Ernst, de Chirico, Masson, Arp, Man Ray, and Pierre Roy. From his autobiographical notes, we know that his neighbors in the Villa des Fusains, rue Tourlac, where he lived for a short time after 1924, were Paul Eluard, Max Ernst, Magritte, and Arp, among the prime movers in the Dada and Surrealist movements.

Although many of these artists and poets may have had a formative influence on Miró, his painting is most strikingly related to the work of Arp. Miró makes laconic reference in his autobiographical notes to the poverty and camaraderie he endured and enjoyed with Arp, recalling a day when they lunched together on "radishes and butter."[19] In correspondence[20] with the author, Arp has, with his customary generosity, refused to acknowledge an influence on Miró, but it is difficult to believe that the younger Spanish artist was not directly affected by the Dada wood reliefs in bright color, and the string compositions on which Arp worked just before and during his early Paris residence. Arp's specific and obsessive iconography of navels, bird masks, mustachioed faces and clock-faces show unmistakable resemblances to various aspects of Miró's imagery of the middle twenties, and Miró took over directly from Arp his characteristic "biomorphic" shapes, and flowing compositions.

One can, of course, deduce other formal and iconographic sources for isolated elements in Miró's radical new style; yet it is to the artist's great credit that his powers of generating form, and an intensely personal poetry, give his pictorial universe remarkable qualities of originality. Throughout his mature career, that is after 1925, Miró reveals striking gifts of adaptability in relation to the most significant art of his epoch. Sometimes he seems simply to mimic and parody, within a more limited register, the devices and metamorphic imagery of Picasso in particular. Yet his own style is so coherent and assured, and his pictorial world so autonomous, that everything he assimilates bends to its rule; his models and sources are magnetized in entirely unforeseen directions. Miró's art testifies both to the unity of modern sensibility, and to its extraordinary variety. Every picture must be won on its own terms, and operate freely under its own energies, even when the impulse that set it in motion can logically be assigned to an outside force. One must also note the continuing references, no matter how extreme their transformation, both to the subject matter and cursive linear energies of *The Farm*, which is as fundamental to Miró's later development as *Les demoiselles d'Avignon* was to Picasso's artistic evolution.

In keeping perhaps with the Surrealists' affection for aberrated and extreme moods, Miró himself has related his radical stylistic change to the added impetus which Masson and the Surrealist poets gave his already sharply developed taste for French literary romanticism: "Masson was always a great reader and full of ideas. Among his friends were practically all the young poets of the day. Through Masson I met them. Through them I heard poetry discussed. The poets Masson introduced me to interested me more than the painters I had met in Paris. I was carried away by the new ideas they brought and especially the poetry they discussed. I gorged myself on it all night long—poetry principally in the tradition of Jarry's *Surmâle* . . . .

"As a result of this reading I began gradually to work away from the realism I had practiced up to 'The Farm' until, in 1925, I was drawing almost entirely from hallucinations. At the time I was living on a few dried figs a day. I was too proud to ask my colleagues for help. Hunger was a great source of these hallucinations. I would sit for long periods looking at the bare walls of my studio trying to capture these shapes on paper or burlap."[21]

Unlike many of the orthodox Surrealist painters, however, Miró never embraced the picturesque tendencies of the movement, its *trompe l'oeil* techniques of illustration and incongruous association. He took over the formal side of Surrealism mainly, its "automatism," its hyperactive principle of analogy and even a certain hermeticism at times. But his paintings are plastic creations first and last, and the data of the Unconscious submits to the control of pictorial logic. The material function of his expressive means has always been uppermost in Miró's mind; ideas and "poetry" are embodied rather than illustrated, and communicate directly through concrete pictorial sensation.

Miró's independent position, and his utter devotion to painting *per se*, have understandably aroused ambivalent feeling in the ranks of the orthodox Surrealists. While André Breton has praised him for his "pure automatism" and said that, on such grounds, Miró "may be regarded as the most Surrealist of us all,"[22] he has at the same time reproached him for his stubborn individualism. In fact, Breton was compelled to invent a special and lesser artistic category to account for Miró in the Surrealist hierarchy, associating him with those essentially permissive artists who merely served as an "instrument of painting." This was in striking contrast to those who actively contributed to the collective Surrealist effort, seeking the establishment of a new order of reality on a sound philosophical basis.

It is characteristic of Miró that he has chosen to remain unaffiliated, and will not allow himself to be circumscribed by the precepts and practices of any single artistic group or movement. Perhaps his repeated reference to "poetry" as the central aim of his art may be best understood as Miró's way of underlining his painting's singularity, and safeguarding it against collective misrepresentation. That jealous regard for his artistic identity opposes, paradoxically, a variety of statements he has made in support of the communal art spirit. In the early thirties, when Miró's art began to show a heightened sense of abstract design, and a clearer unity of organization, in response, apparently, to the general revival of interest in geometric abstraction, he was invited by Mondrian to join his Abstraction-Creation group in a Paris exhibition. But Miró indignantly refused, and later commented rather ruefully on this episode:

"Have you ever heard of greater nonsense than the aims of the abstractionist group? They invite me to share their deserted house as if the signs I transcribe on a canvas, at the moment when they correspond to a concrete representation in my mind, were not profoundly real, and did not belong essentially to the world of reality! As a matter of fact, I am attaching more and more importance to the subject matter of my work. To me it seems vital that a rich and robust theme should be present to give the spectator an immediate blow between the eyes before a second thought can interpose. In this way poetry pictorially expressed speaks its own language . . . . For a thousand men of letters, give me one poet!"[23]

Miró's addiction to the literary, and that self-image of the poet to which he has clung, served him well, however. Clement Greenberg has noted in his excellent monograph: "But Miró profits from almost everything he does. His Surrealist experience supplied him permanently with the conviction of having a message—a conviction that, after his break with realism, seems as necessary to his will to paint as it does to Picasso's."[24] He confronted Surrealism's speculative and philosophical side, its systematic disorders and polished academic techniques with the sensuality of the pure painter; while to his opposite dæmon of abstraction, he turned the face of the poet. His own painting holds in tension these two primary forces of modern painting, and represents perhaps the most radical new departure in the art of the post-Picasso generation.

By 1929 and 1930, when Miró began his first lithographs (plate 1), he had been established in a highly original style for some five or six years. Most recently, after a trip to Holland in 1928, had come a series of Dutch interiors, brilliant in their dense, agitated detail. The large empty spaces, thinly washed surfaces and slack silhouettes of Miró's Dada period gave way to crisper definition, a dynamic complexity of form and movement, and a more objective spirit. Whereas Miró's Dada paintings explored the romantic potential of an echoing spatial void, and the properties of inertia in matter, his new work showed an intense activism of surface. At the same time, as James Johnson Sweeney has noted, he gave evidence, in a series of large drawings on felt paper, of a "new-found graphic freedom and assurance . . . which announce the powerful calligraphy of his mature style."[25]

Miró's first-known, independent lithograph, referred to above, recapitulates, in smaller compass and scale, certain motifs that hark back to *The Tilled Field*. (It is characteristic of Miró to look backward into his own past; he has described his art as one of "recovery" rather than discovery.) Contrasting with the spidery refinement of edge of the more retrospective forms are a few bold, slashing signs, in opaque, greasy black—those graffiti which seem to indicate, like excited stage directions or exclamatory editing, some dramatic action, without, however, disclosing either the protagonists or the occasion.

Miró's habit of summarizing himself before proceeding to new formal adventures is also demonstrated in the four lithographs of the same period illustrating Tristan Tzara's *L'Arbre des voyageurs*. Here the Dada spirit reasserts itself, in the effort to express mixed aural-visual sensation through multiple contrasts of texture, and by a variety of graphic techniques. On one of these papers, a loosely tangled ball of line, suggesting both smoke and hair, is suspended in free space; it is balanced by a gossamer-fine rectangle, and a sequence of nerveless, curving lines, resembling musical half-notes that, lacking some inner tension, have slowly uncurled and seem about to fall off an imaginary staff.

The way in which Miró turned Picasso's conventions to personal account is demonstrated by his first etching of 1933 (plate 4), and by that remarkable expression of volume through a fine, continuous contour line only, the etching of 1935 that appears on plate 3. Picasso's fantastic bathers of 1923, with their dramatically foreshortened limbs and wild, clawing gestures, and the older artist's abstract "bone" figures in the later years of the decade, fore-shadow Miró's forms. But Picasso's stage-box perspective system and sculptural solidity have dissolved in the miraculous fluids of Miró's space. It is as if Miró's solid bodies had been distended by their own accelerated centrifugal movements, until they began to fuse with a flowing spatial environment. Miró does try to preserve some semblance of solidity, and the object qualities of forms, by shading their edges; in the etching on the facing page, however, form is reduced to a simplified calligraphic system of attenuated kidney shapes.

This non-aggressive, purely linear commentary on Picasso's fantastic anatomies suggests a cyclical character in Miró's invention: he has continually alternated between a modified system of chiaroscuro and the linear evocation of form; between flatness and depth; starkness and detailed elaboration; diagrammatic abstraction and elements of descriptive naturalism. Like Picasso, he has at his disposal a complex expressive means, capable of awakening multiple responses without in any way creating an impression of disorder or incoherence. These changes of tempo and inflection are simply different ways of saying the same thing, and remind us freshly that one of the cardinal rules of modern art is the indivisibility of the decorative and expressive impulse, of subject matter and method.

A continuing preoccupation with Surrealist device, as late as 1938, is apparent in the *Portrait of Miró* (plate 23), an etching on which Marcoussis collaborated. The engraving was made the same year that Miró did his large pencil and oil grisaille, *Self-Portrait* (page XI), in the collection of James Thrall Soby, an even more impressive example of the artist's extraordinary ability to build a single, striking phantasmal image from a multitude of small pictorial incident. Perhaps more in the spirit of a *tour de force*, Dali had painted human faces into landscapes, and shown landscape through a face, with that brilliantly perverse anthropomorphism which guided Surrealist sensibility in relation to objective reality. But Miró's painting, and his collaborative etching, are not simply virtuoso exercises, designed to show the interdependence of reality and fantasy, or to pose a riddle. They affirm, rather, the primacy of the artist's expressive means, and suggest that conventional representation can only emerge through his world of creatural forms and calligraphic signs. Hence, the recognizable anatomical features of hands, eyes, nose issue directly from a general formal activity, and grow, as it were, under the etching needle stroke. The work emphasizes the æsthetic autonomy of Miró's pictorial universe, in confrontation with our more fixed and conventional ways of seeing.

Although elements of naturalistic figuration were extremely rare in Miró's art after 1922, they did reappear with unusual emphasis for a time at the end of the thirties. The painting, *Still Life with Old Shoe* of 1937, was Miró's most naturalistic representation since *The Farm*, but, like the self-portraits of the following year, it also used to advantage many of the Surrealist devices of dissociation, as if to expose the underlying hallucinatory character of solid material existence. In Miró's own mind, however, these adaptions of a more conventional Surrealist method represented an approach once more to objective reality, under the pressure of somber events in Spain. "Between the years 1938 and 1940," he has declared, "I once again became interested in realism. Perhaps the interest began as early as 1937 in *Still Life with Old Shoe*. Perhaps the events of the day, particularly the drama of the war in Spain, made me feel that I ought to soak myself in reality. I used to go every day to the Grande Chaumière to work from a model. At the time I felt a need to control things by reality."[26]

With the tragic war in Spain very much on his mind, Miró had painted in 1937 a large mural decoration, *The Reaper*, for the Spanish pavilion of the Paris World Fair. The intensity of this painting, its violence of color and form, suggest that it must have had some special significance for the artist. The torn, dislocated, figure, with its tuberous snout and gnarled, stem-like neck, has many affinities with Picasso's animal-vegetable incarnation of the Dictator Franco, in his etching *The Dream and Lie of Franco*. Miró's figure seems to push its way up out of a malign soil, like some obscene growth, into a flaming, apocalyptic night. Its distortions and clutching gestures also remind us of Picasso's wracked and stricken "weeping women," those preliminary studies-in-anguish which preceded the *Guernica*. Like many of Picasso's images, Miró's lend themselves to multiple interpretations. In an interesting, poetic exposition, Juan Larrea has seen in *The Reaper* "a peasant armed with his sickle,"[27] a heroic symbol of the Spanish people's power to endure; and in the spectral illumination, the promise of a new life.

In all likelihood, however, Miró's figures of the late thirties are neither meant to be heroes nor the symbolic victims of social aggression; and they do not support the distinctions of conventional morality between good and evil. Rather, his paintings and prints seem to reflect and internalize, by their addiction to grotesque genre, the violent public disorders of the period. Such etchings as *The Giantess* (plate 16), *The Awakening of the Giant* (plate 17) and *The Three Sisters* (plate 20) measure the disrupting violence of the age, and of Miró's own feelings, reawakening the artist's sense of the Terrible. Compared with Picasso's inventions, the dramas of anguish take place on a smaller stage and are somewhat more light-hearted in their mocking, derisory accents. Unlike Picasso, Miró doesn't oppose classical figuration and an ideal beauty to the grotesque, and gain expressive force from their opposition and conflict. Miró's ideal world is astral and formal; he exorcises his frightening chimeras by scattering them in the ether where they voyage like disembodied ghosts, forming the constellations of a purely pictorial universe.

In 1939 and 1940 Miró executed only two prints, perhaps because these were climactic painting years for him and the major media once again consumed all his energies. During 1939 he had painted on unsized canvas and burlap mainly, as already noted, allowing the rough surfaces to suggest new forms. The paintings that resulted were more flat and calligraphic in manner, but showed a new expressive intensity, despite the greater standardization of form. This was the period when Miró's elaborate titles often suggested the irrational system of causality in a Rube Goldberg cartoon, as an example, the painting called, *Drop of Rose Falling from the Wing of a Bird Waking Rosalie Asleep in the Shade of a Cobweb*. If these punning titles seemed far fetched, they did capture something of the linking-and-chaining action of Miró's inexhaustible, metamorphic invention.

After the fall of France in 1940, Miró returned to Palma de Mallorca, and stayed there in the early phase of the war. Leading a solitary and "ascetic existence," he read omnivorously in French Symbolist poetry and Spanish mysticism. The decidedly introspective character of his life was in contrast to the controlled objectivity of his new work, a series of gouaches begun in Paris and "based on reflections in water", whose "main aim was to achieve a compositional balance."[28] These paintings reduce Miró's signs to a molecular structure of points, dots and interconnecting, crisp lines; their intensely active surfaces are further animated by bright color accents. The calligraphic scheme, half-Impressionistic, half-Constructivist diagram, seems related to some of Picasso's abstract drawings of 1926 which were later reproduced as woodcuts by the publisher Ambroise Vollard, to illustrate Honoré de Balzac's *Le chef-d'oeuvre inconnu*.

Soon after Miró moved to Barcelona, and he has described a further change in his art that immediately followed: "And as these Palma paintings had been so exacting both technically and physically, I now felt the need to work more freely, more gaily—to proliferate. I produced a great deal at this time, working very quickly. And just as I worked very carefully in the Palma series which had immediately preceded these, 'controlling' everything, now I worked with the least control possible—at any rate in the first phase, the drawing."[29]

Out of this mood, and the need to 'proliferate,' ultimately came the magnificent Barcelona series (plates 24-33) of fifty lithographs in black, which he completed in the early course of 1944, just before his return to liberated Paris. If these lithographs profited from the new freedom apparent in Miró's work, they also showed the results of that concentration in style which had taken place in 1939 and 1940. In many ways, they also recovered something of the anguished, tragi-comic mood of *The Reaper*, and the powerful grotesques of his 1938 etchings. The systematic unfolding of a figurative imagery, with the focus usually centered on dislocated human features and an expressive mimicry of hands, and the many resemblances to the "weeping women" of Picasso's *Guernica*, lead one to assume that violent public events had once again stirred Miró to a high pitch of dramatic expression.

Unlike the etchings of 1938, a ferocity of expression is here matched by superb control of composition and an astonishing richness of invention, even within the more strict formal

limits the artist has set himself. Comparing plates 24 or 25 from the Barcelona suite with the 1938 drypoint in plate 20, one observes both an expansion of style and a more concentrated means. The later prints are more monumental in their scale, without the niggling elaboration of detail which characterizes the preceding work. Forms are not so arbitrarily applied to space, and now seem, indeed, to generate spontaneously their own spatial environment and all those echoing and conflicting physiognomic variations which give them life. If anything, there has been a gain in psychological resonance and in the power to arouse disquieting emotion. Characterization and plastic expression register simultaneously, fulfilling Miró's express aim of reaching the spectator with "an immediate blow between the eyes before a second thought can interpose." If the Barcelona series crystallizes, nearly a decade later, an expressive mood that began in the late thirties, that is typical of the artist's creative processes; Miró reaches the summits of his career, in painting or prints, only after long periods of gestation and experiment.

Like so many of the Surrealists, Miró was never less than candid in his dealings with sexuality. His protagonists in the Barcelona suite are emphatically characterized as male or female; more often his composite images emerge as both, by dint of those metamorphic transpositions of form which scramble identities and project all experience bifocally, under the dual aspect of knowledge and illusion. The prominence of the pudenda in Miró's repertory of images is only matched by the repeated mouths, agape and filled with menacing teeth, multiple eyes and clawing hands. These recurrent themes establish a basic symbolic vocabulary rooted in man's elementary aggressive and instinctual drives. On one level they are a symptom of contemporary crisis, and direct our attention to the predatory characteristics in the individual which have been unleashed by the violence of public life. But they are also part of the modern technique of exposure, an acceptable convention in the campaign against repression and social hypocrisy, which, since the time of Freud, has been one of the rallying grounds of the emancipated spirit. In this connection, Miró has said that the most fruitful goal of modern painting is, "to discover the sources of human feeling."[30] Miró has frequently commented, too, on the necessity of restoring to modern man a magical sense of things; perhaps his emphasis on sexual symbols is also motivated, then, by the fetishistic tendency of primitive art, which equates potency with supernatural powers.

To restore balance in the interpretation of the artist's symbols, Michel Leiris' characterization of Miró's art is useful: "Lightness, *allegria* of his art, where masculine and feminine symbols give to each other the most evident support; without any taste for death, or any of the mustiness of psychoanalysis. White magic, as opposed to so much black magic. A saraband of elves, a Walpurgis night, in the mistless air of the Mediterranean South. All of that in a thoroughly wide awake condition, at the poles from the dream world."

One must note, too, that Miró's subconscious imagery is the occasion of much comedy. He does not treat sex quite with the Rabelaisian gusto of Picasso, but with a more delicate wit, transforming the pudenda into emblematic device, a Freudian heraldry of the Unconscious, enlivened by those dainty, rococo linear flourishes which the eighteenth century would have classified as "gallant invention."

The Barcelona lithographs represented Miró's last effort to delineate a systematic imagery, connected, perhaps indirectly, to man's own expressive gestures and charged with psychological meanings. Even in this series, however, the material function of medium itself is given greater emphasis, as in plate 28, where the central figures are obliterated by a few inky silhouettes and grafitti, and specific dramatic content thereby neutralized. Action and passion are now identified more purely with the immediate physical sensations of media. The artist's energies have broken the confinement of an individualized expression of discrete objects and forms, and function more freely and arbitrarily. From the drama of Miró's *personnages*, we pass on to the drama of matter itself, and to the experience of its pure creative potential. In anticipation of the contemporary Abstract Expressionists, or "action" painters, Miró's art after 1944 reverts to its origins, and reveals artistic form at the source, in the very process of achieving existence and order. To adapt Paul Valéry's discerning comment on the nature of modern poetry, "It enjoins us to come into being much more than it stimulates us to understand." The shifting æsthetic grounds of Miró's expression, from the development of an iconic imagery to a free graphism, became apparent with his renewed interest in ceramics. He made his first large group of ceramics during the period 1944-1946. For the first time, perhaps, the techniques of reproduction and the materials of manufacture with their expressive range of texture and surface, seemed to dictate the form of his art. Also for the first time, "non-artistic" materials (heat-proof facsimiles of pebbles, rocks, and so forth) incorporated into the final æsthetic product were no longer employed in the way of shock tactics, to humiliate appearances and so-called "noble means." The "found" object was promoted from the level of an alien influence, competing with an æsthetic order, and became part of a natural spectacle in which æsthetic and immediate material reality harmoniously interacted. Miró's art moved away from the formal toward the natural, and he seemed content to adumbrate a "way of seeing," finding magical correspondences for his vision in the accidents of natural form. The face of nature and the face of art were no longer distinct, as they had been when he was inventing his *personnages* and setting them in motion on a dramatic stage.

In prints, this process took the form of further and intensified stress on the brute physical facts of medium, in an art which freely mingled visual and tactile sensation. *Acrobats in the Night Garden* (plate 35), a color lithograph of 1948, shows the broadening of Miró's style for decorative and expressive emphasis. His *personnages*, crescents, stars have been reduced to a system of color accents. And the fleshier brush stroke of the lithographic *tusche*, contrasting with the play of line and granulated surface, gives his paper a varied textural range, between impenetrable opacities and transparent washes of tone. The free brush stroke, or graphic mark, is the irreducible unit of design, showing only the barest residual reference to the images and "ideographs" of the past. Miró has begun to neutralize and depopulate his creatural world of forms, in the interests, however, of a more immediate and spontaneous expressiveness. Perhaps *Tall Black Person* (plate 41), a lithograph in black of the same year, will seem to some a disturbingly crude parody of Miró's exquisite gifts of characterization; but its psychological

emptiness, or neutrality, is more than compensated for by the sensuous relish and plastic authority with which the artist smudges, smears, and daubs.

Miró's anti-gravitational impulses, and topsy-turvy space return in *The Diver* (plate 44), but in the form of a deliberately infantile scribble. And the lithographs in black (plates 59 and 66), which formed part of a suite of 13 prints (plates 59-71) published by the Maeght Gallery in 1948, show an abortive revival of the Barcelona series imagery. It is clear, however, that the artist is no longer interested in creating a "world," or in personifying, but wishes to explore the creative potential of a playful, cursive writing for its own sake. The resemblance to oriental calligraphy is no doubt intentional, and jibes with Miró's continuing effort to formulate a universal visual Esperanto of sign and symbol. "I do not differentiate," he once said, "between painting and poetry. I am apt to illustrate my canvases with poetic phrases and vice-versa. Didn't the Chinese, those great aristocrats of the spirit, proceed in this way?"[31]

If Miró has at times appeared to violate the integrity of his medium, by using the lithographic *tusche* as a free brush, he has done no more than Picasso; like his fellow countryman, he has actually extended the expressive range of his materials. It is worth noting, too, that Miró generally avoided the more synthetic textures and virtuoso effects which modern techniques have brought to the printing process. In 1947, when he was in America to carry out a large mural commission for the Plaza Hotel in Cincinnati, he worked briefly with Stanley William Hayter in his New York Atelier. There he completed a number of color etchings (plates 37, 38, 39). The application of a variety of textures, printed through a soft ground, and the use of the more indirect lift-ground aquatint were extremely popular in the Hayter studio; an increasingly skilled control of color printing from multiple screens guided the standard product of the atelier toward labyrinthine invention and a curiously empty technical complexity. Miró, however, apparently used only the direct bite method in the plates which he made at Hayter's studio. The main line in *Little Girl Skipping the Rope* (plate 37) is limp and nerveless, as if a

length of tangled string had been printed on the plate. A similar, though somewhat more crisp, linear impression was achieved in the etchings for Tristan Tzara's *L'Antitête* (plates 47-51). In both cases a burin was used exclusively, in zig-zag cuts, and then the plate was bitten for a long period so that the irregular incision might spread and print to give the impression of a string, or a weathered trace of a crack in a wall. The surface granulation is mainly the result of long biting in a strong acid bath; bubbles of gas in the acid have left the ring-shaped patterns. Miró took advantage of this chemical reaction, and exploited for enhanced textural interest those pits and flaws in the plate which French engravers call *crevés*.

Six years later, Miró employed the direct bite method again for a group of etchings (plates 77-80), printed in a number of color states from a single plate by the engraver Roger Lacourière. In plate 80, the main forms have been "stopped-out" with asphaltum, or some similar hard ground, and then outlined through the ground with the etching needle. After biting, inking, and wiping, ink adhered to the bitten, roughened walls of the plate at the edges of the outlined forms, producing heavy, dark contours in the impression. The varied combinations of color were applied directly to the single plate, and registered in a single intaglio printing for each successive state. The "reverse" impression reproduced in plate 77 was obtained by inking the raised areas and printing in relief, that is, under less pressure than normally used in an intaglio impression. These alternating "positive" and "negative" approaches to the definition of form recall the brilliant black-and-white oppositions of Picasso's rather eerie, spectral Cubism around 1923, and a similar device of dramatic heightening by extreme value contrasts often used by Miró in his paintings, particularly in 1933. Such devices also confirm the double-sidedness of the Surrealists' vision, and their effort to penetrate below the threshold of appearances in search of a phantasmal reality.

Skillfully utilizing mixed media of etching and color lithography (plates 47-51), Miró's illustrations for the third volume of Tristan Tzara's poem, *L'Antitête*, also show the influence of his experience with ceramics in their irregular cuneiform silhouettes and runic scratchings. His outstanding book illustrations of recent years are characterized by an increasing freedom and spontaneity in handling, and suggest far less the archaeological fragment from prehistory. These have been, notably, a group of 72 color lithographs for Tristan Tzara's *Parler Seul* (vignettes on pages VII, XV, XIX, XXII, XXV, XXXI, XXXIII), published in 1950; six color etchings illustrating Michel Leiris' collection of poems, *Bagatelles Végétales* (plate 89), of 1956; and 100 wood blocks in color for Paul Eluard's poem, *A Toute Epreuve* (plate 100-101), issued in 1958. The illustrations for *Parler Seul* represent one of Miró's most successful collaborations with a modern poet, both in relation to text and typography. His brilliant primary colors and rudimentary signs dominate the page in intensity and scale, gaily mocking by their freedom of movement and capriciousness the mechanical regularity of the type block. But their energy, and pell-mell profusion, seem to accord with a principle of spontaneous generation of form embodied in the poem. In *L'Antitête*, Tzara had written: "Under each stone there is a nest of words, and it is out of their rapid whirling that the world is formed." *Parler Seul*, which grew out of Tzara's experience in the psychiatric hospital of Saint-Alban in 1945, continues to emphasize pure verbal creation, and the search for striking linguistic inventions that will restore to the Word its magical and incantatory powers. This poetry of germinations, in which the word achieves autonomous existence apart from its referential meanings, is related to Miró's elementary configurations. In both cases, the end product is determined by the creative process itself, and our awareness of this process is deliberately heightened. The verbal or visual images carry evidence of the route traversed in their making. Michel Leiris' commentary on *Parler Seul* is very much to the point:

"Parallel to the words which are the seeds ('the grain and the harvest,' as Tzara has said) the typographical signs here also show powers of germination. Nothing could be more random, and at the same time more ordered, than this book which represents the birth of a book, or the progressive creation of an object whose impress, on the one hand, and whose vocabulary, on the other, seem to be its entire source of life."[32]

Six color etchings for Michel Leiris' *Bagatelles Végétales* (plate 89) show an increasing expressive freedom and virtuosity in the use of soft-ground etching techniques, with which Miró now manages subtleties and varied depths of tone comparable to those he achieves with the lithographic *tusche*. The artist has enlivened his surfaces by printing in raised relief, or gouging his plate deeply, for a ropy black line. Such emphatic contrasts find their parallel in Miró's paintings of recent years, testifying to the unity of device and expressive purpose in his art, whatever the media, at any given moment of his career.

In 1950 Miró illustrated a book of poems by Joan Cabral de Melo with three wood blocks in color, his first venture in woodcuts with the engraver Enric Tormo of Barcelona. In 1958, 100 wood blocks in color were published as illustrations for Paul Eluard's *A Toute Epreuve* (plate 100-101), a project on which Tormo was engaged for the better part of ten years, Miró has stated. It is characteristic of Miró that he has remained loyal to a small group of expert artisans,

a number of them in Barcelona, over long periods of time, and that he works closely with them, guiding the production of his prints. The wood blocks for Eluard's poem are of a surprising variety and audacity, within a medium obviously more limited in its expressive range than etching or lithograph. It is interesting to note the occasional reminiscences of Arp's woodcuts of the thirties, with their studiedly symmetrical shapes, printed in white on plaque-like, dark grounds. There is no question of derivativeness in a pejorative sense, however, since Miró has utterly transformed his source. Arp's essentially static silhouettes, with their quality of bas-relief, have been set in lively motion, an effect obtained by the use of thin, transparent washes, and by printing color through color in ambiguous depth. The final impression creates an effect of rapid, spontaneous color notation more allied to the water color than the woodcut. Like Picasso's art of the postwar period, Miró's recent expression seems to reflect a new mood of reconciliation, of relaxed playfulness. There is apparent a renewed exploration for its own sake of the inherent expressive possibilities of a variety of media. We are no longer presented with a world of gay grotesques, animal or vegetal, nor are we invited to enter a magical stellar space where the most unexpected events may take place. When the old chimeras and tricks of levitation do reassert themselves from time to time, they are neutralized and robbed of their power to stir us in our affective being. Today, Miró seems to be at the end of those collective passions and adventures that stimulated his invention, and gave it dramatic intensity, throughout that long and sustained period of creative activity which ended with the Barcelona lithographs of 1944.

His prints, and his paintings and ceramics, affirm instead the eternal virginity of the material means themselves. But the freedom with which Miró employs his means have also re-identified his art with a lyrical nature, and in a sense broadened its base. The forms that grow spontaneously, and in floral profusion, beneath his brush, crayon or burin, have become, to adapt the words of Jean-Paul Sartre, "the sensible symbol of nature – this great vague nature, which throws pollen about lavishly and will produce brusquely the flight of a thousand butterflies." It is true perhaps that Miró has ceased to invent, in the sense that he no longer creates a sharply defined and individualized world of *personnages*. Yet, his way of seeing is now so firmly established, and his expression so assured, that even his most rudimentary and slight graphic gestures carry a resonance of residual poetic and plastic meanings. They unmistakably belong to the world he brought to birth, no matter how attenuated their reference to it. And they continue to evoke that primitive wonder and childlike innocence of spirit which has characterized his art from its earliest beginnings. The *genius loci* of *The Farm* still holds sway over Miró's virtually abstract art of today, a hidden presence that we can more easily detect than define. Exhorting the contemporary artist to be guided each by "his own light," that intangible gleam and grace of individual vision which is the mark of distinctive art, Miró has himself perhaps best defined the atmosphere of his style:

". . . everywhere one finds the sun, a blade of grass, the spirals of the dragon-fly. Courage consists in staying home, close to nature which does not take our disasters into consideration. Each grain of dust possesses a marvelous soul. But to understand it, one must find again the religious and magic sense of things, that of primitive peoples."[33]

FOOTNOTES

[1] Albert Aurier, *Mercure de France*, March, 1891.

[2] Dom Willibrard Verkade, O.S.B., *Tourment de Dieu.*

[3] Hans Arp, *On My Way*, "Dadaland", p. 40, Wittenborn, Schultz, Inc., 1948.

[4] Ibid., "Concrete Art," p. 70.

[5] James Johnson Sweeney, "Joan Miró: Comment and Interview," Partisan Review, p. 210, February, 1948.

[6] André Verdet, *Joan Miró*, Galerie Matarasso, Nice, 1957.

[7] James Johnson Sweeney, "Joan Miró: Comment and Interview," p. 208.

[8] Robert Desnos, Cahiers d'Art, Vol. 9 no. 1-4, 1934, p. 26.

[9] James Johnson Sweeney, "Joan Miró: Comment and Interview," p. 208.

[10] Rosamond Bernier, "Miro céramist," (an interview with Miró and Artigas): L'Oeil, Paris, no. 17: p. 46-53, May 1956.

[11] Christian Zervos, Cahiers d'Art, Vol. 9 no. 1-4, 1934, p. 12.

[12] James Johnson Sweeney, "Joan Miró: Comment and Interview," p. 209.

[13] André Verdet, *Joan Miró*, Galerie Matarasso, Nice, 1957.

[14] James Johnson Sweeney, "Joan Miró: Comment and Interview," p. 208. "Then there was the discipline of cubism. I learned the structure of a picture from Cubism . . . ."

[15] André Verdet, *Joan Miró*, Galerie Matarasso, Nice, 1957.

[16] Pierre Guéguen, Cahiers d'Art, Vol. 9 no. 1-4, 1934, p. 46.

[17] Georges Hugnet, "Joan Miró, ou l'enfance de l'art," Cahiers d'Art, no. 7-8, 1931.

[18] Ibid.

[19] Joan Miró, "Je rêve d'un grand atelier," XXe Siècle, no. 2: 25-28, May, 1938.

[20] A letter to the author, dated May 20, 1958, from Marguerite Hagenbach, Arp's secretary:

"Arp would say that you cannot really speak of influence though, of course, Miró was impressed by certain signs and symbols of Arp and perhaps used some of them in his personal way. Miró and Arp saw each other nearly every day in the years 1925/26 when they both lived at 22 rue Tourlac in Montmartre, Paris, in studios formerly occupied for instance by Toulouse-Lautrec.

"Arp believes that Zervos was being polemical when he wrote in one of the prewar Cahiers d'Arts that Arp had influenced Miró. Arp thinks the signs of Miró are closer to those of Catalan folklore and children's symbols."

[21] James Johnson Sweeney, "Joan Miró: Comment and Interview," p. 209.

[22] André Breton, *Le surréalisme et la peinture*, Brentano's, New York, 1945, p. 68.

[23] Georges Duthuit, "Où allez-vous Miró?" Cahiers d'Art, 11 no. 8-10, 1936, p. 261.

[24] Clement Greenberg, *Joan Miró*, The Quadrangle Press, p. 33.

[25] James Johnson Sweeney, *Joan Miró*, Museum of Modern Art, New York, 1941, p. 47.

[26] James Johnson Sweeney, "Joan Miró: Comment and Interview," p. 210.

[27] Juan Larrea, "Miroir d'Espagne; à propos du 'Faucheur' de Miró, au pavillon espagne de l'Exposition, 1937". Cahiers d'Art, 12 no. 4-5: p. 157, 1937.

[28] James Johnson Sweeney, "Joan Miró: Comment and Interview," p. 211.

[29] Ibid.

[30] Francis Lee, "Interview with Miró," Possibilities I, Winter 1947/48, p. 67.

[31] Georges Duthuit, "Où allez-vous Miró?" Cahiers d'Art, 11 no. 8-10: p. 263, 1936.

[32] Michel Leiris, "tu es sorti vivant," Derrière le miroir, 1929/30.

[33] Georges Duthuit, "Où allez-vous Miró?" Cahiers d'Art, 11 no. 8-10: p. 262, 1936.

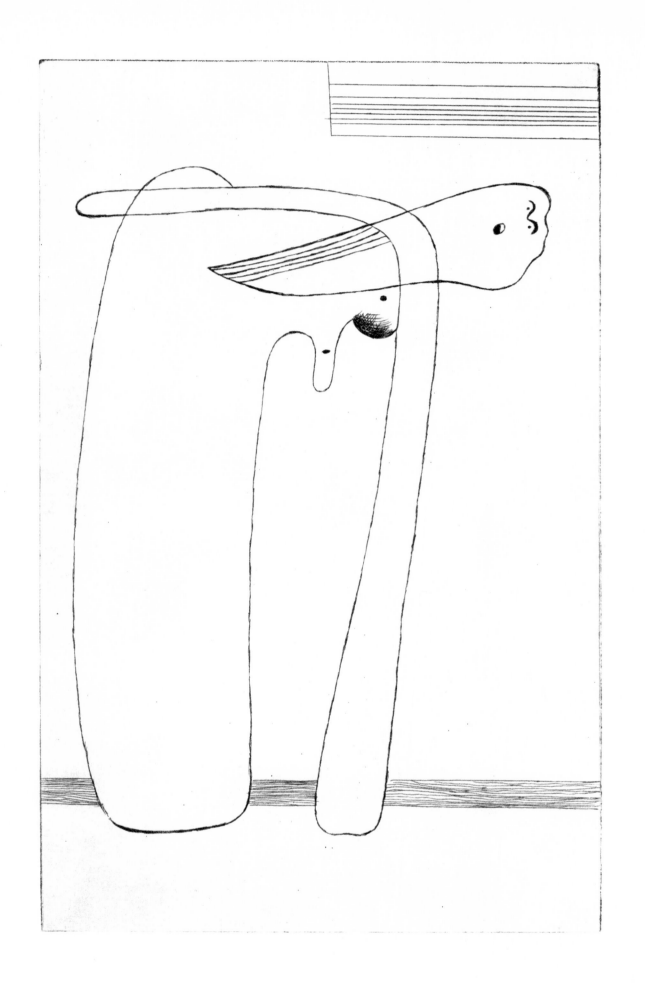

2

3

23

28

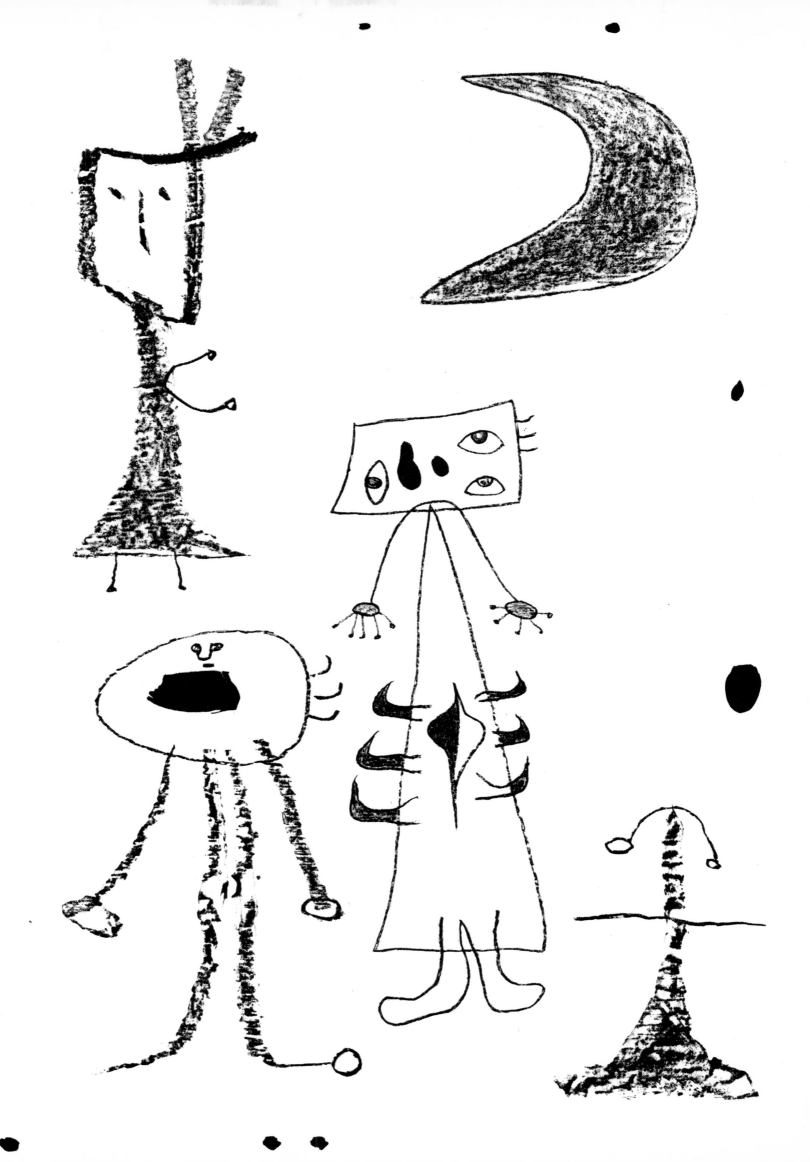

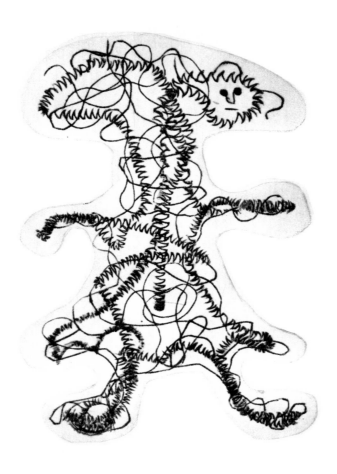

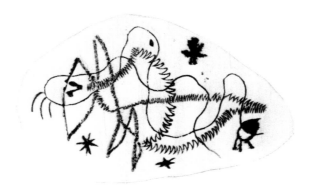

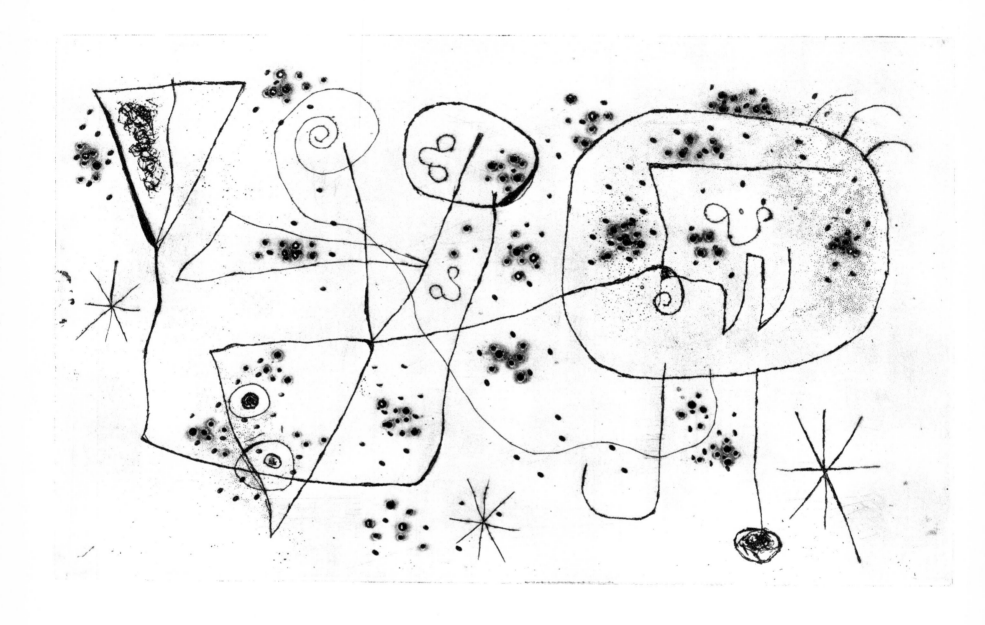

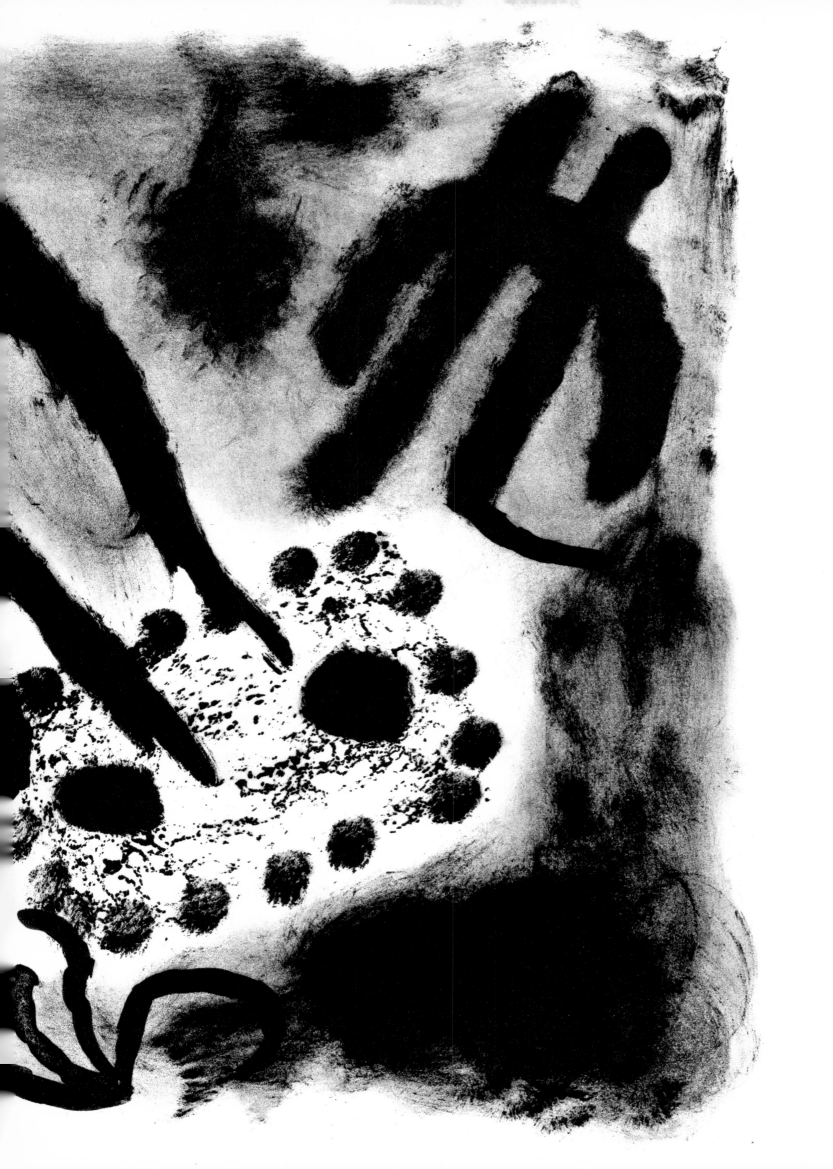

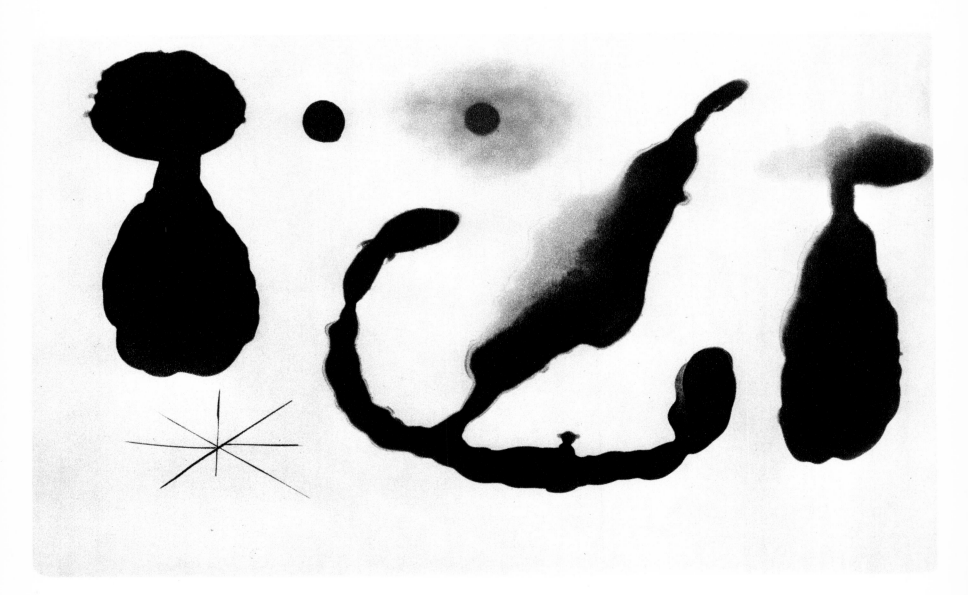

BIOGRAPHICAL SUMMARY

1893	April 20. Joan Miró born at Montroig, near Barcelona.
1907	Enters Academy of Fine Arts, Barcelona.
1910	His parents force him to give up art and to take a job as a salesman.
1912	Miró resumes painting, studies at the Academia Gali, Barcelona.
1915	Leaves the Academia Gali.
1917	Meets the art dealer Dalmau who champions Cubism and encourages modern Catalan painters.
1918	First exhibition (64 paintings and numerous drawings) at the Dalmau gallery, Barcelona (February 16 – March 3).
1919	March. First trip to Paris. Friendship with Picasso.
1920	Moves to Paris. First public appearance of Dada group in Paris.
1921	Exhibition at Galerie La Licorne, Paris. Maurice Raynal writes preface to catalogue.
1922	Completion of *The Farm*, which embodies the results of Miró's previous explorations. Ernest Hemingway buys it.
1923	*The Tilled Field*.
1924	Publication of *First Surrealist Manifesto* by André Breton.
1924–1925	*Carnaval d'Arlequin*.
1925	June: Exhibition at Galerie Pierre, Paris. November: Miró participates in the first Surrealist exhibition. Designs, in collaboration with Max Ernst, costumes and sets for the Diaghilev ballet *Romeo and Juliet*.
1926	Miró's works exhibited in New York.
1928	Trip to Holland. Publication of André Breton's *Surréalisme et la Peinture*, in which Miró is referred to as "perhaps the most Surrealist painter of all." First one-man show in New York (Valentine Gallery).
1929	First exhibition in Brussels.
1930	Miró is represented in the Exposition des Collages, Galerie Goemans, Paris. Preface to catalogue by Louis Aragon: *La Peinture au défi*. Surrealist sculptures *(Objects)*. Lithographs for Tristan Tzara's *L'arbre des voyageurs*.
1931	Sketches costumes and sets for the Diaghilev ballet *Jeux d'enfants*, staged at Monte Carlo.
1933	First exhibition in London (Mayor Gallery).
1937	Large wall painting for Spanish pavilion, Paris World Fair, *The Reaper*.
1938	Wall painting for villa of American architect Paul Nelson at Vergenville-au-Mer (Normandy) where Miró spends several weeks.
1940	Miró returns to Barcelona, then moves to Palma di Mallorca.
1942	Collaboration with ceramic artist Artigas.
1943	Resumes sculptural work.
1944	Executes the fifty lithographs of *Barcelona Suite*.
1945–1946	*Cahiers d'Art* publishes Miró's poem *Jeux poétiques*.
1946	Devotes himself intensively to sculpture; instead of Surrealist *objects* creates elementary volumes.
1947	First trip to U.S.
1947–1948	Large wall painting for the Terrace Plaza Hotel, Cincinnati. Miró moves to Montroig. Frequent visits to Paris.
1948, 1950, 1953	Exhibitions of paintings, sculptures, and ceramics, Galerie Maeght, Paris.
1950	Publication of 72 color lithographs (begun in 1948) for Tristan Tzara's *Parler Seul*. Fresco for Walter Gropius' Graduate Center, Harvard University, Cambridge, Mass.
1952	Series of fetish-like plastic constructions which Miró sets up in his garden at Montroig.
1954	Awarded Graphic Arts prize at Venice Biennial. Exhibition at Krefeld.
1956	Builds large studio at Palma di Mallorca (architect José Luis Sert). Exhibitions in Brussels, Amsterdam, Basel. Exhibition of prints at Krefeld and other German cities.
1958	Completes illustrations for Paul Eluard's *A toute Epreuve*.

Wherever an asterisk (*) appears with the page number, the reproduction is the same size as the original.

*38. *Woman and Bird in Front of the Moon*. Etching. 1947. $4^3/_8 \times 5^7/_8$″. Published in Laurels Album, Gallery Laurens, New York. Edition of 300 copies on *Vélin*, and 5 proofs. Printed by Atelier 17 (Hayter), New York.

*39. Etching. 1947. $6^7/_8 \times 4^1/_8$″. For *Partisan Review* (unpublished). Edition of 5 proofs in two states, each on *Vélin*. Printed by Atelier 17 (Hayter), New York.

41. *Tall Black Person*. Lithograph. 1948. $25^9/_{16} \times 19^7/_8$″. Edition of 50 copies on *Rives*. Maeght Editeur, Paris. Printed by Mourlot Frères, Paris.

42. *Men*. Lithograph. 1948. $25^9/_{16} \times 19^{11}/_{16}$″. Edition of 50 copies on *Arches*. Maeght Editeur, Paris. Printed by Mourlot Frères, Paris.

43. *Women*. Lithograph. 1948. $25^9/_{16} \times 19^{11}/_{16}$″. Edition of 50 copies on *Arches*. Maeght Editeur, Paris. Printed by Mourlot Frères, Paris.

44. *The Diver*. Lithograph. 1948. $9^1/_{16} \times 13$″. Edition of 50 copies on *Pur fil du Marais*. Maeght Editeur, Paris. Printed by Mourlot Frères, Paris.

*46. Color lithograph. 1950. $9^7/_{16} \times 6^5/_{16}$″. Frontispiece for *André Breton, Anthologie de l'humour noir*. (Bibliography 2.)

Etchings. 1947/49. Illustrations for *Tristan Tzara, L'antitête*. (Bibliography 31.)

*47. $4^1/_2 \times 3^3/_{16}$″.
*48. (top) $2^1/_8 \times 3^1/_4$″.
*48. (bottom) $4^5/_8 \times 1^7/_8$″.
*49. (top) $4^5/_8 \times 3^9/_{16}$″.
*49. (bottom) $1^{13}/_{16} \times 2^{15}/_{16}$″.
*50. (top) $4^1/_4 \times 2^{15}/_{16}$″.
*50. (bottom) $3^{13}/_{16} \times 3^9/_{16}$″.
*51. $4^5/_8 \times 3^{13}/_{16}$″.

52. *Persons in the Meadow*. Lithograph. 1948. $8^{11}/_{16} \times 13$″. Edition of 50 copies on *Pur fil du Marais*. Maeght Editeur, Paris. Printed by Mourlot Frères, Paris.

53. *Persons in the Sun*. Lithograph. 1948. $8^{11}/_{16} \times 11^{13}/_{16}$″. Edition of 50 copies on *Pur fil du Marais*. Maeght Editeur, Paris. Printed by Mourlot Frères, Paris.

54. *Young Girl*. Lithograph. 1948. $9^1/_{16} \times 13$″. Edition of 50 copies on *Pur fil du Marais*. Maeght Editeur, Paris. Printed by Mourlot Frères, Paris.

56. *Persons in the Garden*. I. Color lithograph. 1951. $19^{11}/_{16} \times 25^9/_{16}$″. Edition of 75 copies on *Arches*. Maeght Editeur, Paris. Printed by Mourlot Frères, Paris.

Album 13. 1948. Series of 13 lithographs. Additional lithograph for cover, vignettes for front and back of the portfolio, frontispiece, and imprint. Edition of 75 copies on *Pur fil du Marais*. Maeght Editeur, Paris. Printed by Mourlot Frères, Paris.

59. $15^1/_4 \times 11^1/_4$″.
60. $10^7/_8 \times 14$″.
61. $10^1/_4 \times 14^1/_4$″.
62. $10^3/_4 \times 14^3/_4$″.
63. $12 \times 15^3/_4$″.
64. $14^1/_2 \times 10^1/_2$″.
65. $14^3/_4 \times 10^1/_2$″.
66. $12 \times 17^1/_4$″.
67. $10^1/_2 \times 15$″.
68. $10 \times 15^1/_4$″.

69. $10^3/_4 \times 14^3/_4$″.
70. 11×17″.
71. $10^3/_4 \times 14^1/_4$″.

72. Etching for *Series IV* (in two states). 1953. $6^7/_8 \times 10^{13}/_{16}$″. Edition of 13 copies on *Arches* in green, 13 copies on *Arches* in black. Maeght Editeur, Paris. Printed by Imprimerie Lacourière, Paris.

*73. Etching for *Series V* (in two states). 1953. $5^{15}/_{16} \times 4^{15}/_{16}$″. Edition of 13 copies on *Arches* in ocher, 13 copies on *Arches* in black. Maeght Editeur, Paris. Printed by Imprimerie Lacourière, Paris.

*74. Little engraving (in two states). 1953. $2^3/_4 \times 3^1/_8$″. Edition of 13 copies on *Arches* in black and ocher. Maeght Editeur, Paris. Printed by Imprimerie Lacourière, Paris.

Etchings for *Series I* (in eight states in black and different colors). 1952/53. 13 copies of each state on *Arches*. Maeght Editeur, Paris. Printed by Imprimerie Lacourière, Paris.

77. 15×18″.
78. 15×18″.
79. 15×18″.
80. 15×18″.

83. Lithograph. 1948/50. $13 \times 9^3/_8$″. Illustration for *Tristan Tzara, Parler seul*. (Bibliography 33.)

*84. Lithograph. 1953. $12^3/_{16} \times 18^1/_8$″. Supplement to the catalogue of the Miró exposition 1953, Pierre Matisse Gallery, New York. Text by J. J. Sweeney. The catalogue contains two color lithographs. Edition of 1250 copies and special edition of 100 copies with additional lithograph.

87. *The Sad Wanderer*. Color lithograph. 1955. 30×22″. Edition of 50 copies on *Arches*. Maeght Editeur, Paris. Printed by Mourlot Frères, Paris.

89. Color etching. 1956. $9^1/_4 \times 14^9/_{16}$″. Illustration for *Michel Leiris, Bagatelles végétales*. (Bibliography 20.)

90. Etching. 1958. $12^3/_{16} \times 5^5/_{16}$″. Edition of 75 copies on *Arches*. Maeght Editeur, Paris. Printed by Imprimerie Lacourière, Paris.

*91. Color etching. 1958. $6^7/_8 \times 9^3/_{16}$″. Edition of 75 copies on *Rives*. Maeght Editeur, Paris. Printed by Atelier Crommelynck et Dutrou, Paris.

92. *Little Girl in the Wood*. Lithograph. 1958. $22 \times 15^3/_4$″. Edition of 100 copies on *Arches*. Maeght Editeur, Paris. Printed by Mourlot Frères, Paris.

94. *The Sun Eater*. Color lithograph. 1955. 30×22″. Edition of 50 copies on *Arches*. Maeght Editeur, Paris. Printed by Mourlot Frères, Paris.

95. Color etching. 1958. $7^7/_8 \times 11^{13}/_{16}$″. Edition of 75 copies on *Rives*. Maeght Editeur, Paris. Printed by Atelier Crommelynck et Dutrou, Paris.

96. Color etching. 1958. $6^3/_8 \times 10^1/_2$″. Edition of 75 copies on *Rives*. Maeght Editeur, Paris. Printed by Atelier Crommelynck et Dutrou, Paris.

97. Color etching. 1958. $10^1/_{16} \times 13^1/_8$″. Edition of 75 copies on *Rives*. Maeght Editeur, Paris. Printed by Atelier Crommelynck et Dutrou, Paris.

98. Color etching (two states). 1958. $9^3/_4 \times 12^5/_8$″. Edition of 75 copies on *Rives* in blue, 75 copies on *Rives* in bister. Maeght Editeur, Paris. Printed by Atelier Crommelynck et Dutrou, Paris.

Color woodcuts. 1958. Illustrations for *Paul Eluard, A toute Epreuve*. (Bibliography 17.)

*100. $11^1/_{16} \times 8^1/_{16}$″.
*101. $10^1/_{16} \times 6^7/_8$″.

Books Illustrated by Miró

1. Benoit, P. A. *Mon chemin.* Alès, Ed. P. A. B., 1953. 1 engraving on synthetic material (Celluloid). Edition of 21 copies on *Vélin.*

2. Breton, André. *Anthologie de l'humour noir.* Paris, Ed. Sagittaire, 1950. 1 color lithograph (frontispiece). Edition of 12 copies on *Holland,* 25 copies on *Pur fil Johannot.* Printed by Mourlot Frères, Paris. Reproduced page 46.

3. Breton, André. *La clé des champs.* Paris, Ed. Sagittaire, 1953. 1 color lithograph. Edition of 25 copies on *Arches.* Printed by Mourlot Frères, Paris.

4. Char, René. *La fête des arbres et du chasseur.* Paris, Ed. G. L. M., 1948. 1 color lithograph. Edition of 20 copies. Printed by Mourlot Frères, Paris.

5. Char, René. *A la santé du serpent.* Paris. Ed. G. L. M., 1954. 1 color lithograph. Edition of 54 copies on *Arches.* Printed by Mourlot Frères, Paris.

6. Char, René. *Poem.* Alès, Ed. P. A. B., 1958. 2 engravings on Celluloid.

7. Crevel, René. *La Bague d'Aurore.* Paris, Louis Broder, 1958. Collection Miroir du Poète. 5 color etchings and 1 etching on the cover. Edition of 130 copies. Also portfolio containing 22 etchings. Edition of 75 copies.

8. Crevel, René. *Feuilles éparses.* Paris, Louis Broder, 1958. Collection Archives. 1 color etching. In addition 60 proofs with wide margins.

9. *Derrière le Miroir.* No. 14/15. Paris, Maeght Editeur, 1948. 8 color lithographs. Printed by Mourlot Frères, Paris.

10. *Derrière le Miroir.* No. 29/30. Paris, Maeght Editeur, 1950. 4 color lithographs. Printed by Mourlot Frères, Paris.

11. *Derrière le Miroir.* No. 57/58/59. Paris, Maeght Editeur, 1953. 12 color lithographs. Printed by Mourlot Frères, Paris.

12. *Derrière le Miroir.* No. 87/88/89. Paris, Maeght Editeur, 1956. 5 color lithographs. Printed by Mourlot Frères, Paris.

13. *10 ans d'édition.* Paris, Maeght Editeur, 1956. 1 color lithograph. Printed by Mourlot Frères, Paris.

14. Dupin, Jacques. *Les brisants.* Paris, Ed. G. L. M., 1958. 1 color etching. Edition of 50 copies on *Arches.* In addition 15 copies containing 5 states of the etching in different colors.

15. Eluard, Paul. *Solidarité.* Paris, Ed. G. L. M., 1938. 7 etchings by Hayter, Husband, Masson, Miró, Picasso, Tanguy, and Wright. Edition of 150 copies on *Montval.* Printed by Atelier 17 (Hayter). Reproduced page 13.

16. Eluard, Paul. *Un poème dans chaque livre.* Paris, Louis Broder, 1956. 1 color etching. Printed by Imprimerie Lacourière, Paris.

17. Eluard, Paul. *A toute Epreuve.* Geneva, Gérald Cramer, 1958. 80 color woodcuts. Edition of 130 copies on *Vélin,* numbered I–XXIV ("hors commerce"), and 1–106 (trade edition), of which 6 copies (Nos. 1–6) with one set on China and one set on Japan, one illustration with proofs in separate colors, one handcolored woodcut by the artist, and one original woodblock, and 20 copies (Nos. 7–26) with one set on China or Japan and one handcolored woodcut by the artist. In addition, 30 proofs on *Auvergne* with wide margins showing 4 woodcuts. Woodblocks with technical collaboration of Enric Tormo, Barcelona. Printed by Imprimerie Lacourière, Paris. Reproduced pp. 100, 101.

18. Hugnet, Georges. *Enfances.* Paris, Cahiers d'Art, 1935. 3 etchings. Edition of 100 copies, 5 on *Japon Impérial* and 95 on *Arches.* Printed by Imprimerie Lacourière, Paris. Reproduced page 2.

19. Leiris, Michel. *The prints of Joan Miró.* New York, Curt Valentin, 1947. 1 etching black and orange. In the first 50 copies, moreover, the printing in black of the same plate raised with gouache. Edition of 100 copies on *Vélin.* Furthermore 5 sheets in orange and 5 sheets with gouache. Printed by Atelier 17 (Hayter), New York.

20. Leiris, Michel. *Bagatelles végétales.* Paris, Jean Aubier, 1956. 6 color etchings. Edition of 33 copies on *Vergé d'Auvergne.* Printed by Imprimerie Lacourière, Paris. Reproduced page 89.

21. *Le surréalisme en 1947.* Paris, Maeght Editeur, 1947. Les Cahiers de Pierre à Feu. 1 color lithograph as frontispiece. Edition of 999 copies.

22. *L'usage de la parole.* Paris, Cahiers d'Art, 1940. Library edition of the periodical with 1 drypoint. Edition of 25 copies on *Vélin.* The drypoints are decorated with different gouache compositions by Miró. In addition 12 proofs.

23. Melo, Joan Cabral de. *Joan Miró.* Barcelona, Ed. de l'Oc, 1950. 3 color woodcuts. Edition of 125 copies on *Pur fil Guano.* Technical collaboration for woodblocks, Enric Tormo, Barcelona.

24. *Miró Exposition New York.* New York, Pierre Matisse Gallery, 1953. Catalogue with 1 color lithograph, 1 lithograph in black-and-white and cover with color lithograph. Edition of 1250 copies. Moreover, 100 copies with additional lithograph on *Arches.*

25. Paalen, Alice. *Casse–Nuit.* Paris, Ed. Sagesse, 1938. 1 etching in red on pasted yellow paper. Edition of 75 copies on *Arches.* Printed by Marcoussis, Paris.

26. Péret, Benjamin. *Au paradis des Fantômes.* Ed. Henri Parisot, 1938. 1 color etching. Edition on *Vélin.* In addition 15 copies on blue *Montval,* and 9 proofs. Printed by Marcoussis, Paris.

27. Péret, Benjamin. *Anthologie de l'amour sublime.* Paris, Ed. Albin Michel, 1958. 1 color etching. Printed by Mourlot Frères, Paris.

28. Prévert, Jacques/G. Ribemont-Dessaignes. *Joan Miró.* Paris, Maeght Editeur, 1956. 10 color lithographs. Printed by Mourlot Frères, Paris.

29. Spender, Stephen. *Fraternity.* New York, 1939. 1 etching. Edition of 101 copies on *Montval.* Printed by Atelier 17 (Hayter), New York.

30. Tzara, Tristan. *L'arbre des voyageurs.* Paris, Ed. Montaigne, 1929/30. 4 lithographs. Edition of 100 copies. In addition 10 proofs of each lithograph.

31. Tzara, Tristan. *L'antitête. Le 3º volume le Désespéranto.* Paris, Ed. Bordas, 1947/49. (The first two volumes contain original prints by Max Ernst and Yves Tanguy.) 8 etchings. Edition of 200 numbered copies, of which nos. 1–8 on *Japon Impérial,* nos. 9–31 on *Hollande,* nos. 32–200 on *Auvergne.* The first 31 copies contain an additional series of 10 engravings and an original copperplate. Atelier 17 (Hayter), New York. Printed by Imprimerie Lacourière, Paris. Reproduced pp. 47–51.

32. Tzara, Tristan. *Poésie de Mots inconnus*. Paris, Ed. Iliazd, 1949. 1 lithograph in 2 colors. Edition of 157 copies *Ile de France à la cuve*. Printed by Mourlot Frères, Paris.

33. Tzara, Tristan. *Parler seul*. Paris, Maeght Editeur, 1948/50. 72 black-and-white and color lithographs and 1 collage with lithograph on cover. Edition of 250 numbered copies, of which nos. 1–20 on *Montval*, nos. 21–50 on *Arches*, nos. 51–250 on *Malacca pur chiffon*. Nos. 1–50 contain 1 colored pencil drawing. Printed by Mourlot Frères, Paris. Reproduced pp. VII, XV, XIX, XXII, XXV, XXXI, XXXIII and 83.

34. Verdet, André. *Sortilèges de Miró*. Nice, Matarossa, 1958. 1 color lithograph. Printed by Mourlot Frères, Paris.

35. *Verve*. Volume VII/27–28. Paris, Ed. Verve, 1952. *Le chien aboyant à la lune réveille le coq, le chant du coq picote le crane du fermier Catalan posé sur la table à coté du pourron.* 1 color lithograph.

Books on Miró

1941. James Johnson Sweeney. *Joan Miró*. The Museum of Modern Art, New York.

1948. Clement Greenberg. *Joan Miró*. The Quadrangle Press, New York.

1956. Jacques Prévert – G. Ribemont-Dessaignes. *Joan Miró*. Maeght Editeur, Paris.

1959. Jacques Dupin. *Joan Miró*. Harry N. Abrams Inc., New York. In preparation.